W9-AMQ-861

BREAKING THE RULES

Breaking the Rules

The Wooster Group

DAVID SAVRAN

Theatre Communications Group New York 1988

Copyright © 1986 by David Savran

Breaking the Rules: The Wooster Group is published by Theatre Communications Group, Inc., 355 Lexington Ave., New York, NY 10017.

The publications and programs of Theatre Communications Group, the national organization for the nonprofit professional theatre, are supported by Actors' Equity Foundation, Alcoa Foundation, ARCO Foundation, AT&T Foundation, Citicorp/Citibank, Columbia Pictures Industries, Consolidated Edison Company of New York, Eleanor Naylor Dana Charitable Trust, Dayton Hudson Foundation, Exxon Corporation, William and Mary Greve Foundation, Home Box Office, Joe and Emily Lowe Foundation, Andrew W. Mellon Foundation, Mobil Foundation, National Broadcasting Company, National Endowment for the Arts, New York City Department of Cultural Affairs, New York Life Foundation, New York State Council on the Arts, Pew Charitable Trusts, Philip Morris, Rockefeller Foundation, Scherman Foundation, Shell Oil Companies Foundation, Shubert Foundation, Consulate General of Spain and the Xerox Foundation.

All rights reserved. No part of this book may be reproduced in any manner whatsoever without written permission from the publisher, except in the case of brief quotations embodied in critical articles and reviews.

Originally published under the title *The Wooster Group, 1975-1985* by UMI Research Press, an imprint of University Microfilms, Inc., Ann Arbor, MI 48106.

On the cover: Ron Vawter, Kate Valk, Matthew Hansell, Willem Dafoe and Jeff Webster (microphone) in *L.S.D. Part IV:* photograph copyright © 1988 by Paula Court, used by permission.

Library of Congress Cataloging-in-Publication Data

Savran, David, 1950–
Breaking the rules.

Originally published: The Wooster Group, 1975-1985.
Ann Arbor, Mich. : UMI Research Press, 1986.
Bibliography: p.
Includes index.
1. Wooster Group. 2. Experimental theater—New York (N.Y.) 3. American drama—20th century—History and criticism. I. Savran, David, 1950– . Wooster Group, 1975–1985. II. Title.
PN2277.N52W667 1988 792'.097471 88-4894
ISBN 0-930452-82-8 (pbk.)

Cover design by G&H/Soho Ltd.

First Edition: April 1988
Second Printing: July 1991

To my father,
Jack Savran, M.D.

Perhaps . . . we shall still discover the realm of our invention, *that realm in which we, too, can still be original, say, as parodists of world history and God's buffoons—perhaps, even if nothing else today has any future, our* laughter *may yet have a future.*

Friedrich Nietzsche

INTERLOCUTOR: *Tambo, I understand you were at the cemetery yesterday.*
TAMBO: *Yessuh!*
INTERLOCUTOR: *Who died?*
TAMBO: *Everybody in the graves.*
INTERLOCUTOR: *No, I mean what friend or relative was buried?*
TAMBO: *No one.*
INTERLOCUTOR: *Then why did you go to the cemetery?*
TAMBO: *I went there to read the epitaphs on the tombstones.*
INTERLOCUTOR: *That's a funny way of spending your time.*
TAMBO: *That's where I get all my material for my jokes.*

Blackface and Music: A New Minstrel Folio (1936)

The complicity of cultural criticism with culture lies not in the mere mentality of the critic. Far more, it is dictated by his relation to that with which he deals. By making culture his object, he objectifies it once more.

Theodor Adorno

Contents

List of Figures

Foreword

There are many ways to react to the Wooster Group. You can become absorbed in the arcana and minutiae that eventually recombine to form the densely layered textures of their pieces (as David Savran rather remarkably does in this study), or you can just sit back and take it all in as the high-energy show-biz media-blitzed theatrical grandslam that it is. The latter course was tried with great success by uninitiated urban and suburban audiences in Boston a couple of years ago when even the 11:00 p.m. news critics had a great time with *L.S.D.*

And because there is so much detail, too much certainly to be taken in during a single performance, each viewer's experience of the work is quite different. And the pieces themselves are constantly changing—for every performance Liz is busy adding or deleting or speeding something up or slowing it down—less, it seems to me, out of any attempt to get closer to some imaginary ideal of a "finished" performance than simply as an attitude, and a way of thinking and living. I have probably seen *L.S.D.* about thirty times now, and I still get sharply different takes from every performance.

I must admit that my own first encounter with the Wooster Group (it was their especially indigestible *Route 1 & 9*) left me enraged and annoyed—it is hard to say which was worse. Then some months later they mounted a retrospective of their work and I was quite overwhelmed. First off, there are very few companies in our country which can point to a body of new work, manage to revive it across a month, and then have it stand the test of time. But as I saw this body of work, a lyricism and classical repose began to emerge that I had not noticed beneath the busy surface level, and eventually the uncompromising search to confront actual subject matter at the most literal level began to show through. And in how many theaters besides the ballet, opera, and circus can one speak of a spectacular level of *technique* on the part of the performers. In her search for verisimilitude, Liz employs actors with little or no stage experience, children, and a highly skilled core of virtuoso performers. And as with the best work, they do get under your skin and provoke strong reactions. And it's high time. Theater-going in our day has become a predictable act of lip-synching to the hoariest old commonplaces—The Wooster Group restores fire, outrage, *scandale,* and the sensation of something new. Theater as an art form is traditionally twenty to fifty years behind painting, music, dance, and the novel. The Wooster Group is up-to-date.

And I think that whether one likes the work or not is really rather beside the point—it constitutes an event, something that must be seen—it will be important to have been there. Anyone with any interest in theater in the United States of America in 1986 owes it to themselves to know what some of the latest developments are. If theater in the United States is to become large again, the Wooster Group is out there, up ahead, scouting the way. They are inventing theatrical vocabulary that ten and twenty years from now will become the lingua franca of a revivified American Theater. For my money, they are the most important theater company in our country today.

Peter Sellars
Director
American National Theater
May 1986

Acknowledgments

I wish to acknowledge, above all, the unflagging assistance, support and generosity of all of the members and associate members of the Wooster Group. I am especially grateful to Elizabeth LeCompte, who helped and inspired me every step of the way (and who provided the synopses of the pieces herein); Ron Vawter, who gave me invaluable feedback and encouragement; and Norman Frisch, who worked with me very closely and helped immeasurably in developing and clarifying my ideas.

The University of Regina granted me a sabbatical leave to finish the book, for which I am grateful, as well as assistance from the President's Fund in covering my many trips to New York. And I thank my students at the University, past and present, for teaching me to ask the right questions.

I am grateful to *The Drama Review* for allowing me to reprint material that appeared in my article, "The Wooster Group, Arthur Miller and *The Crucible.*"

I am obliged to many people who lent their time and encouragement, including Betty Corwin, Laura Ross, Nancy Campbell, Gabriel Prendergast, Bonnie Jackson, Tim Jensen and my superb editor at UMI, Sundra Flansburg. I wish also to acknowledge my longstanding debt to Bert States. Finally, I must express my heartfelt appreciation to all my friends who nourished me in this effort. I am especially grateful to Paula Vogel, for her enthusiasm and her thoughtful and incisive criticism of the manuscript; David Hult, for giving me perspective; and Ronn Smith, for his patience, watchful eye and unwavering support.

Introduction: Writing History

Among producers of experimental theatre in the 1970s and 1980s, the Wooster Group is unique for its combination of aesthetic and political radicalism with intellectual rigor. From the beginning, its work has been tough—difficult, vigorous and controversial. It has consistently addressed pressing social issues, including the victimization of women, racism and the multifarious processes of dehumanization. It has shocked and outraged a public inured to the unconventional and the daring. It has brought into the theatre material usually considered inappropriate, tasteless or illicit (including pornography, blackface comedy and pirated texts) not for sensational ends, but to explore and challenge middle-class culture, to question its assumptions and mode of operation and to reveal that which it has systematically suppressed. It has once again made the New York theatre a vital arena in which social, political and cultural issues are debated.

The Wooster Group's radicalism is not the result of an anarchic or haphazardly destructive impulse. On the contrary, the Group has examined attentively the culture of which it is a part, and read closely and intently its theatrical landmarks, deconstructing a series of texts, including *The Cocktail Party, Our Town* and *The Crucible*. It has juxtaposed these plays against wildly contrasting material (ranging from deafening disco music to a Pigmeat Markham comedy routine) to perform incisive critiques that expose the contradictions lurking in each text. Coincidentally, it has pioneered a documentary performance mode, a kind of *théâtre verité*, that mixes simple, non-mimetic presentation with a reckless and flamboyant theatricality.

The Wooster Group's theatre did not, of course, develop *ex nihilo*. It is, rather, an outgrowth of the off-Off-Broadway movement. In the early 1960s a number of artists attempted to create alternatives to mainstream commercial theatre. The first wave of experimentation included collectives, like the Living Theatre (under the direction of Julian Beck and Judith Malina) and the Open Theatre (under Joseph Chaikin's direction), as well as individual playwrights such as Sam Shepard, Ronald Tavel and Maria Irene Fornes. In the late 1960s and early 1970s, off-Off-Broadway was further invigorated by the anti-Vietnam War movement and the development of a powerful counterculture. This resulted in a second wave of experimentation which brought to the fore director/playwrights Richard Foreman and Robert Wilson and two collectives, Mabou Mines and The Performance Group. The latter was founded by Richard Schechner in 1967 and served as home base for the artists who began to produce their own work in 1975 under the direction of Elizabeth LeCompte and who would, in 1980, re-form as the Wooster Group.

All of the aforementioned artists rejected the commercial theatre and its mode of production, choosing instead to create their own producing organizations. All worked with performers who had not received formal theatre training and thus had not been assimilated to the ubiquitous Stanislavskian "method." All redefined the performer's responsibilities and altered the traditional relationship between actor and role. All produced a kind of anti-theatre, more closely allied to developments in dance, music or the visual arts than those on the commercial stage. All rejected, to some extent, the traditional division of labor and created a theatre in which the director is the central creative force—a conjoint playwright/designer/director. All questioned the notion that the *mise en scène* must be subordinate to a previously written script and gave more or less equal importance to movement, text, design and music.

Of all the companies, the Wooster Group is the only one to retain its original organization and collaborative working process. Chaikin, Schechner, Foreman and Wilson no longer have their own companies. The members of Mabou Mines do much of their directing, writing or performing independently of the collective. Foreman and Wilson have begun to do a major portion of their work in a traditional theatre situation. Both have developed techniques and styles to use on more conventional material—both have been hired to direct trained actors or singers in a number of classic works, including *Don Juan, Parsifal* and *Medea.* In contrast, the Wooster Group has remained squarely within the experimental arena. It has produced six major pieces, each the result of a lengthy collaborative working process that brings together a variegated body of material from many different sources and filters it through a single consciousness, that of Elizabeth LeCompte.

LeCompte started directing in 1974 while a member of The Performance Group. She had been working as an assistant to Schechner who was then seeking to develop a theatre that would break down barriers: between art and life, between performance space and audience space, and between production elements. This ritualistic theatre was aimed at laying bare and transforming the psyche of all who participated in the theatrical event, both performers and spectators. For most of his pieces, Schechner created a fluid, environmental space and used the raw visceral power of the performer to attenuate the literary and mimetic dimensions of the theatre. He based his rehearsal process on a daily schedule of intensive physical and emotional training, exercises and group psychotherapy.

In 1968 The Performance Group bought the Performing Garage at 33 Wooster Street in SoHo and produced one of their most important pieces, *Dionysus in 69,* a blood ritual of sorts based on Euripides' *The Bacchae.* After seeing and admiring the piece, Spalding Gray and Elizabeth LeCompte joined the company in 1970, Gray as performer and LeCompte as assistant director. They first collaborated with Schechner on *Commune* (1970), an examination of American mythology that juxtaposed a wide range of materials: *Moby Dick,* folk songs, spirituals, Thoreau's *Walden,* the murder of Sharon Tate by the Manson "family," the My Lai massacre and autobiographical texts by the performers.

In working and reworking a succession of pieces with Schechner, Gray and LeCompte developed their own idea of theatre. Gray credits Schechner with bringing him to maturity as a performer; LeCompte describes the five or six years working with Schechner as her apprenticeship, during which she was certainly influenced by his use of disparate texts and acting styles and his development of work through improvisation. In her own theatre pieces she would continue, as he had done, to work in a group situation and to use material furnished by the performers. She would mix cultural analysis with autobiography, combining plays with chronicles of the personalities and preoccupations of the performers.

During her years with Schechner, however, LeCompte became increasingly critical of his methods. She found his *mise en scène* too highly symbolic and ritualistic and his approach to performance dangerously psychoanalytical, urging the performer really to feel—at least in rehearsal—what he was experiencing on stage. She felt that Schechner never filtered the raw material rigorously enough, that he never fully mediated it through himself. She believed that the group situation (in which he enjoyed the role of guru) took precedence for him over the art and that the latter suffered as a result. LeCompte wanted to explore a different kind of theatre and in 1974 she and Gray joined with two members of The Performance Group and other friends to develop their own work through improvisation. The resultant piece, *Sakonnet Point,* broke sharply with Schechner's work. During LeCompte's years of apprenticeship, she had developed her own methods not only from her observation of Schechner—and then often doing the opposite—but from seeing other experimental work being performed in New York.

LeCompte has explained that she was particularly impressed by the work of Richard Foreman and Robert Wilson. She vividly recalls Foreman's *Pain(t)* (1974) which included a fight between two sisters, Rhoda and Eleanor, played by Kate Manheim and her own real sister, Nora. LeCompte remembers it not as a literal representation but as an "abstraction of a fight," featuring recorded voices and postures that suggested a fight more powerfully than anything she had experienced in the realistic theatre. Here she saw violence performed "with no relation to natural gesture and yet so real that it made you believe it was actually happening." Similarly inspirational was Robert Wilson's *Deafman Glance* (1970) which expanded the possibilities she envisioned in using a non-linear structure and "a visual language that was not necessarily psychologically real." In watching Wilson's work, she became attuned to its "musical" rather than logical form and to its "geometric structure": its way, for example, of building an entire sequence upon a single movement drawn by the performers on the stage floor. And she was fascinated by his use of highly suggestive and wistful material, his "almost Wagnerian relationship to the world" and the "deep sadness" that she sensed in the work.

LeCompte was also interested in Stuart Sherman's manipulation of objects on a TV tray, his "super-naturalism," as she calls it, his use of pedestrian, sub-theatrical activity to suggest the arbitrariness and strangeness of the commonplace. She also responded positively to Meredith Monk's *Education of a Girl Child* (1973) which, as a woman's work, was "closer to home" and provided a "tremendous boost."

In the first four pieces that LeCompte directed (co-composed with Spalding Gray and the other performers), the main roles were taken by Gray, Ron Vawter and Libby Howes. Vawter came to the Wooster Group via the U.S. Army. He recalls working downtown in the winter of 1972 as a recruiting officer and passing the Performing Garage on his way home every evening. After hearing, night after night, strange "experimental sounds" coming out of the place, he stopped in to see Schechner's production of Sam Shepard's *The Tooth of Crime* which he was "very taken with." He gradually got to know the Group members and quit the Army in the summer of 1973 to become The Performance Group's administrator. In 1976 he started working with LeCompte and Gray and has since appeared in all the Wooster Group's pieces. Libby Howes, the fourth "core" member of the Group, met Gray in 1974 when he was directing a workshop at the University of Michigan where she was a student. Shortly thereafter she came to New York and in 1975 became involved in the making of *Sakonnet Point*. She continued working with LeCompte and Gray, appearing in the next three pieces and becoming a Group member in 1978. In 1980 she began working on her own and decided in 1981 to leave the Group.

By the late 1970s, that part of The Performance Group working with LeCompte had become more vital than that working with Schechner and it attracted several people who have since become members of the Wooster Group. Designer and technical director Jim Clayburgh first worked with The Performance Group in 1972 after graduating from New York University. He designed the lighting for *Sakonnet Point* and co-designed the setting for *Rumstick Road*. After a two-year hiatus, he continued his collaboration with LeCompte, co-designing *Point Judith* and all following pieces. Performer Willem Dafoe came to New York from Milwaukee, where he had worked as an actor with Theatre X, and joined The Performance Group in 1977. He became increasingly interested in the pieces LeCompte was directing and in 1979 became one of the co-creators of *Point Judith*. He has collaborated on all subsequent pieces and, at the same time, pursued an independent film career. In 1979 Kate Valk, then an N.Y.U. student, started working with the Group (initially to help with costumes for *Point Judith*). The following year she began working on a new piece LeCompte was developing, *Route 1 & 9*, and later filled in for Libby Howes in *Nayatt School* and *Point Judith* after Howes left the Group. Peyton Smith, the most recent full member, came to New York in 1975 from the Provincetown Theatre Company and worked with Richard Foreman in two productions before appearing in The Performance Group's production of *The Balcony* (1979). The next year she became involved in the composition of *Route 1 & 9* and has continued as a member of the Wooster Group. Richard Schechner, meanwhile, left The Performance Group in 1980 and it disbanded, although LeCompte and those working with her retained the Group's corporate status. LeCompte became artistic director of the enterprise and the Group held on to what had always been, in fact, its corporate name: the Wooster Group.

Cognizant of the limitations of a systematic written chronicle, *Breaking the Rules* is a fractured history of the Wooster Group. The present tense runs against the past, juxtaposing documentation and analysis of the collaborative pieces against the Group members' own observations and memories. In the constant interplay, the analysis that proceeds in the present tense provides the text with a basic line of action, interrupted from time to time by voices remembering the past. I have set these voices and tenses against each other; I have interwoven description, analysis, biography and memory in imitation of the Wooster Group's work. I present my own interpretations in counterpoint with the members' stated intentions and interpretations (with which I do not always agree) to expand a series of connotations or to enrich the theatrical with personal associations. Through this polyphony I hope to provide a sense of the complexity of the Wooster Group's work, constituted as it is by a kaleidoscopic interplay of forms, perspectives and voices.

The words of Wooster Group members that interrupt the text, and are not footnoted, are taken from interviews, both formal and informal, that I conducted and edited, most between August and October 1984. Elsewhere, selections from what I call the *Nayatt School Notebook* were extracted from two notebooks containing Libby Howes's records of rehearsals for *Nayatt School.* Because four of the Group's pieces are based on widely performed modern plays, I have included detailed critiques of these plays prompted by the Group's performance of excerpts of each of the "parent" texts. In assembling these disparate materials and interweaving them with my own analysis, I have attempted to create a structure modelled upon *L.S.D.,* the most recent and certainly the most historiographic of the Wooster Group's pieces (also, the piece that was being finished as I was writing this book).

In chronicling the Wooster Group's activity, *Breaking the Rules* focuses on the collaborative pieces directed by Elizabeth LeCompte. This work, however, is not the Group's sole product. Since 1979 Spalding Gray has largely dropped out of the collaborative pieces to develop a series of autobiographical monologues. Although these monologues are closely connected in many and various ways to the collaborative pieces, they fall outside the scope of the book because they are not directed by LeCompte. The only exception is *India and After (America)* which I analyze as an introduction to the Rhode Island Trilogy and to the use therein of autobiographical material.

Since every starting point is arbitrary, since every beginning is both a continuation of and break with the past, I choose not to begin with *Sakonnet Point,* the Group's first piece. Wishing to avoid a strictly evolutionary framework, I disrupt chronological sequence. Thus Part I, instead of offering a measured introduction, provides an analysis of what is arguably the Group's most concentrated and self-contained piece, *Route 1 & 9* (1981). Part II retraces the steps and returns to the earliest work, *Three Places in Rhode Island* (composed of *Sakonnet Point* [1975], *Rumstick Road* [1977] and *Nayatt School* [1978]) and its epilogue, *Point Judith* (1979). It ends with a look at *Hula* (1981), a dance piece composed during a vacation from *Route 1 & 9* rehearsals. Part III is devoted to an analysis of the Group's most recent work, *L.S.D.(...Just the High Points...)* (1985).

In writing this book, I have assumed an ambiguous relationship to the Wooster Group and its audience. As an "authorized" chronicler, I have been made privy to the desires and motivations of many in the Group. I have thus become an insider while remaining a spectator, always outside the Group's activities. My text no doubt reflects my own equivocal position, sitting alongside both spectator and performer, being both the spectator's ally and an intermediary between him and the Group's work. As a result, my text alternates between first and third person pronouns, never feeling comfortable with either authoritarianism, neither the editorial "we" nor the more impersonal epithet, "the spectator. . . . "

For the sake of clarity I have chosen to use the male pronoun to describe the hypothetical spectator or reader. Although its use reflects my gender (and is, thus, an accurate vehicle for my projections) there is a sense in which the convention of privileging the male is grossly out of place here. From the beginning, the Wooster Group has investigated that which is taken for granted and passes unnoticed in our culture. In its work it has questioned the disposition of theatrical forces and the status of the spectator. Writing about this work, I feel almost a sense of embarrassment that rhetorical convention has dictated the use of the male pronoun. In recognizing the relationship between the spectator's stare and the masculine ogle, I am forced to consider the voyeuristic implications of my analytical gaze.

Finally, I would like to record my personal motivation in writing this book. When, in May 1982, I entered the Performing Garage to see the Wooster Group for the first time (the piece was *Nayatt School*), I had no idea what to expect. I knew only that the piece was part of their Rhode Island Trilogy (Nayatt School is, in fact, located some ten miles from where I grew up in Providence). I suspected the work would be contentious because the friend who accompanied me told me of the controversy surrounding the Group's use of blackface in *Route 1 & 9*. I took my place in the front row and listened intently to Spalding Gray's opening monologue, delighting in his irreverent presentation of *The Cocktail Party*. When the curtains opened to begin Part III and the performers descended into madness and chaos, I was enraptured, and I remained so until the end of the piece, carried away by a whirlwind the like of which I had never seen before in the theatre. When the performance ended I walked—or floated—out onto Wooster Street and, in a state of exultation, started running up the street. For me, the act of writing this book has been an attempt to recapture the thrill and the breathlessness of that run.

Part I

Route 1 & 9 (The Last Act): The Disintegration of *Our Town*

Our Town:
(no inflection) "Your mother'll be coming downstairs to make believe, uh, make breakfast."
"Chew that bacon good and slow. It'll help keep you warm on a cold day."
"... his appendix burst on a hunting trip in North Conway."
"There are the stars making the crisscross ..."
"This is the worst piece of shit." "Shut up, I like it, it reminds me of Carousel.*"*
(Lizzie: incredible innocence & the hokey philosopher profound dimensions in downhome and *he's an asshole)*
Nayatt School Notebook October 11, 1977

Elizabeth LeCompte: We began doing Our Town *as a reading, fitting people into parts, rehearsing it during the day and performing it at night. Just as a reading, but excluding the part of the Stage Manager, that voice that connects, so that it would stand as a number of scenes, placed next to each other.*

Kate Valk: When we started working on Route 1 & 9, *it was just* Our Town, *reading* Our Town, *and I was still stage managing. Then I transcribed the Pigmeat Markham records, trying to figure out what they were saying. By the time I finished I could imitate ... I could do all the voices. And that's how I got started performing in* Route 1 & 9, *with the blackface routines.*

Peyton Smith: The beginning of rehearsals was wonderful because the live performance part was dancing. And many of the early rehearsals, before we got into any depth, were spent making this wonderful musical piece that was a lot of fun to do. Of course, then it became more problematic, when we started realizing the intent, and how far it went.

* * *

When *Route 1 & 9 (The Last Act)* opened at the Performing Garage in October 1981, it polarized its audience more radically than any piece performed in New York in at least a decade. By January 1982 it had become the subject of a widely reported controversy. The dispute centered around the piece's juxtaposition of Thornton Wilder's *Our Town* against a reconstruction of a Pigmeat Markham comedy routine, performed by four actors in blackface. The New York State Council on the Arts (NYSCA), which has been a major source of funding for the Group, judged that "Route 1 & 9 contained in its blackface sequences harsh and caricatured portrayals of a racial minority"[1] and, as a consequence, cut funding for the Group by forty percent, the fraction of the grant they believed subsidized the piece. The Wooster Group convened a number of public forums to discuss the piece's alleged racism and in March submitted an appeal to NYSCA, drawn up by Jeffrey M. Jones, aimed at restoring the funding. The appeal contained a thirty-one-page defense of *Route 1 & 9* as well as twenty-three letters of support by a formidable collection of artists, critics and producers. On June 10, 1982, NYSCA rejected the appeal and upheld the reduced level of funding.

* * *

Schema of Route 1 & 9 *(The Last Act)*

Part IA *THE LESSON (Upstairs): In Which A Man Delivers a Lecture on the Structure and Meaning of* Our Town

Video reconstruction of "teaching film"

Part IB *THE LESSON (Downstairs): In Which the Stage Hands Arrange the Stage for the Last Act of* Our Town

"The Lesson" continues
Blind building sequence begins
Black out

Part II *THE PARTY: In Which the Stage Hands Call It a Day and a Telegram Is Sent*

Blind building continues
The "girls" make telephone calls

The Party begins (reconstruction of Pigmeat Markham routine)
Video excerpts from Our Town, *Act II, overlap*

Part III *THE LAST ACT (The Cemetery Scene): In Which Four Chairs are Placed on the Stage Facing the Audience to Represent Graves*

Video excerpts from Our Town, *Act III, begin*
The Party continues "sotto voce"
Ghoul Dance

Part IV *ROUTE 1 & 9: In Which a Van Picks Up Two Hitchhikers and Heads South*

*Video: "*Route 1 & 9*" (Driving sequence)*
Porn

* * *

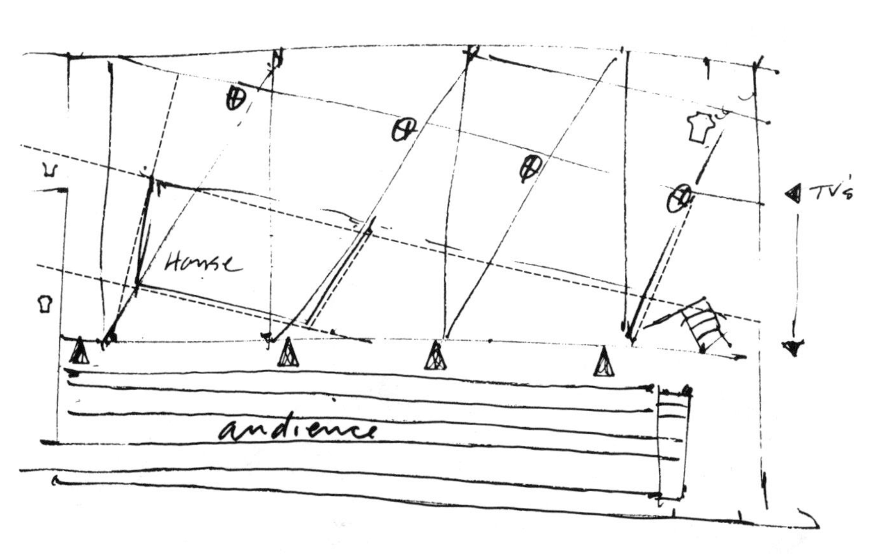

Figure 1. Performance Space for *Route 1 & 9 (The Last Act)* *(Elizabeth LeCompte)*

Elizabeth LeCompte: In the beginning I had an image of the performers in blackface. Wonderful visual thing. I thought of the blackface on them, and the lighting. And I could see, almost immediately, a kind of dance structure, going up and back, along an expanded floor grid from Point Judith. *Usually, that's one of the very first things that comes: a spatial element from the preceding piece, something I couldn't do there, that pushed it too far, or that didn't work, in some way. It's as if each space is an interpolation of the last. Or a rearrangement of the last, or the space*

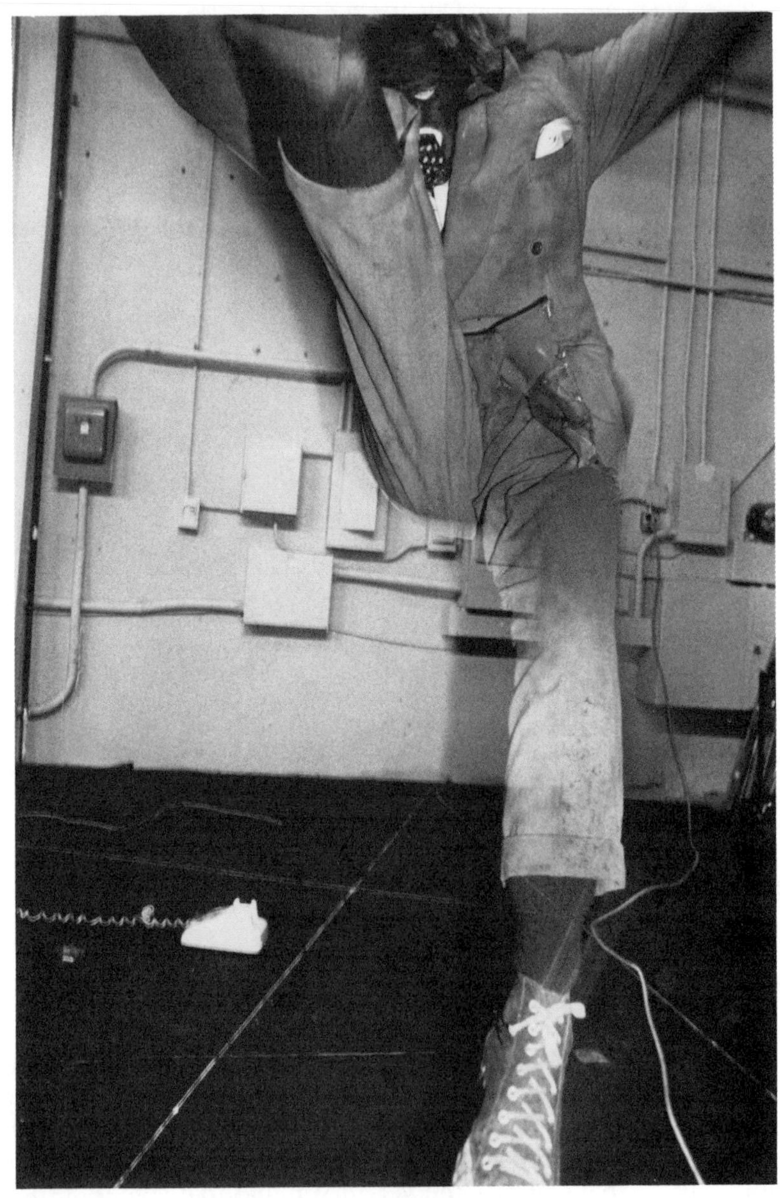

Figure 2. *Route 1 & 9,* The Party
Willem Dafoe, Ron Vawter.
(Nancy Campbell)

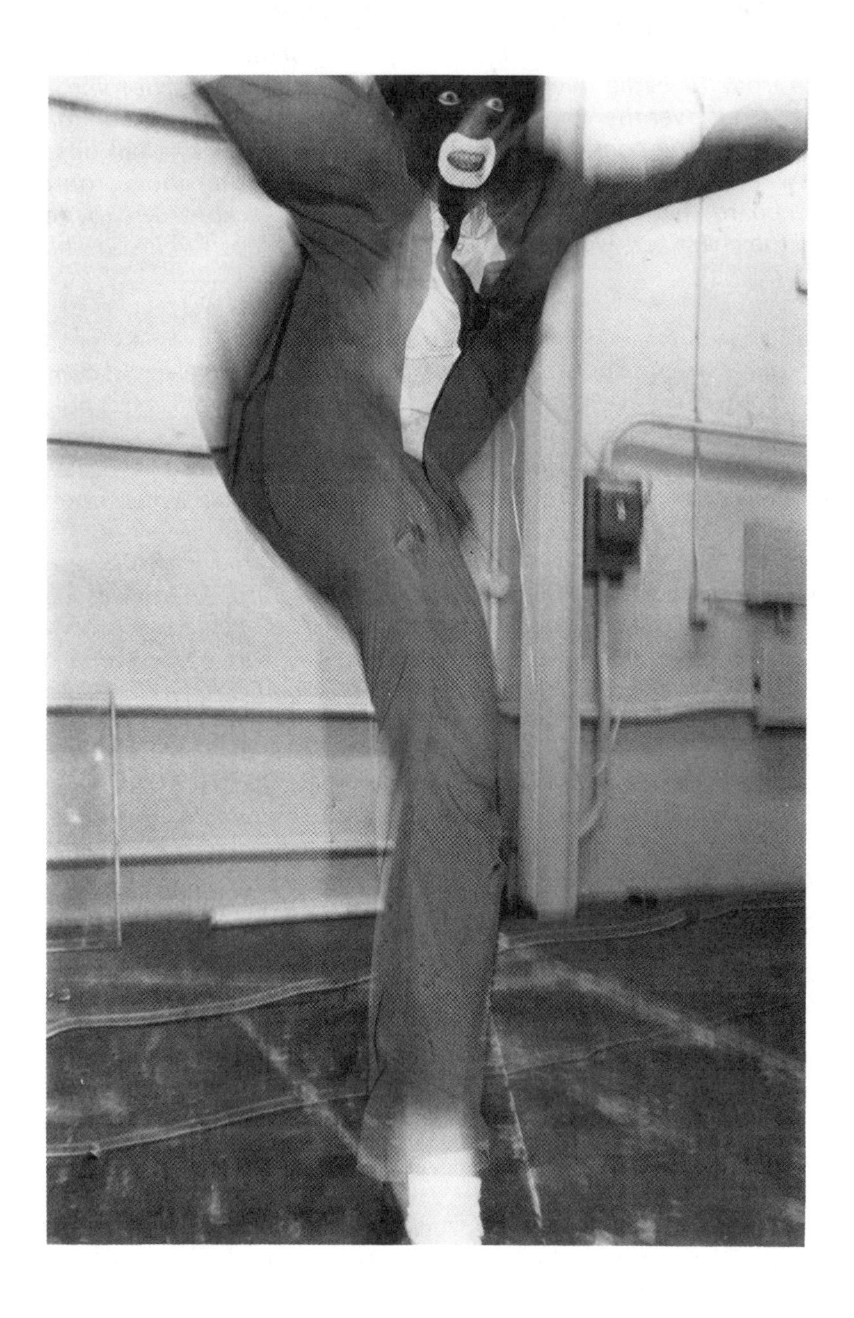

before that. The performance space had been falling more and more into a kind of parallelogram grid. I took the pattern of the house drawn on the floor from the earlier pieces, the parallelogram that it had become, and extended it over the whole space. The tin house would stand on top of the grid. And we constructed dances around that. Like on a chalk board. I knew that the audience would look down from above, onto a blackboard, that I was going to be sketching on a blackboard, so to speak. And the characters would be dancing and sketching in white on a black board.

Ron Vawter: I knew very well that we were unsettling people's feelings, and our own feelings, about racism: racism in ourselves, racism in everybody in the audience, black and white. And it was all about pulling the rug out from under people's secure, liberal and righteous feelings about racism, their own and society's. We were agents provocateurs, saboteurs, working against people's strong feelings of righteousness.

Peyton Smith: Well, sometimes, we got really scared when things got bad. I remember this one night... in the beginning when we got bad reviews, we'd have maybe seven people in the audience. And Route 1 & 9 *is a hard show to do for seven people. Anyway, there weren't too many people this one night. And I went through such a horror. There was a black man in the audience. And he had his coat over his lap. And he would put his hand under his coat. We were doing the part way up front, about the punch and I thought, "He's going to shoot us. He's closest to Ronnie. Well, I love Ronnie but that's the way it goes. I'm going to dive under the seating arrangement." And I had it all blocked out in my mind. And then, of course, nothing happened. So when we went off stage, I said, "Oh my God, I had such a fear." And everyone else saw him. So it wasn't that I was paranoid. It was so odd that we all picked up on it, because he never did anything. He just sat there, but he had this weird look. With* Route 1 & 9, *all the performances were exciting. And I liked that. I liked the controversy. But sometimes it was frightening.*

* * *

Beyond Parody (Part I)

Elizabeth LeCompte: We reconstructed a 1965 Encyclopedia Britannica teaching film starring Clifton Fadiman. For a long time, I didn't know where it would be played, we tried many different places. Finally, I separated it out and put it at the beginning, dovetailing it into the rest of the piece. Clifton Fadiman was the "Stage Manager" of Route 1 & 9, *echoing Wilder's construction in* Our Town. *Then you'd see Ron come back as the Stage Manager, as Clifton Fadiman had played him in the tape. Those kinds of connectors came in late.*

The first part of *Route 1 & 9*, "The Lesson: In Which a Man Delivers a Lecture," is a videotaped lecture on Thornton Wilder's *Our Town*, delivered by Ron Vawter and screened in the upstairs space at the Performing Garage. In the Wooster Group's version, "The Lesson" appears to be a gentle mockery of the banalities of humanistic criticism. For the duration of the tape, the camera holds long static shots of the lecturer and pans portentously as he moves back and forth between a tiny model stage and the ladder to be used in *Our Town* (and *Route 1 & 9*). It zooms in for important "truths" and underscores them by spelling out the catch phrases across the bottom of the television screen. These production devices, combined with jump cuts in the editing (most of which were present in the print from which the Wooster Group worked), suggest that a subtly critical point of view is being taken toward both the speaker and his analysis of *Our Town*. In Ron Vawter's deadpan characterization, the lecturer mouths the formulas of humanistic criticism with a forced informality and playfulness that mask his authoritarian pose. He explicates the play by setting himself up as a

> *Ron Vawter: Fadiman makes these very unwieldly and awkward illustrative gestures. Willem and I studied them very carefully, second by second. When I look at my eyes in the tape, I'm amazed at how glazed over they look. I had done unconscious listening, putting on the audio tape when I was asleep. It's as if performing it reinduced the sleep state I was in while I was digesting it.*

privileged interpreter who speaks for the audience: "He [Dr. Gibbs] uses the word unconsciously, he doesn't notice it, but we do."[2] By so articulating the spectators' emotions ("We've all had that feeling"[3]) he establishes his community with the audience in much the same way that Wilder implicates the spectator as a citizen of *Our Town*.

The apparently ironic stance of "The Lesson" suggests a critique of the universalizing tendencies and the staunchly philosophical (rather than political) pose of liberal humanism. The lecturer, in what LeCompte calls his "extremely white analysis"[4] of the play, would like the spectators to believe that *Our Town* is first and foremost a shared spiritual experience. Adopting the first person plural pronoun, he explains that the play assures the recognition that "all our lives are part of something vast and eternal." He asserts that it "reconciles us to life" and "helps us to understand and so accept our existence on earth." For him, *Our Town*, like "the humanities in general," propounds an unchanging set of

Figure 3. *Route 1 & 9,* (A) The Lesson; (B) *Our Town* Video, Emily Webb; (C) *Our Town* Video, Mrs. Webb
Ron Vawter; Marissa Hansell; Peyton Smith.
(Nancy Campbell)

universal characteristics and all those things that "never go out of style"—birth, growing up, marriage and death.[5] Between 8:40 and 11:00, the time the lecturer allots for a performance of *Our Town,* the Wooster Group reverses these axioms by historicizing the theatrical experience. It lifts the veil of aestheticism that certain artists and critics use to try to shield art from the realities of history and remove it from its political context. In *Route 1 & 9,* the Wooster Group recovers racial and cultural difference. Rather than reconciling the spectator to (social) life, it leads him to become aware of what *Our Town* has repressed and ignored. It suggests that Grover's Corners is but a sweet fantasy and that Wilder's American pastoral promulgates less a universal truth than the ideology of a particular class and culture.

If "The Lesson" were simply a satire, its ridicule of a humanistic interpretation of dramatic literature (and the social values it champions) would unite the spectators "against" these formations. It would thereby repeat the very process upon which the lecturer relies. It would instill a sense of community and superiority among those who can share in the apparent condemnation, a condescension analogous to that enjoyed by Mr. Fadiman, poised confidently between the text he has "mastered" and the audience he "commands." This stratification of points of view is

> *Elizabeth LeCompte: I liked the Clifton Fadiman film, but was bothered about liking it. It touched nostalgic chords of comfort for me that made me angry. It pressed two buttons simultaneously. And I found myself unable to accept either in comfort. I couldn't destroy it, and I couldn't go with it and be satisfied. I wanted to dig more deeply into it.*

subtly undermined, however, by the fact that the analysis proffered in "The Lesson" offers strategic access to the projects of both Wilder and the Wooster Group.

In "The Lesson" the lecturer speaks of the importance of three devices in *Our Town*: music, theme and variations as a formal principle, and the condensed line or word.[6] Wilder used these devices (along with many others) to break with the dominant theatrical style of his time—realism. In the preface to *Three Plays,* he upbraids the realistic theatre for being "evasive," for practicing a "social criticism" that fails "to indict us with responsibility."[7] He notes that a major cause of the theatre's impotence was the box set which, when taken " 'seriously' . . . removed, cut off, and boxed the action," turning the theatre into a "museum showcase."[8] To oppose this convention he delocalized the stage, refusing "childish attempts to be 'real,' "[9] and created performance space.

In a project analogous to Wilder's, the Wooster Group has reacted against the dominant style of its time—realism again. LeCompte notes her own attempts to move the work "ALWAYS AWAY FROM NATURALISM."[10] To accomplish this, the work relies on loud music, not only to create mood, as Wilder does, but to shatter a cohesive dramatic texture and evoke a historical and cultural setting. The Group's attack on linear structure radicalizes Wilder's lyrically episodic technique (theme and variations) to create a violently disjunctive form that breaks sharply with a plot-driven structure. ("I am looking for some substitute for plot. Non-linear," writes LeCompte.[11]) Finally, the art of condensation, or "putting a lot into one small package,"[12] suggests for the Wooster Group the development of complex symbols and actions which resist translation into discursive language.

To renovate Wilder's break with realism, Parts II and III of the piece feature scenes from *Our Town* on video monitors, in what is as much an act of homage as it is a critique. LeCompte acknowledges Wilder as her "predecessor"[13] in American experimental theatre and maintains that she loves "that kind of *Our Town* sentimentality. . . ."[14] For she too has rejected the box set (as exemplified by the miniature stage, the "museum showcase" in "The Lesson") and uses the theatre as performance space. In *Route 1 & 9* she submits *Our Town* to a violent examination but she does so knowing that it has its roots in Wilder's own intentions. Indeed, the closing paragraph of Wilder's preface acquires a particular poignancy in this context, when he writes, "I hope I have played a part in preparing the way" for "the new dramatists we are looking for."[15] Ironically, during a period of retrenchment in the 1980s, in the midst of a revival of realistic playwrighting, Wilder's hope has been fulfilled less conspicuously by new dramaturgy than new performance, and most powerfully perhaps, by a work that uses his own script as a starting point.

By inducing the spectator to read "The Lesson" as satire, *Route 1 & 9* snares the audience in its own smug condescension: it lures the spectator to fall into the very trap that the lecturer himself has fallen into. By the conclusion of "The Lesson," however, *Route 1 & 9* has begun to move beyond parody and call into question the unanimity it has provoked. As the piece proceeds, it cuts through the hierarchy of points of view and makes it increasingly difficult for the viewer to retain a critical objectivity. It works in harmony with Wilder's intent, to ensure that "the social criticism" will "indict" the spectator "with responsibility." It restores the accountability of the individual by leading him to confront his complicity in the maintenance of what is revealed to be a deeply stratified and inequitable culture.

* * *

Kate Valk: I swear, I didn't think the Pigmeat Markham was going to be a problem. I really didn't. All the time we spent working on it, I thought it would be so evident because of the context. My feelings are hurt easily... I'm not interested in offending the audience. Really. I got upset that some people reacted so strongly against the piece. But it was also a very exciting time. Because of the controversy, houses were packed. Also, in this kind of theatre, there is sometimes a lot of distance between you and the audience, not physical distance but... I mean, I'm pretty isolated, working down here. And it was interesting to have so much feedback from everyone. Although I still don't feel that it's been resolved. Because the blackface gives me a lot of pleasure. It's the most fun I've ever had. On the other hand, I hate to do something that I know hurts people or offends them. But I believe in it so strongly... it makes so much sense to me. But nothing tops the time we had in Zurich. Having a few liberals offended at you and getting your funding cut was nothing compared to having 650 people screaming at you. They hated the video. And the blackface, they didn't care about that. They just didn't want video. They were throwing eggs and tomatoes and shaking the booth where the guys were running the equipment. We were all... UUGGHH!!! It was really scary.

* * *

Stagehands (Part II)

Elizabeth LeCompte: We worked with the guys building the tin house blindfolded. That came out of Point Judith, *a whole section of* Point Judith *that I excised, because I couldn't fit it in. I took that section and expanded it for the beginning of* Route 1 & 9*—the comic structure of building the house. I took the idea, really, from vaudeville and comedic films about housebuilding. I remember, particularly, a Laurel and Hardy short in which they play incompetent workmen building a house which, at the end, totally collapses. The idea was to construct some kind of routine with the guys really blindfolded. So we did improvisations around them working, building the house blindfolded, and Spalding sitting above, watching them, talking to them as the foreman. That's where we got the "skeletal house" text that's played in the blackout. We combined the tapes of the improvisations from* Point Judith *with these new tapes and used them as one of the soundtracks for Part II.*

Figure 4. *Route 1 & 9,* Blind Building
Ron Vawter.
(Nancy Campbell)

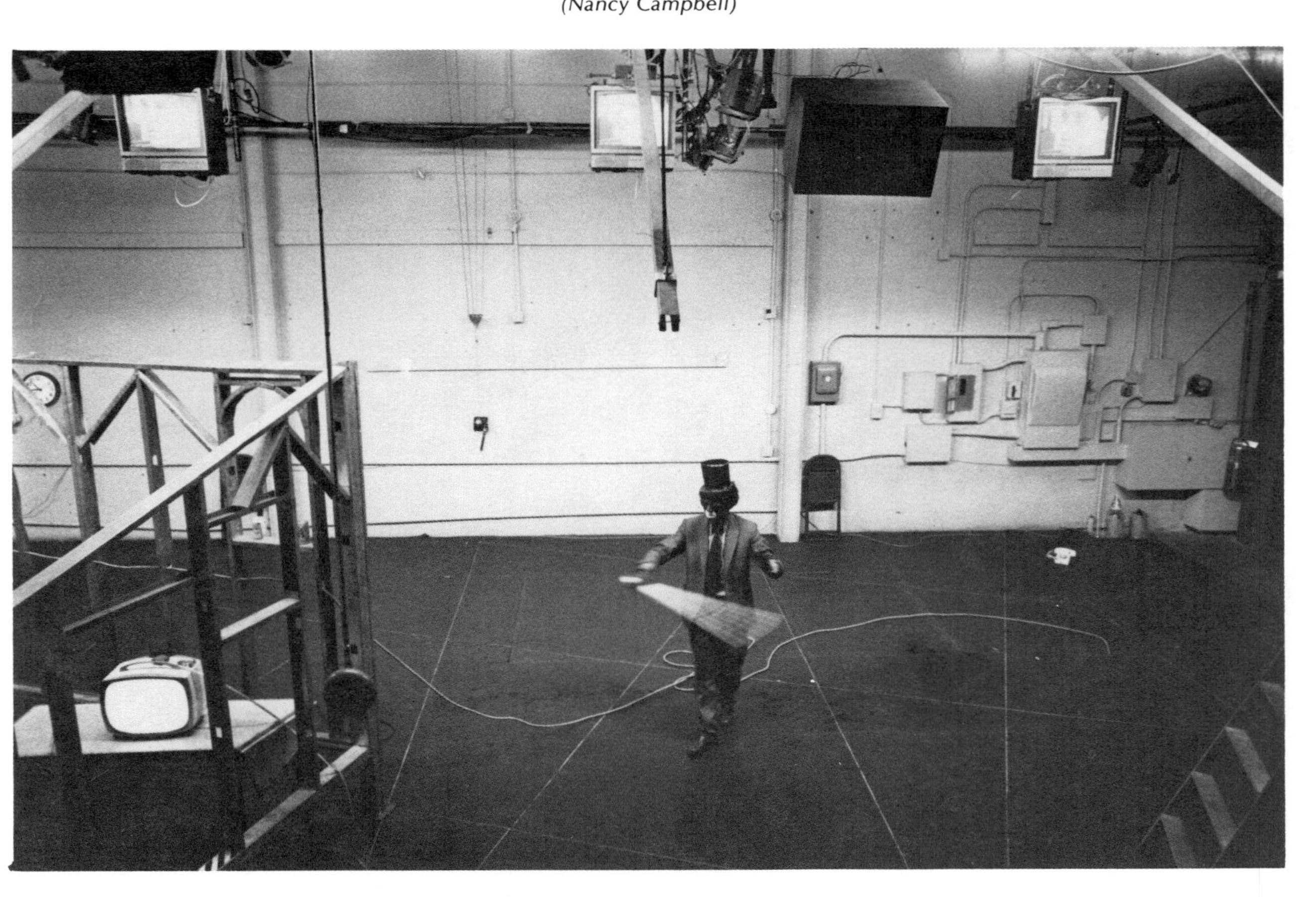

Figure 5. *Route 1 & 9,* Blind Building
Willem Dafoe, Ron Vawter.
(Nancy Campbell)

Part I of *Route 1 & 9* concludes as the audience moves downstairs for the last section of "The Lesson" and the start of a very different kind of performance. The spectators now sit across the length of the Performing Garage, the playing area stretched out immediately before them, four video monitors poised 14 feet above the stage floor. The house lights go to black and in the darkness we hear a conversation between two men (Ron Vawter and Spalding Gray) in which they discuss plans for constructing a skeletal house. In a dialogue which will resonate with one of the final videotapes, Dan (Vawter) explains that there's "quite a call" for these skeletal houses "out in Jersey."

> STEW: What advantage are those skeletal houses?
> DAN: Dan, they're very airy and there's good visibility.
> STEW: How are they heating them these days?
> DAN: Dan. It's organic heating.
> STEW: Organic, meaning what? Over.
> DAN: None.
> STEW: No heat at all. What kind of families could live in a house with no heat?
> DAN: Cold people, Dan.
> STEW: What's that? Come again?
> DAN: Dan. Indifferent people.
> STEW: Do you get those out there, then, in Jersey?
> DAN: They got 'em all over.[16]

U.S. Routes 1 and 9 begin at the Canadian border and meander south, Route 1 along the Atlantic coast and Route 9 along the east bank of the Hudson. They merge in northern New Jersey and proceed south for 30 miles before separating again. A corridor of gas stations, shopping centers and fast-food restaurants, Route 1 & 9 wends it way through one of the most heavily industrial areas in the nation. Like major roads on the edge of every American city, it owes its diversity of offerings to the industrial growth of the past fifty years and the flight of the middle class to the suburbs. For the Wooster Group, this stretch of highway is America's dream landscape of the eighties, the modern counterpart of the Grover's Corners of fifty years before (fictionally located in New Hampshire, somewhere between Routes 1 and 9). It is the thoroughfare for the "Cold people," the "Indifferent people" who inhabit this landscape, the emotional reserve of Wilder's New England Puritans having become a pervasive coldness, sterility, insularity and fear.

Into this evocation of contemporary America, two men in blackface (Willem Dafoe and Ron Vawter) enter, two stagehands who prepare to assemble the reverse forced-perspective skeletal house that will dominate the stage right half of the playing area. After surveying the blueprints in silence they begin to work. As they do, pre-recorded

> *Willem Dafoe: There was a lot of pleasure in* Route 1 & 9, *particularly the blackface building. It's very curious. Because here is a grossly public action, and externally, you have a grossly obvious task doing grossly obvious sight-gags. But you're blind. And it's like you're dreaming. You're out there . . . and it's wonderful, it's the most literal mask you can ever think of.*

dialogue between Stew and Dan from *Point Judith,* instructions for the building of the house, continues over the loudspeakers. The unseen Stew directs the action from afar, a representative of the director and the invisible theatrical apparatus supporting the performers, themselves stagehands of a sort, "the unseen people behind the scenes, the black workers and the maids who scrub at night."[17] Here, the process that makes visible what in the theatre is customarily invisible will reach as far as Grover's Corners and reveal all that lies buried there. Besides forming a link with the earlier piece (LeCompte sees her activity as "creating a body of work, a continuum"[18]) the construction of the skeletal house sets forth a provocative "what if . . . " What if the laborers from *Point Judith* were to be taken out of context and placed in entirely new surroundings? What if, instead of being inserted into *Long Day's Journey into Night,* they were made to collide with and become part of a critique of the quintessential paean to white, middle-class American life and death, *Our Town*? What if, to accentuate their contrast with the Webbs and the Gibbses, they were presented as black?

The transformation wrought upon these two characters places them, within the confines of American culture, at the opposite pole from the characters in *Our Town*. Like the latter, presented in soap opera close-ups, the two stagehands emerge not from the "real" social world but from a theatrical tradition, here vaudeville, blackface minstrel shows and silent films. Like virtually all of *Route 1 & 9*, they are quoted, wrenched out of context to collide with Wilder's lyric ghosts.

At this point in the piece, the spectators' attention is turned toward the "antics" of the two stagehands—none of *Our Town* has as yet been screened—and the grotesque and unsettling figures that they cut. They install a wall upside down, spilling a can of beer fastened to one of the supports, and fumblingly light a cigarette in the middle. Working several feet from the front row, they are close enough for the audience to scrutinize their deep black make-up and exaggerated white lips. Their appearance is monstrous, as distorted as the face of a performer in *Rumstick Road* when a color slide of another woman is projected on her. These characters are also projections: now a white man's image of black men. Their routine is a transformation of burlesque in which, as LeCompte notes, the "humor comes from out-of-control destructiveness."[19] Here, however, as Laurel 'n' Hardy become Amos 'n' Andy become Stew 'n' Dan, the humor has evaporated, in part because of the black blinding glasses that force the men to perform their routine at half-speed, drawing the comedy out so far "you can see the holes in the joke."[20]

The gulf between white and black culture is widened as the women, also in blackface, begin a series of live phone calls, broadcast over speakers in the theatre. Willie (Kate Valk) invites Ann (Peyton Smith) to her birthday party—a celebration which will contrast violently and poignantly with Emily's twelfth birthday. She then phones a number of fried chicken outlets in an attempt to get food delivered for her party. The calls are live and, of course, change from night to night. They are, in part, "about the distance between uptown and downtown," as LeCompte explains.[21] Most of the outlets Willie calls are in Harlem and most won't deliver. When she does find one that will and gives Wooster Street as the address, the answer invariably comes back, "Oh, we don't go down there." (The elaboration of cultural schism is again based on a division within Grover's Corners, where a "Polish Town" lies just "across the tracks."[22]) The breach between black and white culture is underscored by the audio/visual paradox the phone calls induce. The audience sees Willie, a white woman in blackface, call a fried chicken

Figure 6. *Route 1 & 9,* Blind Building
Willem Dafoe, Ron Vawter.
(Bob Van Dantzig)

Kate Valk: The public forums were fascinating. It's interesting to go back and listen to the tapes, because of what you can tell about people from their voices. I spoke once and my voice is... it sounds like I'm crying. More emotional than articulate. And Liz was kind of clenched, angry but very articulate. And Richard Foreman, very articulate about the whole thing. And listening to one of the critics, you can hear the hatred in her voice when she attacks Liz.

outlet and, adopting a black dialect, "jive" with a man at the other end of the line. Rather than forging a link, the ruse only accentuates the schism.

Willie continues her calls while the men continue their work and scenes from Act II of *Our Town* play on the monitors. After telephoning two bars, she finally reaches the men—now Kenny and Pigmeat (in the process of constructing the house they have constructed new identities for themselves). She asks them to come to her party and bring some liquor: "We don't have no liquid entertainment. That's right. We need some liquor for the punch. So listen honey, bring anything—whiskey, gin—anything you can get your hands on...."[23] Now transformed, the men pick up the liquor bottles and join the women for the birthday party. "ALL RIGHT. LET'S GO,"[24] Willie yells as the song "Hole in the Wall" explodes over the speakers. There follows the reenactment of the Pigmeat Markham routine and another radical change in the tonality of the performance. The loose, improvisational style is suddenly replaced by a wildly theatrical revel, a vaudeville of comedy and dance. But the abruptness of the change will only account for a small part of the inevitable shock.

* * *

Willem Dafoe: One night, of course, Kate did the telephone thing. And early, she was having a lot of success at getting stuff delivered.
David Savran: From uptown?
Kate Valk: There used to be a place on Grand Street.
Willem Dafoe: Well, various places. But on this particular night, in the heat of performance, we probably got about twenty people in the audience. And it's very early in open rehearsals. And the order of the show is scrambled. We got mostly the blackface stuff, and maybe we show the porn film at the end uncut, or something like that. But it's a mess, as far as how it's structured. Well, Kate gets on the phone and she calls up Cattleman.
Kate Valk: Under Dial-a-Steak.
[Laughter.]
Willem Dafoe: And she does the whole thing about, "Oh, yeah, four of

those, and get me some of them." And she really started stacking it up.
Kate Valk: I ordered barbecued chicken and ribs and potatoes and salad.
Willem Dafoe: Dial-a-Steak, like any convenience...
Kate Valk: I never asked the price.
Willem Dafoe: Well, I'm standing near the door, getting ready to go out to dance or something. And I hear a knock on the door. And there I am in blackface. And I open up the door and there's the biggest fucking black guy you've ever seen in your life with, dig this, one of those accident collars on. [Laughter.] This guy was mammoth, I'm not kidding. And it was winter, I remember he had one of those big sheepskin coats on. And he had two enormous shopping bags full of food. And he said something like, "Cattleman, sixty-eight dollars."
Peyton Smith: It was eighty. It wasn't sixty-four dollars.
Willem Dafoe: So he said, "That'll be sixty-four dollars." And I kind of, "Um, sir...."
Peyton Smith: In blackface.
[Laughter.]
Willem Dafoe: In blackface. And we had about twenty bucks.
Kate Valk: And there was nobody in the audience. We didn't have any money.
Willem Dafoe: And it was all done like, "Wait, wait..." until I realized there was nobody to go to.
Kate Valk: And the show's still going on.
Willem Dafoe: So I grabbed the NYU volunteer who ran the box that night and said, get the box office!! I had no choice. And I had him run upstairs and rifle through the drawers to get the money. And we're, like, practically shaking. We hardly had enough money for a tip, or anything.
Michael Stumm: Well, did you eat the food?
Elizabeth LeCompte: Yes.
Kate Valk: It was delicious!

* * *

The Blackface

Elizabeth LeCompte: I'd been interested in early recordings and films of comedians, mainly Laurel and Hardy and Abbott and Costello. Then I came upon some Pigmeat Markham records, a year or so before I started working on the piece. I had been working with stand-up comedy in Point Judith *and I wanted to take it one step further, with Pigmeat Markham. The routines interested me because of their performance tone and because of the idea of blackface. On a conscious level, it was a visual idea, an exercise in performance, a device to give the performance distance.*

Blackface offered a physical mask, as well as the throwaway vaudeville style and the "non-acting" we had explored in porn films for Nayatt School. *The structure of set-up and delivery offered a verbal mask that was interesting to me. The jokes offered a cultural mask and seemed extremely simple but were like parables. They seemed so elemental, so basic. There's no ironic play or psychologizing. They're very simple situations, the kind that I've always been attracted to.*

The remainder of Part II consists of a reconstruction of a Pigmeat Markham comedy routine originally performed at the Howard Theater in Washington, D.C. around 1965. Kenny arrives first, spilling the contents of a huge liquor bottle into the "punch," that is, onto the floor immediately in front of the spectators. Pig then arrives with his bottle and explains: "I went to the back of the drugstore, heh, heh, I know that the back of the drugstore was dark in there. I don't know what I got, but whatever it is I'm gonna pour it in. . . ." He pours the contents onto the floor and, taking a look at the label, exclaims "CASTOR OIL?!! Well, I'm a son of a gun, I done put the castor oil into the gals' punch."[25] They dance and scream toasts over the punch:

> PIG: The woodpecker pecked on the school house door.
> KENNY: Yeah.
> PIG: He pecked and he pecked till he couldn't peck no more.
> KENNY: Yeah.
> PIG: He come back the next day to peck some more.
> KENNY: Uh huh.
> PIG: He couldn't peck no more.
> GIRLS: Why?
> PIG: Cause his pecker was sore.[26]

They continue dancing until, one by one, they stop because each has to go "send a telegram." At the end of the sequence the meaning of the phrase becomes clear when Pig defecates in his pants and provides the skit with its punchline:

> PIG: Oh, me.
> WILLIE: Pigmeat.
> PIG: Oh, ho, ho, oh ho.
> . . . .
> WILLIE: Whatsa matter Pigmeat?
> PIG: Whadya mean?
> WILLIE: Don't tell me you gotta go send a telegram too?
> PIG: No, no, I done sent mine.[27]

Figure 7. *Route 1 & 9,* The Party
Kate Valk, Willem Dafoe.
(Bob Van Dantzig)

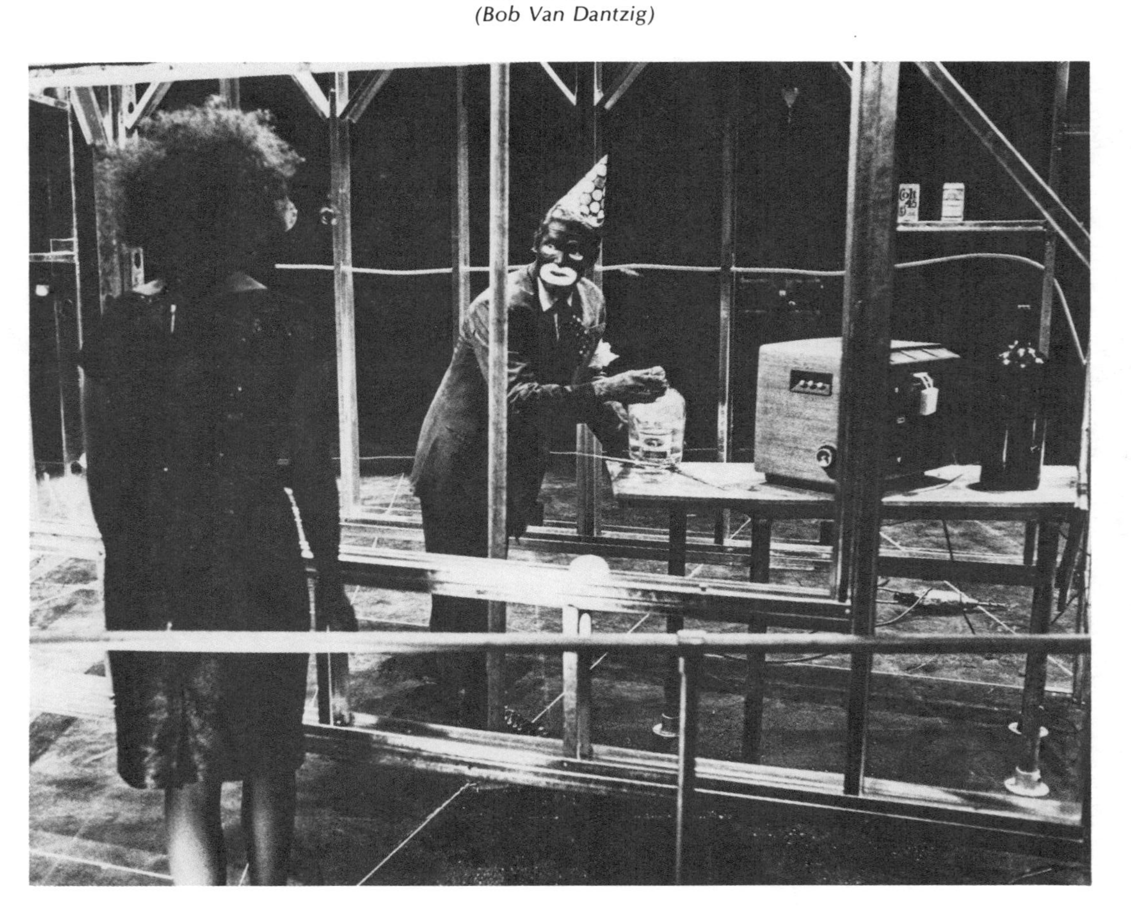

Figure 8. *Route 1 & 9,* The Party
Peyton Smith, Kate Valk, Willem Dafoe, Ron Vawter.
(Nancy Campbell)

Dewey "Sweet Papa Pigmeat" Markham (1904–1981) was a well-known black entertainer who began working in 1918 and performed almost exclusively for black audiences (late in his career, in 1968, he did have a "crossover" success with the song "Here Comes the Judge"). From the thirties to the fifties he played the vaudeville houses in blackface, mingling comic routines and songs. As in the minstrel show, his black characters were depicted as dim-witted, fun-loving and benignly criminal. By the late sixties his sexually explicit and scatological comedy was being supplanted by the more sophisticated and politically militant comedy of Godfrey Cambridge, Dick Gregory and others. These latter, having emerged in a period of racial turmoil and rising political consciousness, worked to replace the old stereotypes with more positive images.

Blackface was first used in mid-nineteenth-century minstrel show entertainments by performers who blackened their faces with burnt cork. Originally devised for the white man playing the servile black, it became an emblem of servitude, incompetence and submission. Ironically, however, in black vaudeville from the thirties to the fifties, written and performed by blacks for a black audience, Pigmeat Markham, like many of his contemporaries, chose to blacken their faces further and to whiten their lips. They appropriated the convention but reversed its meaning by using it in a different context, transforming the once-oppressive images into a source of irony and amusement.

In contrast with sophisticated black comedy, Pigmeat Markham's is politically ambiguous. To a white audience, it will appear to reinforce racist stereotypes. By portraying blacks as inept and carefree, it will seem to justify blacks' subordinate roles in society and allow oppression to remain hidden under the guise of paternalistic compassion. By alleging an innate servility, it will suggest that blacks will never rise to challenge the hegemony of an oppressive society. A black audience, however, will read these same stereotypes differently. Rather than accept the racist mythology, it will, to some extent, turn it against the ideology that created it. It will see the stereotypes as fictive rather than real. It will use laughter to ridicule and undermine the images of oppression.

As a political phenomenon, blackface remains deeply equivocal, either racist comedy or critique of racism, depending on one's perspective. In *Route 1 & 9* it works much as it does in Markham's comedy except that it turns its critical sights against both white and black stereotypes. Next to *Our Town,* the blackface comedy is an act of liberation. In contrast with the Puritan restraint of the Webbs and the Gibbses, the revels of Pig and his friends show a tremendous vitality. Their unbridled enthusiasm brings the coldness of Grover's Corners into sharp relief and holds Markham's comedy up as a life-affirming

> *Ron Vawter: One of the wonderful techniques that Liz chose to use, to shake you up, was uproarious comedy, that would really make you double over and laugh hard. And then when you were getting ready to take the next suck of wind in, you realized what you were laughing at.*

alternative to Wilder's graveyard meditation. The problem with the piece's reception arises because the images themselves, taken out of context, are undeniably racist. This fact is responsible, in large part, for the work's censure by NYSCA and others (including critics for the *New York Times* and the *Village Voice*). The allegation that the piece is racist, however, ignores the function of blackface in the piece as a whole and overlooks the possibility that its use might extend Pigmeat Markham's own implicit critique of its racist content. For both Markham and the Wooster Group, the blackface does not designate a real black persona but indicates that a theatrical convention is being deployed, a performance style which frees the performer to revel not in social reality, but in its unreality. As LeCompte explains, "The blackface is not sociological. It's a theatrical metaphor."[28] It sets the performer at liberty and unleashes a Dionysian revel which celebrates what is repressed in Grover's Corners: sexuality and organic process.

As Elizabeth LeCompte admits, the performance of the Pigmeat Markham routine remains deeply ambivalent: "The blackface is both a . . . painful representation of blacks and also wild, joyous, and nihilistic and, therefore, freeing."[29] This ambiguity is not limited to the blackface sequence but is ubiquitous in *Route 1 & 9.* Throughout the piece ethical, political and aesthetic phenomena resist any single interpretation which would derive from a polarization into two opposite formations, the one "good" and the other "bad." The piece may, at first glance, appear to be structured around an antithesis (Wilder vs. Markham), and yet the more closely one examines the interplay between the terms, the more useless and deceptive the antithesis becomes. Any interpretation of the work which places Wilder, white culture and Puritan restraint on one side, and Markham, black culture and raw vitality on the other, does so by erecting a sharp line between oppressor and oppressed. The performance undermines this duality to reveal the blackface, for example, as being simultaneously the sign of victimization and liberation, blindness and recognition. The deconstruction cuts through the dualist metaphysics that has produced these categories and implicates the spectator in the performance as both black and white, free and enslaved. It offers no ideological haven from which the action may be watched with impunity.

This strategy contrasts sharply with our pathway through the dialectical structure of *Our Town* (with Wilder as chaperon), in which

Figure 9. *Route 1 & 9*, The Party
Kate Valk; Willem Dafoe.
(Nancy Campbell)

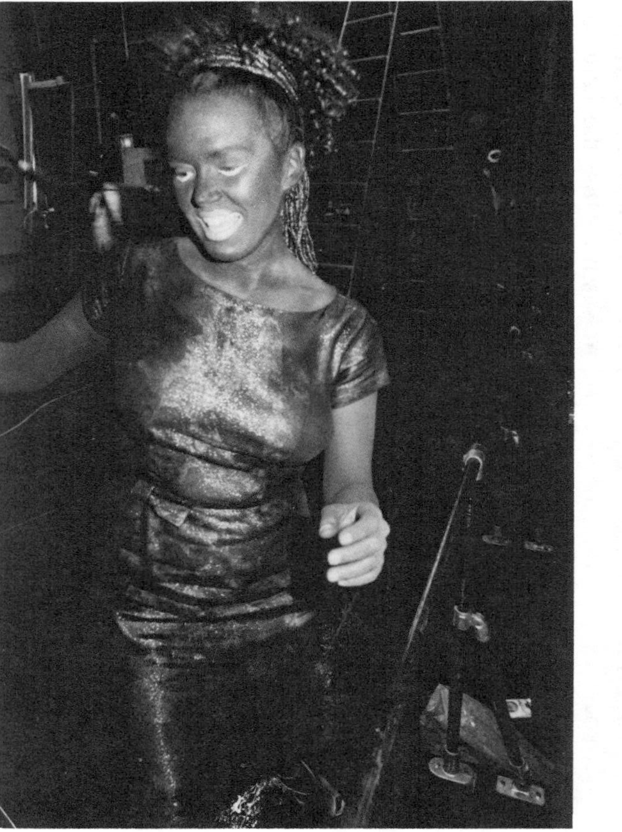

each act transcends the previous one and defines an ever-wider point of view. Act I presents the community, the collection of individuals which comprises the social, religious and economic fabric of Grover's Corners. Act II lifts George and Emily out of that fabric through their courtship and marriage and, at the wedding, brings the community together to accept a new dyad into the ever-revolving temporal cycle. The last act, in turn, leaves the temporal behind and reveals each individual to be part of something eternal and universal, the community of man. Like humanistic drama generally, *Our Town* moves from surface difference to inner identity; it strips away the mask to reveal the face of undifferentiated Man beneath. It will discover a common humanity *in spite of* (rather than *because of*) superficial differences. In *Route 1 & 9,* this metaphysics of face and mask is subsumed by a politics of non-hierarchical variance which corresponds, on the social level, to a vision of radical egalitarianism.

The transformation of *Our Town* into *Route 1 & 9* demands the development of an alternative way of perceiving personal and social dissimilarities. The perspective of liberal humanism constructs a vertical metaphor of depth—one penetrates through surface difference to discover inner identity. In the Wooster Group's work this is replaced by a metaphor of diffusion through a horizontal space—one sees individuals spread out through a social field. The former erects a sharp line of demarcation between outer and inner man, while the latter erases boundaries imposed by categorization along racial, religious or cultural lines. The former, in echo of the lecturer, perceives humanity as theme and variations, the latter sees only variations. The former constructs a stratified geological cross-section of human relations, the latter a surface map. Now, the very desire of humanism to penetrate the blackface is revealed to be an indignity, because it assumes that the humanity beneath is white.

* * *

The Death of the Dead (Part III)

Elizabeth LeCompte: I'd come to the public readings of Our Town *and listen to the performers read and sing hymns. The play stood alone for a long time, probably for three or four months without my touching it. I knew we were going to work with televisions—I wanted to work with televisions. And, in fact, we bought four monitors and a deck before we had any idea of what was going on. I just knew how they would look in the space, that they would start far away from the audience and come very close. And they would mirror the physical actions of the dances down below. Or the dances would mirror the physical action of the monitors descending from above. And sometime, in the middle of the process, I realized that when you took the Stage Manager out of* Our Town, *it became a soap opera. So I took the last act and worked with Willem on separating it into scenes, close-up scenes with a soap opera feel. We did improvs around soap opera style, using TVs. And we watched soap opera. I would time the segments in between the ads. And from that, we got a kind of rhythm. The actors' pacing is soap opera but the visual image is more "portraiture," the actors speaking directly to the camera which serves as point of view.*

Part III is "The Cemetery Scene: In Which Four Chairs are Placed on the Stage Facing the Audience to Represent Graves." Jim Clayburgh lowers the four monitors into their foreground position, about seven feet above the stage floor, and the focus shifts from the live performers to the television screens. The alarm bell rings for 30 seconds and Wilder's

> *Jim Clayburgh: There was one great cameo role in* Route 1 & 9 *which everyone forgets: the WASP preppy cranking while the black people danced.*

elegiac last act rises above the plaintive dissonance of Ives's "The Housatonic at Stockbridge." On the monitors the excerpts unfold gently, in powerful contrast to the Pigmeat Markham routine just completed. The quietly understated performances, replicated four times through the space, combine with the sweetness of the language and the emotions expressed to acquire an almost hypnotic power. The juxtaposition against the blackface, however, suggests another interpretation of Wilder's last act: musing on life and death, the characters, now in their graves, articulate less the specificity of temporal existence than the end of the culture they represent. Now the subtitle of the piece *(The Last Act)* comes into focus as the sweet dream of an American community, the humanist idyll of transcendence, of life after death, passes before the audience's eyes, as though for the last time. Like the newly dead of Grover's Corners, the spectators have been rudely and unexpectedly awakened, watching the four live performers who are trying not to disturb the television ghosts (whose number includes their own whitefaced selves), while the Stage Manager's warning words echo through the space, "You not only live it; but you watch yourself living it."[30]

* * *

Reading Our Town

Kate Valk: Route 1 & 9 *was really Liz's meditation on death. Her father had just died that summer. The death of the dead in* Our Town. *And then, sure enough, right after we opened the piece, Pigmeat Markham dies. It just seemed like a wild coincidence. Liz and I went to his funeral. It was really neat, in a way. It was so weird because I'd never seen him. I'd only listened to his records. And then, to see him in person when he was dead.... It was weird. But the people there were wonderful. All these old, old black entertainers from the Apollo, when it was in its heyday. It was really very interesting to see all these people. Like this real tall, skinny woman, black woman, with a big blond wig on.*

Because of the new context in which Wilder's last act is placed, its ostensible subject—death, also a last act—is necessarily presented quite differently from the way it would be in a live production of the complete play. The dead are now placed, not in ordinary chairs, but on television screens in extreme close-up. Quietly philosophical, they have bid farewell to the world and are now detached from the passions of life. Emily arrives among them, her already ironic comment acquiring both a new irony and a new veracity: "Live people don't understand, do they?...They're sort of shut up in little boxes...."[31] Both dramatically and ideologically, Emily has found her final resting place. Newly coffined, she comments on the confinement of the living, failing to recognize that she is now literally shut up in a little box, the 21-inch repository of white middle-class culture, reaching into every home. The four characters below, meanwhile, now threefold alive in contrast with the "dead" characters, culture and medium, do not understand Emily (the old black-and-white television on the table in their house is turned off). Lost in their own world, they neither listen to her nor mourn for the dead who hold power above them.

In *Route 1 & 9* the relationship between life and death, black and white, man and woman, live and recorded media is defined less as a static polarity than as an insistent crossing over. Just as Emily "crosses over" in the last act, so the live performers cross over racially when, at the end of Part III, they wipe off most of their make-up, and sexually, when the men put on women's clothing. At the same time, they cross over into the earlier work by donning costumes from the preceding pieces. And all four cross over into *Our Town* since they are each given a role to play in the videotape. In the early minstrel shows (where white male performers enacted all the roles) racial and sexual boundaries were transgressed in order to reaffirm their fixity. With the Wooster Group, on the contrary, the act of crossing over recovers its disruptive potential, threatening both the highly stratified society living along Route 1 & 9 and the television-style realism that it cherishes.

At the end of Part III the performers momentarily take on the most powerful and suggestive mask in *Route 1 & 9*—the vampire. Just before their transformation, George's face is shown on the monitors, sobbing, while the women, off-screen, comment laconically on his pain and castigate him for his show of emotion: "Goodness! That ain't no way to behave!"[32] Suddenly "Jump on the Line" sounds and the four, in what remains of their blackface, begin to dance furiously, shaking their skirts wildly, a horrible grimace on their faces. They approach the audience, blood streaming down their faces, their mouths gaping open to reveal vampire fangs. The restrained emotionality of *Our Town* and the constraints placed on the live performers to remain quiet during the video now explode into a frenzy of blood lust and rage. Finally, all that has been contained bursts forth in the passion of these vampires. They are the shells of Markham's characters, after the life has been sucked out of them by the roles they assume, unleashing their rage in what remains of their blackface. Simultaneously, they are the occupants of Wilder's cemetery, now revealed as the bloodless undead, shaking their skirts obscenely and releasing their repressed desires in a fury of murderous passion. The emblems of an impossible union between life and death, Pigmeat and Emily, they enfold oppressor and victim into a grotesque unity. They have returned to native soil, to dance wildly on the graves of the dead. They have come home, the true gods of that stretch of highway, Route 1 & 9, the quintessential humanists who, in their lust for blood, would make the world over in their own image.

In *Route 1 & 9* the vampire sets loose all those desires and fears, most notably sexual ones, which, to some degree, are repressed in white middle-class society. Act II of *Our Town* may be concerned explicitly with courtship and marriage but the treatment of these rituals is radically de-sexualized. Just before the wedding Mrs. Webb (in a speech shown on the monitors in Part II) confesses that she has never told Emily anything about sex: "I hope some of her girl friends have told her a thing or two. It's cruel, I know, but I couldn't bring myself to say anything. I went into it blind as a bat myself." The failure to recognize the role of sexuality does not, of course, reduce its impact on human relationships. On the contrary, its repression effects a displacement which, by making desire unmentionable, transforms it into fear, and not only fear of physical contact. In *Our Town* the impossibility of acknowledging desire produces a sickness, a *Weltschmerz* (as the lecturer might say), to which the women, as sexual beings, especially fall victim. To the end of her speech quoted above Mrs. Webb suddenly adds, "The whole world's wrong, that's what's the matter."[33] Shortly thereafter as Emily, "frightened," is brought to the altar she says, "I never felt so alone in my whole life. And George over there, looking so . . . !" She prefers to leave the sentence incomplete rather than choose between "desirable" and "terrifying." In this context of sexuality repressed, the two words have come to mean the same thing, just as "love" is now transformed to its opposite: "I *hate* him. I wish he were dead."[34] The synonymy of desire

Peyton Smith: It was amazing, the number of people who didn't see the pornography. Because it was down on the stage floor and they'd just look up at the color monitors. "It doesn't exist," they'd think. "I'm just going to stare up there. I don't want to be a voyeur."

and terror has become the mark of a guilt and self-loathing that is never purged. In the last act, it may be for more than the sake of pathos that Wilder has Emily die in childbirth.

In *Our Town* death denotes less the end of being than the end of passion. The dead sit forever serenely and coldly in their straight-backed chairs suffering the termination of and punishment for desire. In relationship to this "heaven" of renunciation and sterility, the revels of the four live performers (which take place before the transformation into vampires), as muffled as they are in Part III, appear as the deepest desecration. ("We are trying to be quiet. We are ostensibly trying not to interfere with the last act of *Our Town* playing on the upper monitor system."[35]) Below they dance, drink and kiss, crack jokes and laugh, Pig/Ron blows his nose, while above Mrs. Webb is directed to embrace

Elizabeth LeCompte: Gradually it evolved that the scene would be the continuation of Willie's party. We constructed it slowly, running improvs next to the video, until they got more and more set, and the scene had a tempo. We used the video as the "music."

and kiss her daughter "in her characteristic matter-of-fact manner."[36] All the bodily functions that have been repressed at Emily's twelfth birthday are celebrated at Annie's party. The floor is slippery with spilt booze while the four carouse, snot in their noses and shit in their pants. In *Route 1 & 9* this intense physicality betokens a life far more material than Emily's and, by implication, the necessity of a death far more conclusive and blank than that dramatized in *Our Town*. In fact, Wilder's last act is not really about death at all. It offers, rather, the repressive and ultimately

Figure 10. *Route 1 & 9,* The Last Act
Willem Dafoe, Peyton Smith, Marissa Hansell on monitors.
(Bob Van Dantzig)

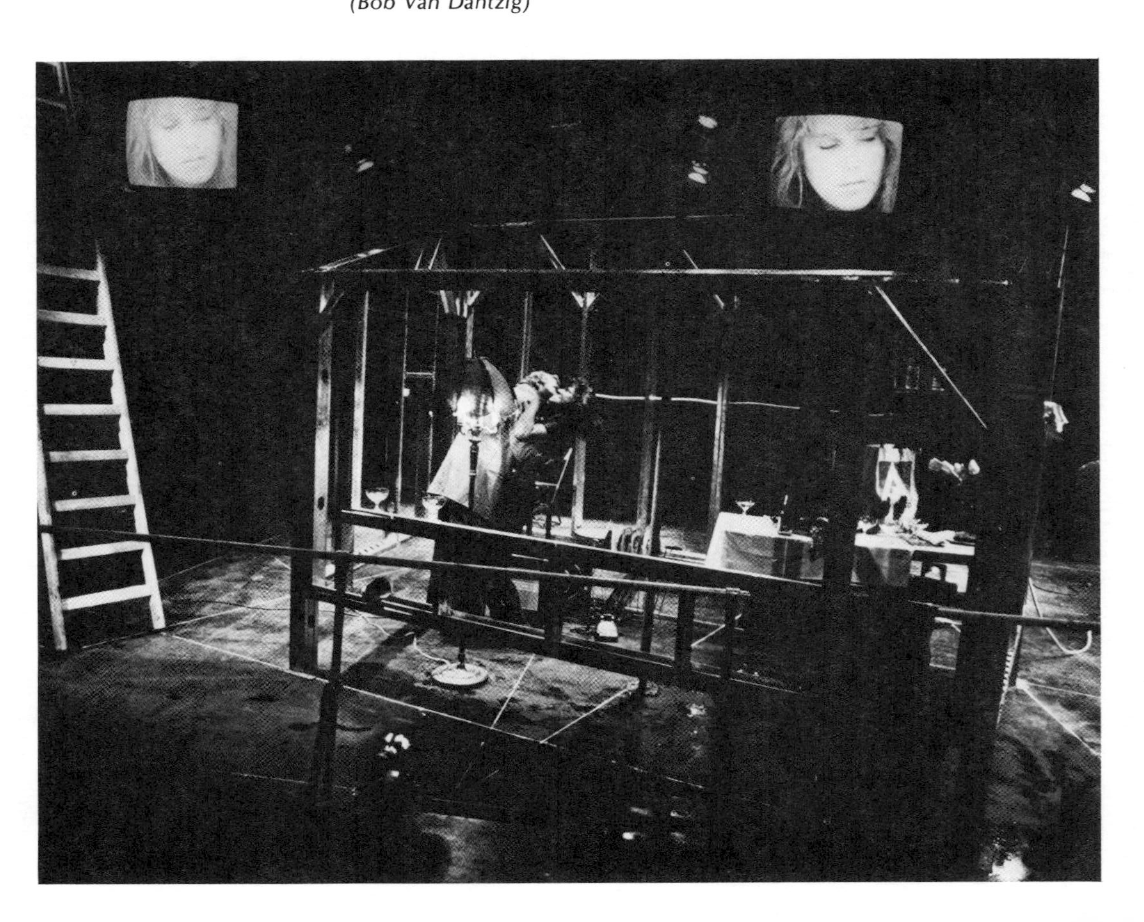

romantic mythology of a life free from passion which disallows a confrontation with death. Against this, the Markham routine is a terrible affront because it everywhere assaults us with the inevitability of death. Pig's failure to control his bowels is a scatological profanation in the rarified world of Wilder's dead because it evokes a fear of a death now seen as the conclusive loss of control over one's own body. As LeCompte explains: "The defecation joke is funny and disgusting. There's a wonderful ambivalence because it's a horrific social no-no and at the same time an elemental thing that's part of us. It's not just obscene. The joke is a way of laughing at death."[37]

What is most disturbing about the blackface sequence is less the quotation of racist stereotypes than their use to reveal what has been repressed in the culture that created them. For a society that imposes a schism between intellect and emotion, soul and body, man and woman, white and black, and prioritizes the first of the pair, *Route 1 & 9* comes as a horrifying violation of decorum. Not only does the piece reject these priorities, it rejects the very act of prioritization. The blackface, the "imperfect superposition of one identity over another," like the cross dressing, deliberately dissolves the frontiers, subverting the polarities. As Jeffrey Jones explains in the *Appeal*, "Images which express the furtive desire to dissolve these boundaries evoke the greatest cultural anxiety, and are either suppressed altogether or tolerated briefly. . . . "[38] Blackface and drag threaten the separation between races and sexes and create a hybrid (like the vampire) that blurs the distinctions that have been so carefully erected. The possibility of successfully crossing over, of a white person being taken for a black, is unnerving to those who cherish these cultural boundaries. And note here that the specific example of alleged racial ridicule singled out by NYSCA, Willie's series of telephone conversations, is the one time in the piece when a white person did indeed "pass" as black.[39]

In the end, *Route 1 & 9* does not exonerate its audience. The exposure of so much that lies concealed in American culture also brings

> *Kate Valk: After doing* Route 1 & 9, *everybody's heads were spinning. Because Liz couldn't say, "No, it's not racist." Yes, it is racist. Yes, I'm racist. You're a liar if you say you're not. That's what it was about. And then, to be censored. It just seemed that suddenly the issues were burning.*

to light assumptions and emotions that we harbor regarding racial difference. (Here, the first person pronoun becomes crucially operative.) As members of a "liberal" or, at times, a professedly "radical" community (either the theatre or the university), we devotees of experimental theatre take a certain pride in what we believe to be our non-racist attitudes and practices. It is precisely this pride that the piece attacks. For despite the great racial diversity of this country, the vast majority who read this book will be, like the Wooster Group's audience, white. "Maybe once every two or three performances we have a black person in the audience," LeCompte notes.[40] The theatrical and educational communities are, for the most part, as polarized along racial lines as the society to which they belong. In an America only three or four generations removed from the emancipation of black slaves, it is virtually impossible not to hold racist attitudes. Perhaps the most powerful effect of *Route 1 & 9* is that it leads admirers and deprecators alike to re-examine racial attitudes, not simply on a gross cultural level, but in one's minute personal interactions, not with a view toward an impossible escape from racism but toward an understanding of how it functions and how it corrupts us.

In an article in the *Village Voice* in November 1981, Elizabeth LeCompte is asked about the racial politics of *Route 1 & 9*. She explains that she realizes that there are

> white people in America who would consider themselves not racist. . . . You may consider yourself not subjectively racist, but objectively if you exist and make money in a culture that is obviously living off a third world people, you [are participating in racism]. In that sense, I'd say yes, this piece is racist. Right down the line.[41]

As LeCompte understands, racism is deeply inscribed in American culture—not simply on the level of attitude, individual and collective, but in the workings of the economic infrastructure. The more we look about us and examine all that we take for granted, the more conscious we must become of a racism to which we may be an innocent and unwitting party but which, regardless, plays itself out through us. As members of a culture that trades in signs, we hope to abolish racism by erasing its symbols—like blackface—in the belief that this action will erase the underlying fact. In the end, however, the refusal to recognize racial difference, less than erasing the fact, suppresses the awareness of the results of racism. As we blind ourselves to difference, with the best intentions, we fail to notice the institution of disparity in the social sphere, in opportunities, education and pay. If *Route 1 & 9* is to leave its mark, we will, at some point, look around us and echo Emily's line from the last act: "So all this was going on and we never noticed."[42]

* * *

Elizabeth LeCompte: In the controversy over Route 1 & 9, *one of the things that was said was, "There is no distance on it." In other words, it was racist, because there wasn't a character or voice of authority saying, "Look, this is a horrible thing. This is racist." I suspect that if Spalding had been off to the side saying, in one way or another, "I deplore this," it would have been alright. Everyone would have said, "Oh, this guy is dealing with his racism on the stage," instead of the audience having to deal with the racism unmediated.*

Peyton Smith: It seemed to me quite obvious what we were doing. I was shocked. But I've been shocked by the response to everything we've done. Because we are self-contained, and we aren't very aware of what the outside... I mean, how do you know? I thought when we started that blackface was... illegal. We all laughed at that. But I was quite shocked that the piece was ever perceived that way. And then you sense the distance, even more strongly, from the whole community.

* * *

Alternate Routes (Part IV)

Elizabeth LeCompte: The first part of the piece we made was the porn film. We did that before I'd even known we were going to make Route 1 & 9. *I took that material, after the fact, and attached it to the end of Part III, without dovetailing it or cutting it in. We made the film as a story: a drive out of the City to a house where the porn was shot. What I did with the footage was cut it in half and run the parts simultaneously, rather than sequentially. So the elements that went into the piece were: Clifton Fadiman, the building, Pigmeat Markham,* Our Town, *and the porn film. They gradually grew into each other. I took the part where the guys were building, added the girls' phone calls in over that, and then spliced it together with the girls suddenly calling the guys. Connection. But the lives started out separately, both artistically and literally. Gradually, I just overlapped and scissored. But that wasn't until just before we opened. With* Route 1 & 9 *I decided not to judge what material was relevant and what was not. Anything that we were working with would enter into the dialogue. So the porn film came in as a dialogue with the piece itself, in a way. Whatever we work on,* that *is the piece that's happening, because that's what we're thinking about.*

Part IV, "Route 1 & 9: In Which a Van Picks Up Two Hitchhikers and Heads South," consists of two videotapes, transferred from super-8 film, played simultaneously. Above, the four monitors feature the tape described in the subtitle, an escape from New York along the New Jersey Turnpike to the exit for Route 1 & 9. Below, the old black-and-white television is rolled out of the frame house and on it is shown a tape of a man and woman having sexual intercourse. The videotapes provide a pseudo-documentary epilogue that breaks with the highly theatrical style of Part III and directs the spectator's attention, like Willie's phone calls, to the world outside the theatre. The cool, unassertive presentation offers a meditative counterpoint to the wildness of "The Cemetery Scene." It initiates a leave-taking but in no way offers a resolution. The distance that *Route 1 & 9* charts, between Markham and Wilder, black and white, uptown and downtown is extenuated by the unsettling juxtaposition of a drive on the New Jersey Turnpike against a "porn film," of the fine color monitors against a television that looks like it was salvaged from a junk yard (it is, in fact, a 1964 English television). Eschewing the final synthesis provided by Wilder (in transcendence) and Markham (in a punchline), Part IV oscillates between points which, like the distance between the integers 1 and 9, are as far apart as they can be.

The distances in Part IV are not simply physical and ideological but interpretive as well, since both videotapes defy a straightforward or unequivocal reading. Seven feet above the floor we watch the driver (Elizabeth LeCompte) as she leaves the darkness of the Holland Tunnel (whose entrance is but a few blocks from the Performing Garage) and emerge into the bright morning sunshine. The van moves along quickly and silently (there is no soundtrack) as a man inside (Ron Vawter) smokes a cigarette and sips a cup of coffee (the camera is mounted alternately in and on the van). There is a sense of liberation here, of taking control of the future and the space into which one is headed. For LeCompte, driving provides a sense of comfort: "I have no anxiety, because my purpose is to drive, and you don't drive unless you're going somewhere."[43] Certainly, after the horror of the vampires the trip may indeed be a liberation which (literally) dispells the darkness. The sun, low on the horizon, glistens on the Manhattan skyline and beams into the van. As the spectator studies the gas stations and the Holiday Inn, however, he may be reminded that the horror stretches far beyond New York and that the suburban sprawl through which the van passes is as much home to these spirits, both Wilder's and Markham's, as the City itself. He may also recall that New Jersey was designated, at the beginning of Part II, as the home of the "cold" and "indifferent" people who populate Route 1 & 9. As the drive proceeds, the one "event" in the tape, the stop to pick up the hitchhikers (Willem Dafoe and Libby Howes), produces the same sense of uncertainty as the drive itself. The offer of a ride may be an act of kindness to two strangers but it also may evoke anxiety: What if, to articulate this fear, the hitchhikers are dangerous? What if the driver has plans of his own for them?

* * *

Peyton Smith: And then, the pornography upset audiences terribly here, too.
David Savran: Really?
Peyton Smith: You didn't know that?
David Savran: I guess I heard about it, but it seemed so overshadowed by . . .
Peyton Smith: By the rest.
David Savran: Liz did tell me she thought initially that that would be the problem.
Peyton Smith: Right. In terms of the debate, the pornography wasn't a big issue. Although it was brought up in the discussions. But in performance, we'd do the whole party scene and the wild dance and then we'd go sit down and the pornography would come up. So we would be on stage, but passive. And people would start talking. And they didn't talk during the blackface. But they'd start, "Oh, come on!" And, "Is this it? Is the play over? Do we have to sit and watch this? I'm not gonna watch this!" And we were supposed to be sitting there passively. We weren't supposed to look at the audience, we had to keep our eyes down, because Liz didn't want it confrontational. And I wanted to look up so badly, to see who's angry and wants to walk out. [Laughs.] I wanted to know so badly.

* * *

The silent videotape shown below features the performers who played the hitchhikers going through a series of sexual turns. The lighting is angular (much like the sun over New York City in the tape shown above) and the camera rarely allows a glimpse of the faces. The stark black-and-white footage captures the play of light over the soft curves of the bodies and the darkness of the crevices on which the attention of the performers is focused. The sex sequences are graphic, the couple trying various positions. They are less concerned with performing for the camera than allowing it to oversee them, much like a voyeur. The "director" (Ron Vawter) is occasionally visible, holding up a microphone, and there are several brief shots interspersed showing a few people seated at a dinner table in another part of the room.

As screened on the old black-and-white television, the "porn film" (like late night cable TV) provides yet another release after the repressive atmosphere of Grover's Corners. Following the last act of *Our Town*, it is a cemetery desecration, a dance on the graves which, like the high kicks of the vampires, further defiles Wilder's Puritan romanticism. (It also, like the blackface, raises questions of exploitation and censorship.) Its mixture of eroticism and death, liberation and defilement may be heightened by the spectator's realization that the man in the tape, Willem Dafoe, plays the part of George Gibbs in the video of *Our Town* (LeCompte, however, did not intend the identification). Regardless, the "porn film" visualizes the fantasy that George and Emily finally "rut," dispelling the sterility of Grover's Corners, as the rest of the family waits dinner for them. It is both a flashback and epilogue to *Our Town*

Ron Vawter: We wanted to create this very private and possibly obscene image that's very lively, but small, on the TV, against the end of the graveyard, the meditation on death. Literally, a little procreative act.

("Goodness! That ain't no way to behave!"), both end and beginning, the consummation of the courtship in Act II and the action which will assure Emily's death in childbirth. Here, the triumph of the body, shut up in a little box, restores the ambiguity of that seventeeth-century euphemism—death—fusing in the shudder of orgasm, the climax of passion with the rattle of death.

Finally, the force of *Route 1 & 9* stems not from its conclusive analysis of an "object" (be it racism or humanism or pornography) but from its examination of our role in the creation of these "objects" and our complicity with forces of dehumanization. In this sense, the transformation of *Our Town* into *Route 1 & 9* by no means dismisses the impact of the first person plural pronoun in Wilder's title. What in *Our Town* designates a universal community of which we are all a part, becomes, in its deconstruction by the Wooster Group, the mark of our immersion in a network of relations that renders each of us simultaneously victim and victimizer.

The screening of the two videotapes in the final part of *Route 1 & 9* signals the intersection of past and future, the juxtaposition of a flashback (the "porn film") against a flash forward (the exit from the Performing Garage, SoHo and Manhattan). It thereby imitates the process of contemplation that is about to begin when the spectator leaves the theatre and, immersed in new activity, remembers what has passed before him. Watching the two tapes, he may feel disoriented, faced with the impossibility of taking in the monitors and the old television at the same time, looking up and down, catching only fragments of each and losing the continuity. But this feeling will be dwarfed when he walks out into a night which holds far more potential disorientation and

Elizabeth LeCompte: I used the driving away to show that New York exists here. And New Jersey's over here. It's like some kind of placement in the world that I need. And in the most literal sense, it gives a perspective, quote unquote, capital P.

uncertainty than anything the darkness of the theatre may shelter. No longer will he be able to sit back unseen and watch the performance in silence. For now, as *Route 1 & 9* ends just as the van prepares to climb the exit ramp to Route 1 & 9, the action is about to begin, as he leaves the theatre and enters a cold and indifferent world.

* * *

Ron Vawter: It was very difficult for a couple of years because we thought we'd really gone too far. We were told that you can't confront, not only the audience, with such volatile possibilities, but you can't confront yourself with it publicly either, as artists. That was even more damaging than the problems we had with the audience: that we were being punished for exploring our own attitudes. Now that is censorship in the worst sense. We are artists working in a public forum, so the only place we can show our work is in public presentation. I think, also, it was a bad time. A lot of people were just in the wrong . . . in different spaces. I think when we bring it back people are going to say, "Oh my God, this was such a wonderful thing. Why four or five years ago . . . ?" I think it will be so clear what our intentions were that there won't be any offense. But at that time nobody was taking any risks. That we should examine racism in ourselves, and in the audience . . . well, it just frightened everybody.

Elizabeth LeCompte: The material is the important thing. I always go back to that as a way of interesting myself in a process, so that I have something objective, something outside myself that I'm dealing with.
David Savran: And all the material that you use is marked by an internal contradiction, a conflicting response on your part.
Elizabeth LeCompte: Yes, it gives me great pleasure. But, of course, it always evokes a conflicting response in the audience. To very few people does it give the same. . . . I'm saying that I get great pleasure from that contradiction. I get great pleasure in facing it off, almost as an enemy. Conquering it by facing it.
David Savran: So it's the material you're confronting, not the audience.
Elizabeth LeCompte: Yes—but with the audience as witness. Obviously, for many audience members, it's not pleasurable. I don't think that that's what you necessarily go to the theatre for. In fact, I don't know where you go for that. . . . It's a very hard thing. But I think that's the politics of the piece.

Figure 11. *Nayatt School*, Part III, The Chicken Heart
Libby Howes, Spalding Gray.
(Bob Van Dantzig)

Part II

From the Rhode Island Trilogy to *Hula*: Simple Demonstrations of the Laws of Physics

Most perceptive students... must see through the fundamental misrepresentation in the typical lecture-table "experiment," in which a subtle and beautiful phenomenon is distorted beyond all recognition in order that the ephemeral visual clues can be amplified for the benefit of people seated at a distance. They must be aware of the fact that demonstrations tend to wrench phenomena from their natural context in order to make a "main point" stand out clearly before the average student. And the most interested and intuitive students must be very uncomfortable when... the attention is displaced from the real effect to a substitute or analogue, so that a gross model... becomes the means of discussing a basic phenomenon... without giving the class a glimpse of the actual case itself.

Gerald Holton, "Conveying Science by Visual Presentation"

Representation

Elizabeth LeCompte: The initial design for Rumstick Road *had the booth in the center, on top, because of the picture I have here in "Conveying Science by Visual Presentation." Every night I'd go home and get into the bathtub and sit with this book, so it's all buckled. I'd read it over and over again. Later, I had an idea, coming off this thing of lecture-demonstration, that we would do a science experiment in* Nayatt School, *but it never came to be. And it carries over through all the pieces.*
David Savran: In Nayatt *the huge jar of maraschino cherries looked like pickled lab specimens.*

Elizabeth LeCompte: That's all the leftover stuff from those ideas. But it's just the leftover, because originally I had all kinds of ideas about wonderful science experiments that we'd do, actual ones that are done in high schools and colleges, just to demonstrate different things.
Ron Vawter: The laws of physics. Simple demonstrations of the laws of physics.

* * *

The lecture-demonstration never fully analyzes or explicates experiential reality, for it always transforms what it attempts to explain. Either it isolates a phenomenon in an experimental situation that bears little resemblance to its natural site, or else it replaces it altogether by another one, of a completely different nature, on a completely different temporal and spatial scale. Thus, as an explanation of the movement of waves, the water-wave tank may be a useful visualization, illuminating the *principles* of wave interaction. But the demonstration itself will not, if only because of its scale, provide a realistic representation of the play of ocean surf. Or yet again, Brownian motion (the random movement of microscopic particles in a gas or liquid) can be represented by using a tray of mechanically agitated steel balls. This visualization may help the viewer understand what Brownian motion is, although it operates according to entirely different principles. In both examples, the demonstration is no more than a metaphor for the original.

In the classroom, a phenomenon to be studied is removed from nature and the network of contingent events which comprises its context. It is analyzed either as a self-contained, discrete event, or else is represented analogically by a model that bears no more than a casual likeness to the original. In either case, the naturally occuring event is nowhere to be seen. Instead, a replacement is manipulated to a predetermined end: the demonstrator knows from the beginning the physical laws that the presentation has been designed to prove. His energy is directed toward explaining scientific principles to the curious onlookers—not by showing the richness and complexity of the phenomenon, but by simplifying it, by reducing it to a straightforward and wholly visible process.

When Elizabeth LeCompte speaks of her activity as lecture-demonstration, she does so fully aware of the complexity of the phemonena she studies and the distortion requisite to all representation. As a result, her work is less a simple demonstration than its deconstruction: a representation turned back upon itself and offered as a critique of the assumptions, goals and methods which have allowed it to come into being. In the Wooster Group's work, the demonstration is problematicized; it is revealed to be an activity highly charged with ideology, dependent upon a certain mode of linear thinking and the belief that phenomena can be isolated and re-presented and yet retain their uniformity and stability. The work challenges the "neutrality" of the scientific method to reveal that the phenomena under investigation will always be transformed in the process of presentation by a demonstrator whose credibility is always on the line.

All of the Wooster Group's pieces use certain characteristics of the lecture-demonstration but call them into question in the very act of appropriation. The performance of *Rumstick Road,* for example, presents a complex phenomenon in an apparently objective, scientific way, using documentary material and a performance style suggestive of the cool statement of fact rather than the expression of an impassioned or opinionated subjectivity. In the end, however, the mode of performance is revealed to be part of the "problem," as the work's apparent objectivity is linked to the questionable therapeutic methods it is examining. Like *Rumstick,* all of the pieces present a complex phenomenon by manipulating people and production elements with smooth efficiency. And like spectators at a well-rehearsed demonstration, we search for the elusive original phenomenon by trying to unravel the counterpoint of disparate elements.

The search comes to a halt once we recognize that LeCompte's sleight of hand turns the demonstration inside out. The focus is no longer solely on the represented phenomenon, but on the elements that encourage us to intuit its presence: light, sound, film, video, scenic environment, texts and performers. Because we are habituated to consider the theatre an imitative art form, we expect that these physical elements will work together to represent an absent subject, the tapes and slides in *Rumstick Road,* for example, conjuring the several absent members of the Gray family. To believe, however, that these absent ones form the main subject of the piece is to overlook the complexity of the live action and the Wooster Group's incessant questioning of the theatre's mimetic capability. The aggressiveness of the performance focuses the spectator's attention on the incessant interplay between the absent subjects (among them, the Gray family) and the means used to produce them, more as optical illusions than dramatic characters. The theatrical means dissolve the referents, in much the same way that Mary Tyrone's beloved fog shuts out the world in *Long Day's Journey into Night*: "You feel that everything has changed, and nothing is what it seemed to be."[1] *Rumstick Road* confronts the audience not with the transparency of language and spectacle, but with their opacity, and with the knowledge that these revenants exist only in image and sound. It leads the audience to recognize that the performance can be no more than a similucrum that transforms utterly the people and things to which it refers, that the theatrical representation is necessarily a *mis*representation.

* * *

Text

Elizabeth LeCompte: When I choose texts, they're random in a way. I feel I could use any text. That was something that started very early with Spalding. I could pick anything in this room and make a piece that's just as complete as L.S.D. *I could take three props here: the printing on the back of that picture, this book, and whatever's in this pile of papers, and make something that would mean as much, no more nor less, than what I've constructed in the performance space downstairs.*
Spalding Gray: It comes from living in a space and having it your clubhouse. I mean, just look around this room and think of the possibilities.
Elizabeth LeCompte: So you don't have to worry about meaning, it's all here. It's like this space is an extension of our lives. I think we've been very lucky to be able to work this way because most people are dislocated and have to choose their props.
Spalding Gray: Right.
Elizabeth LeCompte: We don't have to choose them.
Spalding Gray: And that carried over to my monologues. Because what I do is found poetry. I simply work with the stuff that comes, that's in the room, in the life.
Elizabeth LeCompte: Remember when you auditioned for Williamstown?
Spalding Gray: Right.
Elizabeth LeCompte: And you had that prepared stuff?
Spalding Gray: I had all this prepared stuff that I was going to do for Williamstown Theatre Festival and they kept me waiting so long, I got very frustrated and took the instructions and used them as an audition. I said, "If we cut you off, that doesn't mean that we don't like you. . . . " And this was enough for them to see me and bring me back. They didn't know me at all.
Elizabeth LeCompte: Finally, it's not about that text, it's about a different relationship to meaning and text than we'd been working with before.

Elizabeth LeCompte: The reason why I keep something . . . for instance, someone will say, "This doesn't work here. Ronnie getting up [in Part III of L.S.D.*] and going over and touching the house doesn't work here because he's got to be over there, to tune his drums, or something." But by chance, in an improv, Ronnie has done that. And I take that chance occurrence and say, that is the* sine qua non, *that is the beginning, that is the text. I cannot stray from that text. As someone else would use the lines of a playwright, I use that action as the baseline. I can't just erase it. He's made that text by that action and I must adjust around it. It's an action-text that may have nothing to do with any thematic thing we're working on. I call it chance work, like throwing a handful of beans up in the air. And when they come down on the floor, I must use that pattern as one pole against which I work my dialectic. I cannot alter it unless, somehow, another structure, another bunch of beans that I throw up in the air, comes into conflict with the first. Then one bean must move, one way or the other. But only at that point.*

All of the Wooster Group pieces begin with a body of found "objects" much as the lecture–demonstration always begins with a phenomenon or case in point as its subject. These raw materials are of five different orders: first, recordings of private interviews or public events, such as, in *Rumstick Road,* Spalding Gray's interviews with his father and grandmother, or in *L.S.D.,* the excerpts from the Leary/Liddy debate; second, previously written dramatic material, either from "classic" works such as *Our Town,* or from comic skits, or from plays written specifically for the Group, such as Jim Strahs's "Rig"; third, prerecorded sound, music, film and video, such as the video of *Our Town* or Ken Kobland's film, "By The Sea," as used in *Point Judith*; fourth, the performance space that is left from the last piece, containing various architectonic elements that will be used in the development of a new piece; and finally, improvised action-texts: gesture, dance and language to be used either as an independent strand in the work or as an elaboration of material from one of the other categories.

Like a maker of collages, LeCompte takes up a found object, a fragment, that comes onto the scene without fixed meaning, and places it against other fragments. The interwoven network of objects that results is a text, within which the component object is newly produced (or re-produced), the result of active process, fabrication, work. A sense of the object's arbitrary nature is preserved, however, by virtue of its *dis*location within the text. Rather than being cemented to another, each is tied to the others loosely by a kind of noise, both sonic and gestural, a constantly changing background interference. Thus bound, it remains discrete, its casual nature now evident as a causal disjunction, a separation induced by a rupture of the laws of cause and effect.

The textual network of which every Wooster Group piece is composed is never simply an elaboration of a single pretext, since none of the floating fragments, regardless of its size or prestige, ever becomes a fixed center around which a piece is built. Even *The Cocktail Party,* once it is incorporated into *Nayatt School,* stands as both far more and far less than a pretext for the latter work. For all its metaphysical weightiness and dramatic solidity, the Eliot play, as performed by a group of children, and set off against a sketch about an ever-growing chicken heart, is used not to center the piece but to question the possibility of a balanced, centered structure. Rather than quoting it, properly and demurely, the piece pulls *The Cocktail Party* apart and offers it as a sacrifice, much like Celia Coplestone herself:

> And then they found her body,
> Or at least, they found traces of it.
> . . . .
> But from what we know of local practices
> It would seem that she must have been crucified
> Very near an ant-hill.[2]

In *Nayatt School* Eliot's play is meticulously dismembered and its "traces" inserted into a larger, open-ended network. It is sacrificed to a performance that litters the playing area with shards of countless other texts, celebrating the very insanity that Eliot judiciously places offstage. It becomes merely one morsel to be devoured by a text that remains radically plural and irreducible, a text that defies a single reading.

* * *

Interpretation

Elizabeth LeCompte: If you analyze the actions of Sakonnet Point *you'll see they are extremely abstract. They were developed without words and with people who didn't know Spalding's past. So the projection becomes more problematic.*

David Savran: Then the introduction of content comes in large part retrospectively, from the later pieces, and the fact that objects like the red tent acquire resonances throughout the Trilogy.

Elizabeth LeCompte: We had very little to work with and we wanted to show that you don't need much to work with. If you worked with objects and things, then they took on special meaning which they didn't have before because you handled and dealt with them. The red tent was something that was here in the Garage because we were living in it. We took it downstairs. I saw it as a beautiful hovering red bell.

Ron Vawter: It's really more like the way a musical phrase is repeated in a symphony, and it gains meaning because it's used, and variations are played upon it.

Elizabeth LeCompte: It's not to say the psychological content isn't important, it's just that it's definitely after the fact. It's only one strain, one element in the work; it's not the core around which the piece is built. The core is always dispersed.

Ron Vawter: Bernard Berenson wrote a monograph on Piero della Francesca, it's called "The Ineloquent in Art." I read it when I was a student and was very, very impressed by it. And I remember thinking about it when I first saw Sakonnet Point *and was so attracted to it. Berenson was saying that the great works of art that meant anything to him were the ones which weren't trying to say something or convey a meaning, but literally just were there. He was talking about Piero della Francesca's figures that just sit there and don't seem to be trying to express anything. He also talked about the seated Buddhas . . . that these allowed him to be engaged because they weren't busy trying to speak to him.*

Elizabeth LeCompte: Yes. And it's interesting that Piero della Francesca is often considered cold.

Ron Vawter: And only concerned with form . . .

Elizabeth LeCompte: Which was one of the complaints about Rumstick Road.

Ron Vawter: I think one of the reasons why audiences project onto it so heavily and why there's such massive interpretation is because you are discreet in that way. . . .

Elizabeth LeCompte: I want as many interpretations as possible to co-exist in the same time and same space.

Ron Vawter: You'll reject something that's too pointed.

Elizabeth LeCompte: It would make a meaning. Not that the meaning is wrong, I just can't see one meaning. I want many, many meanings to coalesce at the same point.

Ron Vawter: Just recently you were saying, "We can't have Jeff Webster play Proctor and Leary, [in L.S.D.*] because it's too much of a . . . "*

Elizabeth LeCompte: It makes a "literary" interpretation too dominant.

Ron Vawter: An event which can be interpreted only one way inhibits and limits the possibility. It's not that we're deliberately trying to make pieces which are mute. Just the opposite. I often see a piece as an opportunity for meaning, rather than an expression of a single meaning.

In gathering fragments of action, drama, film and video, the Wooster Group produces a kind of performance that is quite different from most scripted theatre. It does not begin with a theme or message, external to the work, but rather an immediate and concrete desire ("we wanted to show that you don't need much to work with"). *Route 1 & 9* was not intended to be an analysis of racism, any more than *Rumstick Road* was intended to be an indictment of psychiatry. Ideas and themes which emerge from the pieces do so only in retrospect, as a residue of the textualizing process, much as, in a chemical reaction, solid flakes precipitate out of solution. And for all the pieces, the reagent is the spectator. Each will see a different piece, much as each, in the laboratory, would see a different configuration of chemical flakes. Here, however, the work breaks with Newtonian physics, which assumes the uniformity of the phenomenon under scrutiny regardless of vantage point. Instead, the Wooster Group initiates what could be described as an Einsteinian project that celebrates the multiplicity of perspectives and only one certainty: that the phenomenon will be different for each member of the audience.

As with any piece of theatre, each spectator will be assured a different chain of associations and way of making sense of the action. The Wooster Group's work is carefully designed, however, to accentuate the indeterminacy of performance (like the work of a number of contemporary playwrights: Kroetz, Nelson, Churchill, et al.). Certainly, there are many factors which make for the open-ended structure of the work, including those that reach beyond the work itself to its social and aesthetic context (and which remain operative in any act of interpretation). Leaving the latter aside, we can specify three reasons why the work authorizes multiple interpretations: first, the lack of a clear-cut narrative spine. In structure, *Route 1 & 9* could not be more unlike a play such as *Our Town,* which is built upon a highly delineated plot line, with clearly drawn, idiosyncratic characters whose development carries the emotional weight of the piece. In its place, *Route 1 & 9* offers a non-linear structure, a collage of forms from different cultural traditions. The characters are drawn in a two-dimensional cartoon style, heavier with idea than psychology, and change radically from scene to scene, medium to medium.

Second, the structure of the Wooster Group's work is not bound by the laws of cause and effect. The transformation of the four live performers into vampires in Part III of *Route 1 & 9* is not a direct or obvious result of a line of action. Rather, the connection between events is what Kenneth Burke calls associative or qualitative, in which "the presence of one quality calls forth the demand for another."[3] Thus, the violence sublimated in the racist stereotypes in Part II evokes the desire for the eruption of that violence. In Part III, the Wooster Group provides it: in the vampires' frenzy, an immediate and visceral explosion.

Third, none of the Wooster Group pieces provides an unambiguous frame of reference or offers a clear signal of meaning. At no point in *Route 1 & 9* does LeCompte make clear what attitude she wishes the audience to adopt toward the blackface. As she notes above, she avoids placing a performer outside the action to condemn racist stereotypes, not to obfuscate the issue, but to hand it to the spectator as a reality to deal with. In *Rumstick Road* questions about the nature of Bette Gray's insanity are raised many times by the people being interviewed and by Spalding Gray himself in the phone call to his mother's psychiatrist. But finally, the piece (for many reasons) refuses to pass judgment or to take a

> *Elizabeth LeCompte: I've had people who loved* Rumstick *who said, "I see, you're saying that psychiatrists are really horrible people." And I'd say, "No! Somebody else saw this and said the psychiatrist is the only one who really tried to help her." I think the piece leaves the possibility for both interpretations always open.*

stand regarding her treatment. To pass judgment, the spectator (or creator) must place himself *above* the material, clearly delineating the issues and separating subject from object, as in a typical lecture-demonstration. Rather than strike this detached "scientific" pose, the work dramatizes the impossibility of assuming an objective point of view.

All of the Wooster Group's pieces insist on a complexity of vision and refuse the moral high ground, thereby depriving the spectator of the frame of reference with which to separate the ironic from the non-ironic. Instead, each piece mobilizes a free-floating irony, one whose drift constitutes the work's plurality, or enunciates the various opportunities for meaning. The Group thereby questions both the self-containment of the work and the marginality of the spectator. It urges the latter to make the kind of choices usually considered the province of the writer and/or performer. As a result, each piece must be considered only partially composed when it is presented to the public, not because it is unfinished, but because it requires an audience to realize the multitude of possibilities on which it opens. As each spectator, according to his part, enters into a dialogue with the work, the act of interpretation becomes a performance, an intervention in the piece.

Figure 12. *Sakonnet Point,* Spalding and the Woman with the House
Spalding Gray, Libby Howes.
(Ken Kobland)

* * *

Sakonnet Point

David Savran: What was the initial spark for Sakonnet Point?
Spalding Gray: I think the spark was simply being in the room, as a group, the ones that wanted to work together. There was a period when we had the Garage as a workshop and all of us felt we wanted to be doing something that wasn't just a series of exercises, but that led to a piece. There was no central theme, no central person. I remember I got frustrated and I asked Liz to help because I thought she'd be a good director. So I asked her to watch it and take notes. Thinking back, I can't remember that there was an initiating idea, anything beyond the fact that we would improvise, in that space, and begin to set things.
Elizabeth LeCompte: In those days, too, that was really common to do, and I think it came from . . .
Spalding Gray: It came from the [Robert] Wilson stuff. I'd been dancing a lot up at the Byrd Hoffman School. We all knew, through improvising, that if you work every day, after you do warm-ups—because Richard [Schechner] had done that with Commune, gone around with a microphone—and you watch and you pay attention, that something would take shape organically that would be expressive of that space, of the history of that space.
Elizabeth LeCompte: It was a simple process, it was just being in the space.
Spalding Gray: And the piece was a simple piece. I was interested in displaying myself as a dancer, not talking, and I needed someone to help me work that out.
David Savran: At what point did the title come? Because the title introduces a certain content: autobiography, the whole summer motif.
Spalding Gray: I think it came just before we opened, when we knew we needed a title. And I'm pretty good at titles, for some . . . whatever reason. It's reminiscent, certainly, of childhood. I thought that was obviously true and then my younger brother compared it to To the Lighthouse, which got me into reading that book.
David Savran: So then, all the content of the piece really came afterwards.
Spalding Gray: It's a projection. The ideas were a projection. Much of the so-called content of summer themes and lost childhood was audience projection.
Elizabeth LeCompte: It was a series of improvisations with different personalities, Spalding being the central one, the hub of the wheel. What I remember doing was putting Spalding together with others. Spalding would bring the props and sometimes the other people would too, and

they'd get together. And we'd have certain records that were picked by one or another of the people in the group.
Spalding Gray: The Tchaikovsky Concerto. *Also I found a lot of the props in the dumpster, those little trees... found objects.*
Elizabeth LeCompte: Found objects, but not with any specific point...
Spalding Gray: Five-and-dime stuff.
Elizabeth LeCompte: Not an intention, really, other than to get things together in a space.

Sakonnet Point (1975) was the first collaborative creation by the group of performers that would become the Wooster Group. Gray explains that when he began working with LeCompte and the other performers in the spring of 1974 he "had no conscious objective themes or ideas from which to work." He would bring props into the empty rehearsal space and "perform certain silent associative actions with them."[4] The others would join in, one at a time, while LeCompte stepped aside to direct. As the piece evolved in rehearsal, she coordinated the visual and sonic elements, structuring and editing the piece, giving a "meaningful theatrical structure"[5] to the raw material furnished by Gray and the other performers.

Sakonnet Point was conceived months before the idea of *Three Places in Rhode Island,* the Trilogy, of which it is the first part; it remains strikingly "innocent" (the word is Gray's)[6] in relation to the two other pieces. The title evokes an oceanside town in southern Rhode Island where Gray spent his summers as a boy and the piece is suffused with the atmosphere of childhood remembered. The traumatic material of the later pieces is kept at a distance and a "romantic nostalgia"[7] envelops the performance. Sounds of nature (birds and crickets) and rhapsodic music (Tchaikovsky's *First Piano Concerto*) predominate along with images from childhood: a miniature airplane, a toy village, a game of catch. Like a summer at the beach, the piece unfolds in slow and measured rhythms, awash in a sea of anticipation and regret, of self-sufficiency and loss.

> *Spalding Gray: I wanted to juxtapose a real place against an abstract association, to concretize it. So very literal-minded people have come from Rhode Island to see the pieces and were totally confused.*

* * *

Spalding Gray: It was about an innocent, a primitive kind of working that I was doing. I was interested in dance and I wanted more and more to move away from spoken word and text. And I really wanted... I refer to it as body ego. My ego had gone into my body and I wanted to display myself. I was doing a lot of t'ai chi exercises and taking some free-form dance. And so all of that was new, therefore innocent, in a sense, and primitive, because... I was taking a radical departure from the way we had worked with Richard, following a story line. Sakonnet Point *was a very fragile mood piece. And it had the light changes and the long fade at the end. We knew the piece was about innocence... because it was the first time. And it had a kid in it. And it was very... gentle. And, I guess, Liz and I were testing... testing the ground.*

Elizabeth LeCompte: For me, Sakonnet Point *was the primordial mud out of which the rest of the work arose. It was more dance than theatre and it defined the use of action and set out the iconography, the ongoing visual landscape—houses out of grid patterns, for example. I was thinking of Cézanne and trying to find a form analogous to his painting, but in another language.*

* * *

Schema of *Sakonnet Point*

Spalding and the Boy

Spalding and the Woman with the House

Spalding and the Woman with the Fan

Spalding and the Woman with the Blanket

Spalding and the Woman with the Sheets

* * *

In *Sakonnet Point* Gray and LeCompte create a theatrical vocabulary and a lexicon of objects, both of which carry through into the subsequent pieces. They refuse an initial written text, using instead the dynamics between performers in rehearsal as the found material. The resultant piece is structured much like a still life, fixing a seemingly casual grouping of objects into a rigorous and highly formal composition. Just as the late paintings of Cézanne dissolve three-dimensional space into a shimmer of surfaces and planes, *Sakonnet Point* fragments action, space, and characters. It suggests, by juxtaposing multiple vanishing points, that the spectator's ever-changing perceptions fabricate a world of objects and people, and that form is less an intrinsic property than the onlooker's projection.

In stark contrast to Richard Schechner, LeCompte, Gray and the other performers did not attempt to frame a coherent narrative. They did not plan a piece about Spalding Gray, childhood, autobiography or performance itself. The original impulse was a desire to explore: the self, the other and a space. The piece developed out of (and represented) the concrete relationships among participants in a real space. If the spectators desire a narrative, they must construct it. If they want to read the piece as a memory of childhood summers, they may provide the appropriate associations. If they care to see the piece as the introduction to a Trilogy, as that which sets up certain patterns and images, they are free to do so. In any case, they must grant themselves the freedom to credit their own responses, to "have a dialogue with themselves,"[8] out of which the piece will emerge, less an object of contemplation than an immediate, performative experience.

Willem Dafoe: Emotionally and personally, the Trilogy was really about a way of working.

* * *

In the Performing Garage, the spectators sit on platforms set at different levels on three sides of the large atrium-like playing area. On the fourth side, atop a 14-foot platform, stands a large, red dome tent, lit from within, whose occupants cast shadows across its luminous skin. Inside, two women play the Tchaikovsky *Concerto* on a small phonograph and softly converse. Below, the volume of space is defined by a large black tarpaulin which stretches diagonally from the platform to the floor and by three clotheslines running from the platform to the wall opposite. The floor itself is marked by V-shaped taped lines extending across the playing area and a pool of light in its center.

Within the vertically oriented performance space, the red tent, high on its platform, comprises neither foreground nor background. Rather, it seems to undermine a clear distinction between these two spatial categories. Lit for the duration of the piece, unlike the playing area below, it is lifted far away from the spectators to remain a constantly glowing presence above a world of shadows. The incessant muffled dialogue and music issuing from it draw attention to a spoken language that is always kept at bay in *Sakonnet Point,* much like the adult world it evokes. The 14-foot separation signals the distance in the piece between a discursive and mysterious adult domain and a realm of play; between experience and innocence; between the grown man, Spalding Gray, and the eight-year-old Boy, played by Erik Moskowitz.

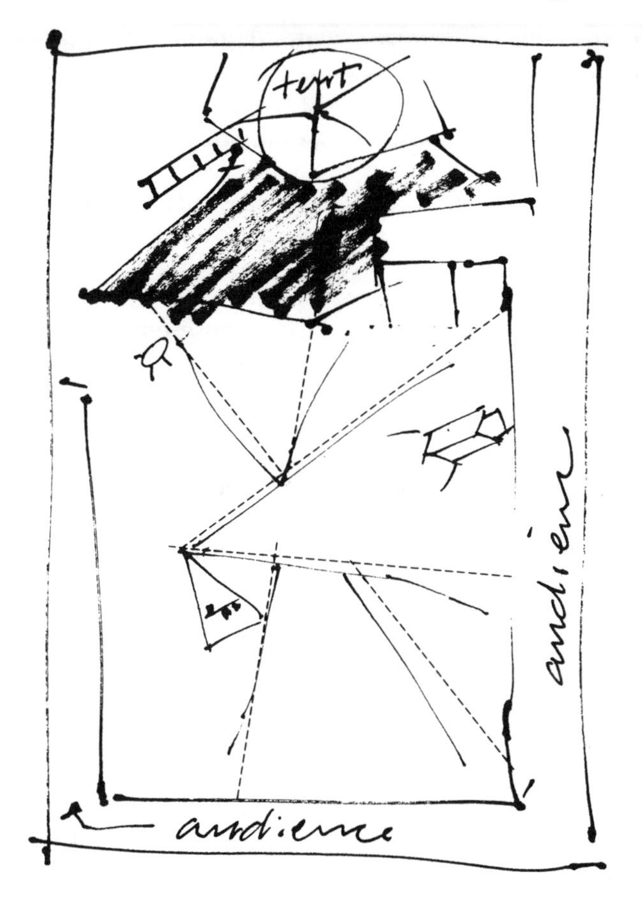

Figure 13. Performance Space for *Sakonnet Point* (Elizabeth LeCompte)

* * *

Spalding Gray: Regarding the movement of the pieces, Sakonnet Point *was for me the dumb show, the child. Then* Rumstick Road *and the tapes: listening to the relatives talk through the door, as a child first learns to speak. And then in* Nayatt School, *sitting at the long table and speaking myself, in the first monologue. I get my voice. And then,* Point Judith, *a farewell, essentially, and a return to the actor.*

If we follow Spalding Gray's conception of the pieces as a representation or simulation of "the development of a child," *Sakonnet Point* becomes the rediscovery of early childhood. It summons up a pre-verbal world of action without reflection, "images without thought." In the progression of pieces in the Trilogy, it marks the first stage in a movement from silence to language. The warm summer day of *Sakonnet Point* antedates speech and evokes, rather, dance: a language the body uses "to speak without words."[9] Dialogue recedes and the whole body comes into play: a challenge to the schism that characterizes adult experience in the Trilogy—between thought and emotion, mind and body, experience and contemplation.

Although *Sakonnet Point* may offer a glimpse of the unity of experience and sensation, it suggests that a representation of this unity is impossible. Throughout the piece, wholeness is evoked through a representation that is always an image of division, in which the "character" Spalding resonates between a reflective adult self and an active child persona. The piece commemorates wholeness only as a separation—as a reflection upon childhood which, conscious of its contemplative stance, is always already stripped of innocence. In this beginning, a divided consciousness speaks the only language it knows, the language of representation, in which it finds itself both subject and object, apportioned between present and past. The exigencies of performance (which institutionalize schism) guarantee that *Sakonnet Point* will be less about immediate experience than its reflection, less about the unity of childhood sensation than the impossibility of summoning up that unity. As LeCompte has acknowledged, "The piece isn't about the past, it's really about us thinking about the past,"[10] from a perspective, we might add, which renders that past irrecoverable and (literally) unspeakable.

For Gray and LeCompte, *Sakonnet Point* dramatizes the realization that the theatre, as it has been handed to them—whether by the Western humanistic tradition generally, or Richard Schechner, specifically—is necessarily a site of schism, of separation between actor and character and between the invisible director and technician (who regulate the mechanics of the performance) and the visible performer. Like all the Group's pieces, it does not so much reject the theatrical apparatus—and Schechner's working methods—as undermine them from within, by exposing their particular mode of operation and the way they transform non-theatrical material. Rather than taking the theatre for granted, it underscores the autonomy of individual production elements. Gesture, sound and lighting no longer work in sychronization to create a unified whole. In its place, a performance unfolds marked by discontinuities and dislocations, by collisions between different energies, personae and media. The performance space itself is fragmented and multiple, both an interior and an exterior. It remains an undisguised theatre at the same time that it becomes a place for childhood explorations, studded with platforms and tents, places to hide, fantasize, and bask in the sun. Foreground and background meld. Language recedes but sound is everywhere: from Tchaikovsky to the old hymns, from a thunderstorm to "Sounds of the American Southwest," vividly rendered and, at the same time, filtered through a haze of memory.

* * *

Spalding Gray: I think, finally, that everyone is playing themselves. There is a huge misunderstanding on the part of people who aren't involved in acting. They think (as they do of a fiction writer), "Where do they ever get those crazy characters from?" Just inside, they simply look in, or they don't look in and they just do it. It's just an intuitive thing—this is the right voice, this is what comes—like a child playing. It's no different from a child playing.
David Savran: And you always use yourself or the world around you.
Spalding Gray: Who else? Who else is there? How do you ever escape from yourself? Never. There are certain mystics who claim that they do, but I think that they're still in their body and they're still coming from themselves.

For Spalding Gray, all performance is autobiographical, not because it re-creates the performer's past, but because the performer can play only himself, can project only the diversity within. In *Sakonnet Point* he breaks with realistic acting and instead celebrates a fragmented psyche and the reflexive nature of consciousness. Ironically, it was his training in traditional acting that led him to reject it. He used the "method" to find an alternative to it and become a creator of autobiography (using the self as text) rather than a re-creator of someone else:

> My college Stanislavskian training had taught me to find and observe the "other" in the streets of Boston, the physical place I was living in at the time, but somewhere in this process I came to realize that I could only guess at knowing this "other," I could only pretend. The other person was always a thing, an object. His subjectivity, with its inner freedom, escaped me. This observation of the other, as a study for a role, froze and congealed any fluid essence. I realized that I could not, and did not want to, reduce others to that object, that study for the stage. I wanted to explore myself as other. I wanted to investigate my actions. I no longer wanted to pretend to be a character outside myself. The streets where I encountered this other were in my body and mind. The "other" was the other in me, the constant witness, the constant consciousness of self.[11]

The Wooster Group's work proceeds not from the self-identical but from division within consciousness and explores the "other" within the self. It performs a schismatic which does not simply divide mind from body, thought from emotion, along traditional metaphysical lines. Instead, it begins with *difference,* with a difference which ensures that the self will be less a dualistic construct than a multiplicity of masks, "a play of moods, energies, aspects of self." It defines the self as "the many-in-the-one" and performance as the pre-condition for being.[12]

Gray's articulation of the ground of difference is one point of departure for the Wooster Group's deconstructive project. In its above formulation, it undermines concepts of self and other, and of performance understood as secondary or derived activity. *Sakonnet Point* registers a break with the mimetic tradition by positing the self—constituted by a freeplay of forces and moods—as always already immersed in performance, in schism: representation to, of and by self. The agents multiply and coalesce. The character Spalding and the performer Gray both appear before us, not to reinforce a distinction between the "theatrical" and the "real," but to demonstrate that the former is necessarily inscribed within the latter. His eight-year-old double is not simply an alter-ego or secondary self, but the diffusion of the "many-in-the-one" through the performance space, the re-presentation (i.e., multiplication) of the fragmented self.

> *Elizabeth LeCompte: In the beginning we were all attuned to a certain kind of reticence and a certain kind of non-acting: task oriented and non-psychological. And people who were interested in that gravitated to us.*

* * *

Spalding Gray: All the performers were struggling to give themselves over, to be servants to the action. And by filling that action—whether it was given to you arbitrarily by the director, by Liz, or was something that you discovered in improvisation—you were filling up your body with this energy, and projecting it. And it would take on meaning, make a kind of sense. It couldn't always be interpreted, but it had a presence, just the way a piece of abstract art has a presence because of its color or its design. This had a presence because of its energy. Even if the members of the audience didn't know all the time what was going on, they were always (if they were open) in something, in a rarified atmosphere. They were in, the way you're in a space when you're riding in a car, and colors are flashing by in the landscape and it's taking you. But you can't grasp it.

To represent the dance of selves, the interplay of facets of personality, Gray uses what he calls "personal-abstract" movement. Developed through improvisation work at Robert Wilson's Byrd Hoffman School, it is not an expression (literally, a squeezing out) of hidden emotions. Gray describes it as "a constitution of personal energy rather than a psychological exploration of personality."[13] For the performer it is always a concrete action with a clear intent, a specific improvised response to the space or another action taking place therein. Furthermore, since it arises as a physical impulse it is never conceived of as a manifestation of hidden desires or psychological obscurities. To the spectator, personal-abstract movement may appear abstract and ambiguous because he does not share in the performer's chain of associations: he is deprived of the contingent activity and the original context in which the movement was developed. For him, the action enunciates opportunities for meaning rather than a fixed denotative value.

Near the beginning of *Sakonnet Point* there is a section which well illustrates personal-abstract movement and the particular way it reverberates with implications:

> The Boy pretends to strangle himself with his hand. He struggles and falls down and plays dead. Spalding examines The Boy. He listens for his heartbeat. He feels for his pulse. The Boy plays dead. Spalding tickles The Boy. He picks him up and spins him in his arms. The Boy's body goes rigid during the spinning. The Man emerges from behind the black tent. Spalding hands The Boy to The Man, and The Man carries him away.[14]

* * *

David Savran: I'm curious about the section in Sakonnet *where The Boy pretends to strangle himself and you tickle him, Spalding. I saw that as the beginning of the doctor persona for you. Did you ever think of it in those terms?*

Spalding Gray: I may have when I was doing it each night, but I'm not really aware of it now. It was an action that seemed intuitively right, that Liz liked as a director, and that agreed with me. There was no discussion of it. I was like a dancer at the time, in the sense that I was only concerned with executing the movement and doing it with full concentration in my body.

Elizabeth LeCompte: It was just a nice move. I liked it. I saw that Erik liked to play with his wrists. So we asked him to do things with his hands. And always, with kids, the fun thing to do is to pretend something's strangling you. So he did it as an improv. He liked to do it. Kids like to pretend they're dying.

Among the various possible interpretations of *Sakonnet Point* in general and this sequence in particular, lies a reading that uses Spalding Gray's autobiography as a guide. This choice, which Gray himself has often taken, and which has formed the basis for most critical exegesis of the Trilogy, is as arbitrary as any other choice. (How can one assume that the spectator will be familiar with the details of Gray's life? LeCompte maintains that other performers in *Sakonnet Point* didn't know his history.) The autobiographical critic will see in this sequence an echo of a real suicide, that of Margaret Elizabeth (Bette) Gray, Spalding's mother, which forms the subject of the next piece, *Rumstick Road.* In *Sakonnet Point,* however, the suicide is never mentioned. Regardless, one may see its prefiguration in the piece's sense of foreboding, in the atmosphere of waiting, or even suspense, that the piece creates. The less autobiographically inclined critic, meanwhile, may interpret these same qualities by seeing in the juxtaposition of performers, the dark intimations of an adult world that lies beyond the realm of the innocent self.

* * *

Elizabeth LeCompte: With the performers, I try to take the first thing they do and work with that.
Spalding Gray: The first and the best thing.
Elizabeth LeCompte: I don't go looking for the right text. It's what comes up.
Spalding Gray: You take the original performance space as the universe.
Elizabeth LeCompte: That's right. And that's hard for me, because Spalding's very... I'm not a narcissist, so I can't take the material from myself. I have to take it from the performers and what they bring me, and from what happens to be lying around. So I'm really a scavenger.
David Savran: I think of your work on this material as being architectural.
Elizabeth LeCompte: I would, too. [Laughs.] That's from my point of view. Architectonic is the word I would use.

By developing *Sakonnet Point* through improvisation, Gray and LeCompte avoid defining the *dramatis personae* in a way that suggests Spalding Gray's family. All the events in the piece were the result of dynamics between the performers in rehearsal. The five sections of the piece do not develop a plot line but function like architectural components—arches, windows, curtain walls. They each present the interaction between Spalding and another performer, first with The Boy, then with each of four Women who appear, respectively, with the House, Fan, Blanket and Sheets. Each of the Women establishes a highly particularized relationship with Spalding, based on her own persona.

Despite the suggestion of the later pieces, the four woman are not, separately or together, impersonating his mother: "We were just trying to make scenes out of who we were in the room."[15] The actions each couple performs neither tell a story nor initiate an investigation of the mother–son relationship. They become, rather, discrete moments in a personal-abstract dance, a cross-section of a concrete relationship.

Because LeCompte has documented the way she fragmented the third part of *Sakonnet Point,* the sequence provides a good example of her method for structuring improvised material. In this section, the most overtly confrontational part of the piece, Spalding interacts with the Woman with the Fan (Ellen LeCompte). At the beginning of the scene she enters the playing space, slamming the door behind her. She then takes a black ball out of her pocket and proceeds to bowl down the plastic tree forest. She fans herself with a Japanese paper fan while Spalding whips the air by spinning a length of zip cord. She puts on a record of children's song, goes around the space piling up objects on a green towel and drinks a glass of milk, letting the milk drool from the sides of her mouth. Both performers then take off their shoes and socks while Spalding spins the laces. The Woman lies down on the floor in a splayed position and puts the corner of a red bathing cap in her mouth, allowing the rest to spill out across her neck and onto the floor. Spalding walks over to her, looks up at the ceiling and then down at her frozen figure. He claps his hands over his face, covering his eyes.

The sequence described above is based on the initial rehearsal dynamic between Spalding Gray and Ellen LeCompte: "When Ellen presented herself in the space, she destroyed the space." At first, the confrontation had been structured as a series of actions leading up to a crisis. Elizabeth LeCompte explains:

> We broke it up, decided to take away that linear story line of them coming into conflict, coming into confrontation and subsiding. So we took the confrontation and put it first, then put in the middle of that one of the subsiding moments, then put another confrontation in the middle, then another subsiding. To break that pattern.[16]

In this sequence the emotional dynamic is highlighted at the expense of plot development. The fragmentation of the action, the absence of a causal connection between the events, erases the immediate provocation, leaving only the aggressive impulse behind, as a tension rather than an analyzable conflict between two highly particularized "characters."

In being about the past, but refusing to recreate it, in being about loss, but refusing to specify what exactly has been lost, *Sakonnet Point*

Figure 14. *Sakonnet Point*, Spalding and the Woman with the Fan
Spalding Gray, Ellen LeCompte.
(Ken Kobland)

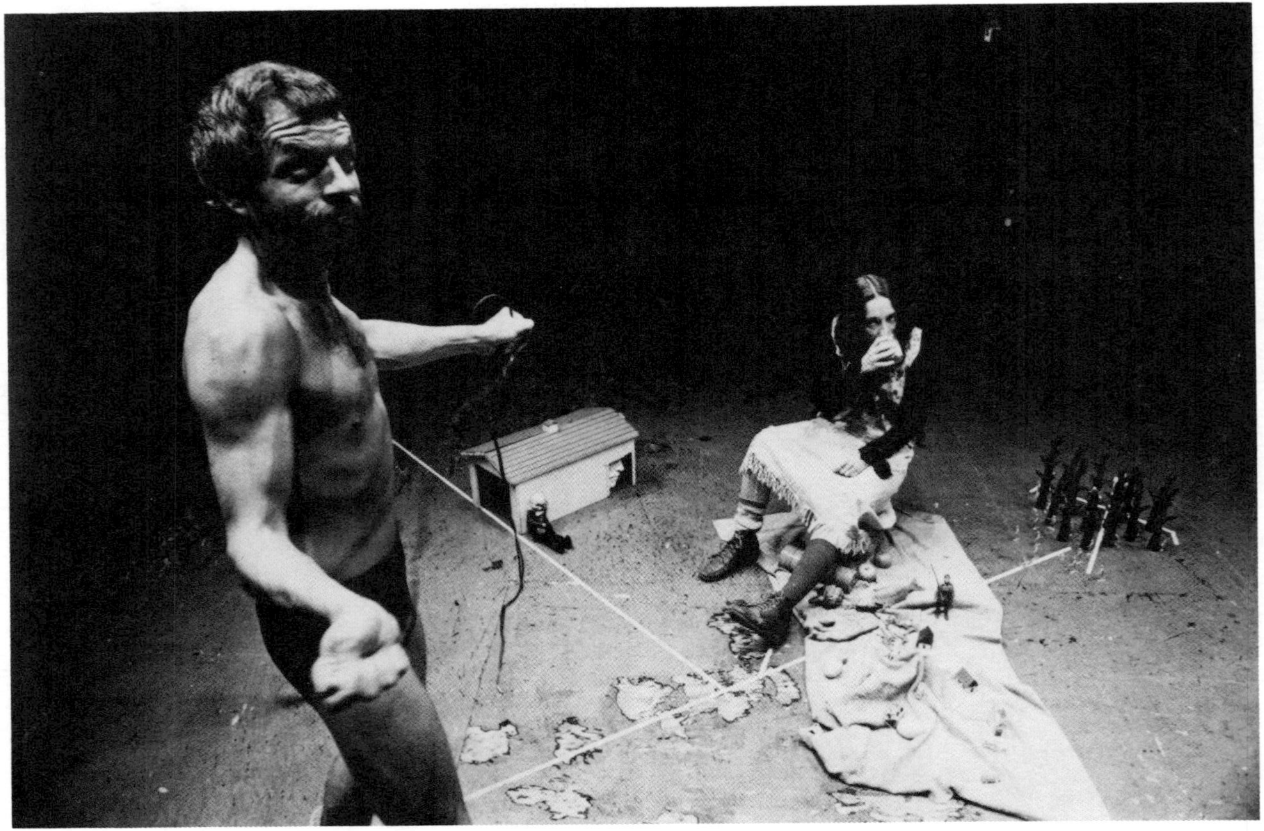

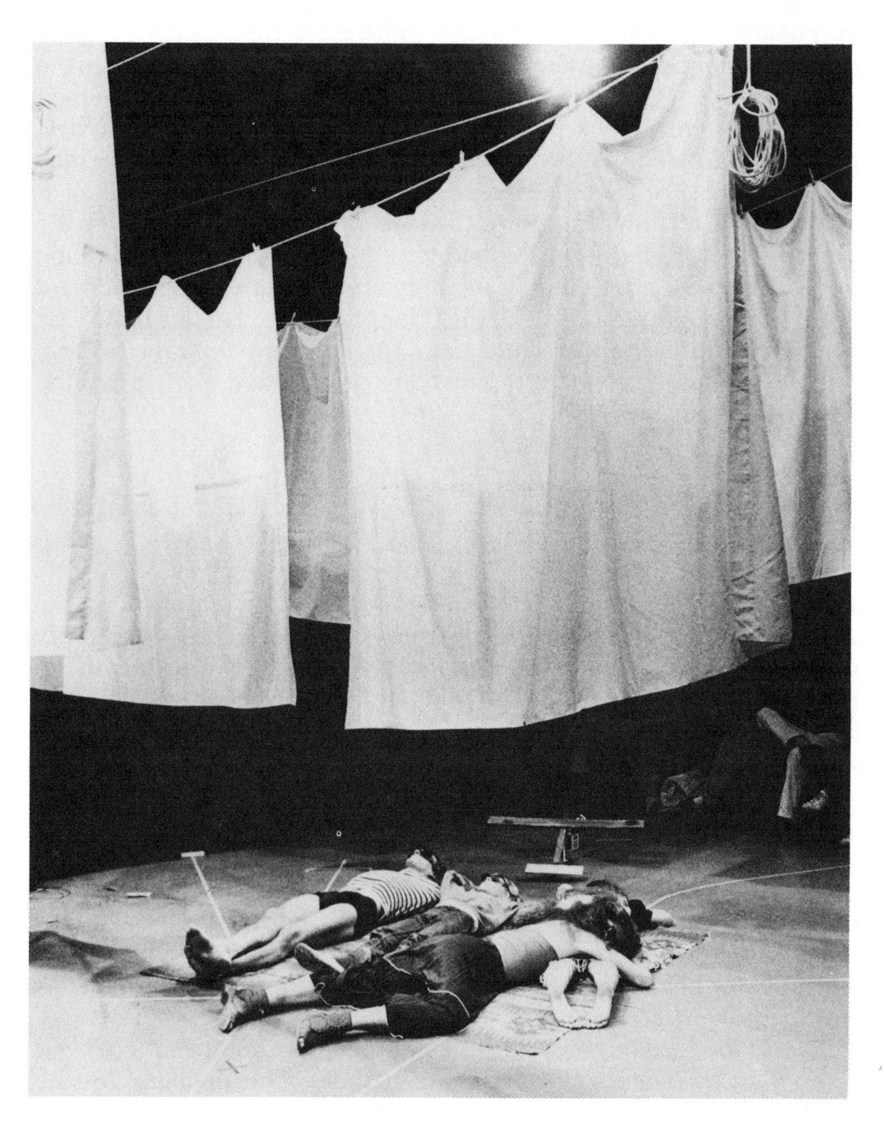

Figure 15. *Sakonnet Point,* The Sheets
Spalding Gray, Erik Moskowitz, Libby Howes, Ellen LeCompte.
(Bob Van Dantzig)

opens up a field in which past and present, innocence and experience, presence and absence resonate freely. It does not aim at recapturing childhood, knowing that such a project would be both a falsification and a dispossession, a wresting of the past from the one for whom it remains a memory. When Spalding Gray writes that the piece, like the others in the Trilogy, "reflects" upon themes of loss, he alludes more to its method than its content. By dispensing with "character" and psychology, *Sakonnet Point* refuses to be tied down to a particular loss, thereby becoming "not just about the loss of my mother but about the feeling of loss itself."[17] Certainly, the ending of the scene described above, with the Woman lying on the floor, the bathing cap spilling out of her mouth, evokes the horror of a violent death. But the effectiveness of the moment is not dependent upon symbolic identification, that is, upon the spectator's substitution of Bette Gray for the Woman with the Fan. Instead, it becomes a spur to our own imagination and, perhaps, to the memories of our own past.

* * *

Memory

Spalding Gray: The Trilogy isn't really about memory. My own impulse came, in part, out of memory but the pieces themselves are not memory pieces. They're art pieces, they're not referential. They were built in the space. And they were spun off innuendo, which was my personal memory, which is what I used to fuel myself. Every person had a different way of fueling himself, a different drive in making the piece. When we were in rehearsals, we worked with open narrative and images that were dreamlike and, therefore, could have a number of interpretations—non-psychological. They produced different memories in different people. For me, for instance, there's a memory of Sakonnet Point, going up on top of the highest hill there and seeing the houses by the sea and assuming that they were the size that I saw them. And that memory came either after or before putting the little houses on the floor in the light. It's hard to know where in the circle the memory comes. Which produced which? So they are memory pieces and they're not memory pieces and memory is a tricky thing. It's always the memory of the memory. There's an interview with Borges in which he talks about his father thinking of memory like piling coins. So he's talking about an incident in Argentina in the morning and then talking in the afternoon about the same incident, but through the filter of that morning's memories. So it's constantly, constantly changing and evolving. And history to me is such a fiction, finally. . . .

In the Rhode Island Trilogy and its epilogue, *Point Judith,* Spalding Gray's memories occupy a pivotal position. *Rumstick* and *Nayatt* are in part about his own experiences and make extensive use of personal documents. The four pieces, however, do not attempt to recapture or represent particular moments from Gray's past. Instead, *Sakonnet Point,* in its disposition of the physical environment, turns memory into a three-dimensional space, as if it were delineated by a play of recollection and forgetting. Like that ideational expanse, it is arrayed with a collection of disparate objects, on different scales, organized in clusters of varying densities. The space is not uniformally illuminated but is defined, rather, by a play of light and shadow. Certain scenes and images come into sharp focus while others recede into the darkness. *Sakonnet Point* is a memory piece because it concretizes the theatrical metaphor associated with the act of recollection: it performs the play of memory.

As Spalding Gray realizes, memory functions as an ever-shifting filter through which the past is screened. As he recalls *Sakonnet Point,* he no longer remembers whether his associations were a cause or result of the action of the piece. The play of recollection thus defines not only the past that the piece itself "remembers" but the performer's own memories of producing the work. The chain of cause and effect is doubly disrupted ("Which produced which?") and the artifact further entwined with its interpretation. As the difference between primary and secondary discourse is broken down, the writing and reading of the piece become coextensive. As Gray remembers the work, he transforms it, filtering it through his present experiences and thoughts, in effect, staging it again. And the process is the same for all of the members of the Wooster Group. As they recall the composition and performance of the pieces, as they re-read their own activity, they rewrite the work.

* * *

India and After (America)

Spalding Gray: I don't think there's any one reason for my mother's suicide. And there was no one reason for my collapse after India. It was a collision of events, including diet, that sometimes happens in peoples' lives. And if they're young enough, they're resilient. I think that death is often about that, many things colliding. For my mother, many things collided over a two-year period. And for me it was over a two-year period too, '76 and '77, the life experience from which the material for the monologue, India and After, *was taken. It was a very intense period for me. It was very... very chaotic and just one of those... big change periods, a metamorphosis.*

When Spalding Gray returned from India in 1976 after the Performance Group's tour of *Mother Courage,* he was in great emotional distress. He became "deeply identified with the memory of [his mother's] madness" and started experiencing many of the same symptoms she had experienced during her periods of manic-depression. He dealt with his distress, in part, by working with LeCompte and the other performers to make the second part of the Rhode Island Trilogy, *Rumstick Road,* which directly addresses his mother's madness and suicide.[18] The period itself is commemorated in one of Gray's monologues, *India and After (America),* composed in 1979.

The piece is unique among Gray's monologues because of the way it is fragmented. An assistant (originally Meghan Ellenberger) sits behind a desk, stage left, with a dictionary and stopwatch in front of her. Next to her, in the middle of the space, hangs a large clock. Gray sits stage right. The assistant then chooses a word at random, reads the definition and allots Gray a specified number of minutes in which to relate a part of his narrative, associating on the chosen word. His stories deal with the trip to India and his first few months back in the States. His tone is never grave but remains characteristically wry and anecdotal. Although at several points in the monologue he makes a reference in passing to his emotional difficulties, he communicates the severity of the crisis less through the content of the stories than through their fragmentation.

In the videotape of a performance of *India and After* made by Dan Weissman and Brad Ricker, Gray is given thirty-eight words on which to structure his monologue. Some of the associations are quite literal, some metaphorical and others more obscure, more private. He makes no attempt to begin at an obvious beginning and, for most of the piece, he keeps the stories separate and unconnected. Roughly, the stories can be divided into seven groups, each focused around a particular event or activity: performing *Mother Courage* in India, taking mescaline in Kashmir, having an audience with a guru, visiting an Indian fishing village, returning to New York, going to jail in Las Vegas and making a porn film.

The spectator's attention is directed toward several different phenomena. Listening to the content of the stories, he attempts to piece them together and make sense of them. As if watching a television quiz show (the contestant searching for the right answer, trying to "beat the clock") the spectator shares both the speaker's anxiety and the thrill of the game. Gray, however, differs from the typical contestant because he is unable to watch the clock, let alone "beat" it. As the minutes pass, he works his stories in and out of the allotted slots, sometimes fitting one sleekly into the time limit, ending on a particularly final note, or even a punch line. Other times, he's cut off abruptly by the bell. By the end, it becomes clear that there remain too many stories to tell and too many connections to be made. The piece can never be complete, just as the experience of which this monologue allows a glimpse cannot be all told. There will always be fragments left over, unexplored and unexplained, that elude the play of rationality and the game of chance, loose ends that resist incorporation into this cunningly constructed artifact.

* * *

Spalding Gray: The structure of India and After *came about because I was too close to the material. It came out like a travelogue. I didn't know how to fragment it by chance. All the other pieces had been fragmented by memory. Memory creates its own frames. So when I performed it, it was a real bore for me. It just droned on and on. For whatever reason, it didn't work the way my mind was working at the time that I was going through it. Since I was interested in building my vocabulary, I took the dictionary and asked Meghan to be a timer and to break it up by her design. That gave it a structure and pushed it further into the past.*

India and After is not so much *about* Spalding Gray's emotional crisis as it is a translation of the crisis into another medium: it puts the spectator in a position similar to that of the monologue's distressed subject. The former is forced to work to make sense of what is happening, to remember the different narrative strands and the various personages. As the monologue proceeds, his task becomes easier only because he has become familiar with Gray's strategy and the different story lines.

Spalding Gray is never at leisure to communicate his emotional state directly because he must split his attention between the stories and the external structuring device. He does, however, allude to it several times simply by recounting what happened. In the videotape, on the twenty-seventh word, *prime mover,* Gray tells of his visit to a psychiatrist in New York. On the twenty-eighth word, *termite,* he talks about being suspended in a harness from a banyan tree while performing *Mother Courage* under a fall moon and remembers his consciousness at that moment: "the out-of-tune harmonium, Miriam, me, India. No past, no future, I couldn't make sense out of it all."[19] Despite the subject matter and the method, he never loses control of the proceedings; he is never at a loss for words, except once. *Turndown* is the twenty-ninth word and he is given one minute. He starts to think of a story but then, unable or unwilling to speak, he slowly looks up at the spectators for the rest of the minute, simply watching them watch him.

After the last story, the assistant reads all of the words back in sequence. In the course of the monologue, their denotative meanings have become secondary and the words are now heard primarily as cues for the narrative fragments. When, for example, the spectator hears *termite* in the final roll call, he may remember less the insect than the description of Gray suspended in a banyan tree. The recapitulation thereby provides a retrospective index of how meanings change through personal associations, of how a private trauma has been transformed into a structured public event, and of how pain has been translated into a memory.

* * *

Rumstick Road

Ron Vawter: When we came back from India, Spalding was in very bad shape. He was obsessed and involved, in the throes of his mother's suicide in '67. And he wanted to continue working in the theatre. Liz was dealing with him and she wanted to direct again, so they thought they would organize Spalding's thoughts into a piece about his mother's suicide. Libby Howes was here and we started working upstairs. We worked all through the fall and winter of '76 on Rumstick Road.

Spalding Gray: Rumstick Road *grew out of a need on my part to make something, to try to understand . . . to concretize some of the fears I had after getting back from India: that I was identifying with my mother so much, that I had inherited the genetic quality of manic-depressiveness. And those fears provided a terrific drive for me to make that piece, to get that out in the open, to explore. It's not that the piece grew out of* Sakonnet Point.

David Savran: When you started working on Rumstick Road, *you used many of the same objects from* Sakonnet Point.
Elizabeth LeCompte: That was a painter's idea of taking a still life and rearranging it, repainting the same scene from a different angle.
Spalding Gray: Taking the little white house from the floor and opening it up.
Elizabeth LeCompte: And suddenly, either the house had gotten very big or you, as an audience member, had gotten very small. It's just a change in perspective. Probably more in a cinematic way, drawing into a close-up. Very early on I had a vision of the two rooms next to each other, in perspective. And then I wanted to fill the rooms with something.

David Savran: With Rumstick Road, *the tapes came first, didn't they?*
Elizabeth LeCompte: Yes, Rumstick *is the one piece where we had most of the text before we started. It was a contained, one-voice text in the sense that it was all taken from the same material, with the exception of Ron's improvisation around the doctor. It was all text from Spalding's family, which gave it a certain unity. I was working with the idea of a lecture-demonstration, a science lecture. I was trying to present the material as clearly as possible, with as little interference from other people's egos, other people's personas ("characterizations"), as possible. What would be best? When would it be best just to listen to the tape and when would you need someone to "sit in," to show you, for example, how far away the speakers sat during the interview? It started from that.*

Rumstick Road (1977), the second part of the Trilogy, is an exploration of the madness of Bette Gray and her suicide on July 29, 1967. The process of assembling the piece began in 1975 when Spalding Gray decided to speak to his two grandmothers about their lives. For "no particular reason," finding it was "more fun" to talk in the presence of a "witness," he brought along a tape recorder to preserve their memories and observations.[20] The next year, after his trip to India, Gray returned to Rhode Island and made a long tape with his father, Rockwell Gray, Sr., which included a discussion of his mother's nervous breakdown in 1966 and her suicide the next year. As Gray explains, all of these recordings were made quite innocently: "There was no plan or direction in the making of the tapes. I was not conscious of doing anything . . . other than asking questions as they came up."[21] Back in New York he and Elizabeth LeCompte listened to the tapes in their loft many times. Together, they began to select the parts they found especially interesting and use them as background for physical warm-up exercises and improvisations at the Performing Garage with Libby Howes and Ron Vawter. The rehearsal work began in September 1976 and ended in the first performances of *Rumstick Road* in April 1977.

Elizabeth LeCompte has explained that she used Renaissance illustrations of anatomical demonstrations as a starting point for *Rumstick Road's* scenic concept. In these pictures, the instructor sits "high on a balcony over a table" while "the demonstrators, the people who handle the corpse" are placed in the middle. "The doctor is above, and on either side, facing him, are the students."[22] In *Rumstick Road,* the central

Schema of Rumstick Road

Room (Stage Right)	**Room (Center)**	**Room (Stage Left)**
Part I		
	Direct Address	
	Letter from Alice Mason	
Tag	*Tag*	*Tag*
Dance With Gun		
The Pick Up	....	*The Ghost*
	The First Examination (On Table)	
Part II		
	Direct Address	
House Slide		
House Dance	....	*House Dance*
		Interview with Dad in Tent
		Flying the Tent
Part III		
	Direct Address	
	The Scientific Statement of Being	
Scene Change (The Move)	....	*Scene Change (The Move)*
Slide Show		
Letter From Mom		
		Interview with Dad in Chairs
Telephone Call (With "Dr. Bradford")	....	*Woman in Tent*
	The Second Examination (With Gram Gray tape)	
Part IV		
	Direct Address	
	Letter from Dad	
Family Snapshot	*Family Snapshot*	*Family Snapshot*

* * *

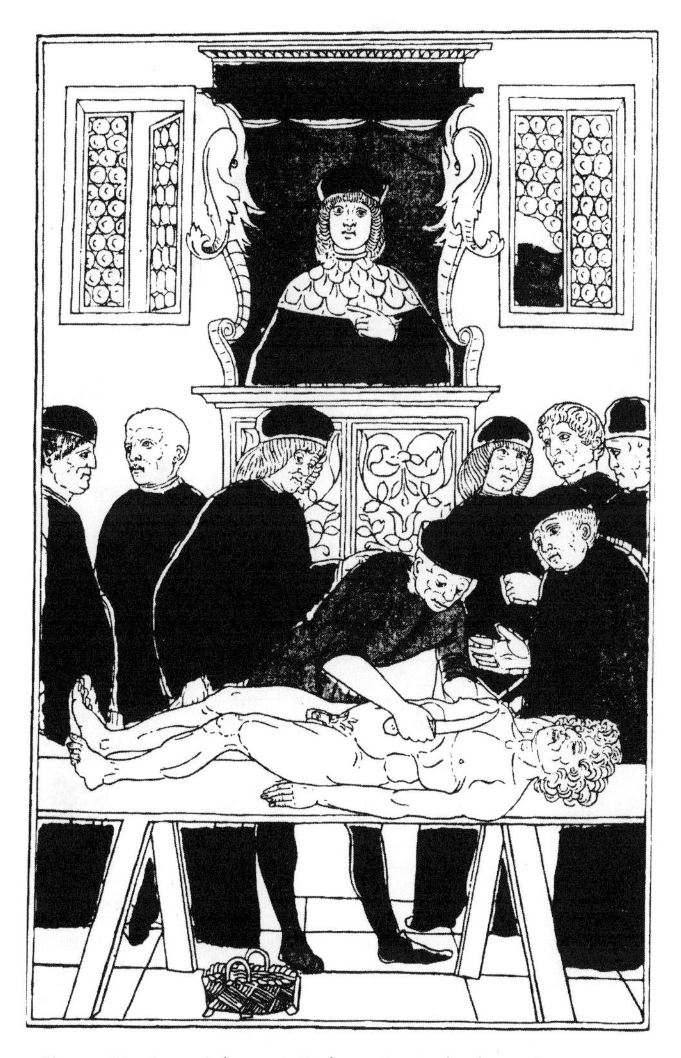

Figure 16. From Johannes Kethan, *Fasciculo di Medicina,* 1493

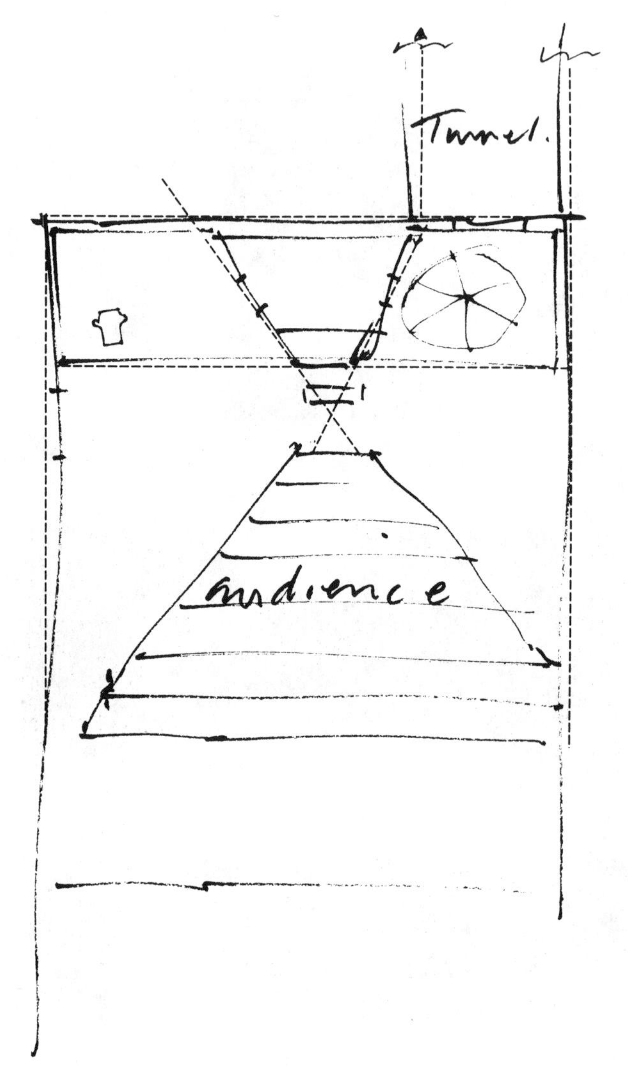

Figure 17. Performance Space for *Rumstick Road* (*Elizabeth LeCompte*)

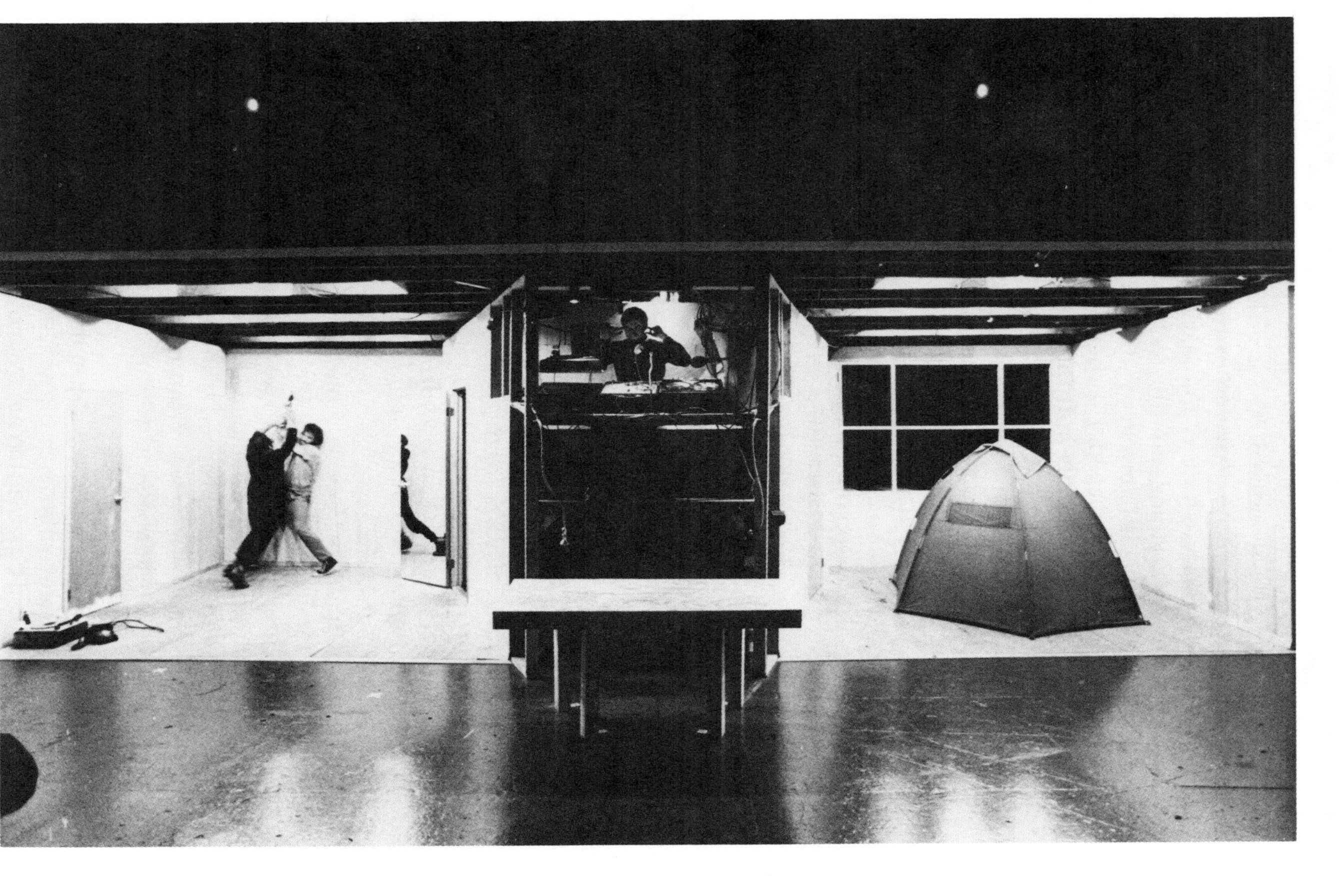

Figure 18. *Rumstick Road,* Dance with Gun
Ron Vawter, Spalding Gray, Bruce Porter.
(Ken Kobland)

control booth serves as the demonstrator's pulpit, dividing the performance space, and flanked by two large recesses. Stage right, the two side walls are bisected by wooden doors. Stage left has only one door and features a large, dark niche, covered with a glassless six-pane window. Behind it, the miniature house from *Sakonnet Point* glows, as if in the distance. Above everything sits the technical director (Bruce Porter, later Jim Clayburgh), his figure lit for the duration of the piece, controlling the many tapes to be played. The spectators sit on a triangular bank of seats whose apex lies directly in front of the control booth.

While arrayed much like a Renaissance anatomical demonstration, the performance space for *Rumstick Road* also suggests a horizontal section of a human face.[23] The two recesses become eyes separated by the control booth, the bridge of the nose. Seated before this tripartite setting, the spectators study the giant face and the two enormous eyes—or three, the control booth is also an eye—which in turn study them. The gaze of the spectators is focused on the center stage area, occupied by the control booth and a slab of wood resting on four legs which is used as an examination table twice during the piece.

* * *

Elizabeth LeCompte: I went through such a hard time with Rumstick. *People would say, "Oh, that's such a sad story about Spalding's mother's death." I felt at the time that they missed the point. Spalding was so central that they saw him, but not the piece. It's not that he wasn't the center of the piece, but that it was not about Spalding's mother. And many people immediately felt sorry for this person who's revealing what actually happened. Certainly his presence was at the heart of the piece's power. But I felt that* Rumstick *was more confrontational, more ambiguous, less judgmental than many people thought it to be.*

Given the presence of Spalding Gray on stage and the use of interviews with members of his family about his mother's madness and death, the wooden slab down center would appear to be a dissection table and the lecture-demonstration, an autopsy. Guided by these presumptions, an interpretation of the piece would proceed from the hypothesis that the corpse to be dissected is Bette Gray's. From that it would follow that *Rumstick Road* will be an analysis of the multifarious causes of her suicide. Immediately, a problem arises.

There is no body. There is no Bette Gray in the piece, no performer who plays her. Spalding Gray appears as himself, as Spud, but the other performers are labeled only as Man, Woman and Operator. They are never identified as members of the Gray family. In Part III they are associated with several of the latter, but not in the way that an actor is usually identified with a character. Rather than impersonate one of the Grays, the Man or Woman simply allows the voice or features of one to be superimposed over him or her. The Man, for example, mouths the words of Rockwell Gray, Sr. in a recorded interview performed in lip-sync. Shortly thereafter, for a recorded conversation between Spud and Gram Gray, he dons a mask of an old woman. The Woman is aligned with the image of Bette Gray only once in the piece, when a slide of the dead woman is projected on her. Both Gray and LeCompte insist, however, that the Woman is *not* impersonating Bette Gray. Libby Howes herself explains, "I am not Spalding's mother, I am Libby."[24]

Rumstick Road does not attempt to represent Bette Gray but rather to question any representation that would try to enact her madness or suicide. It examines the similarity between the gaze of the spectator and that of the physician, between the forces that produce alienation in the theatre and in the practice of medicine. It explores the process that turns people into objects, both onstage and off. It suggests that impersonation will be a dehumanizing act, violating both the performer, who will be robbed of her subjectivity and identity, and Bette Gray, who will be reduced to a vehicle for arousing pathos.

Gray and LeCompte explore the suicide, but not through impersonation, the analysis of a psyche, or the construction of a cathartic narrative. They exploit it less as the raw material for a family tragedy (in the manner of Eugene O'Neill) than as a metaphor for social and psychological dislocation, a focal point for a cultural investigation. They do not attempt to represent, but to explore what it means to represent, to hold up for examination, to submit to the diagnostic gaze. They refuse to impersonate Bette Gray because they realize that the playing of roles, both in and out of the theatre, is never politically innocent. They do not attempt to construct a coherent narrative, suitable for the representation of an event with clearly defined causes, but to reassemble a broken chain of texts. Cause and effect lose their contingency. Language itself becomes suspect, in league with a deceptive rationality. The theatre is indicted as the site of disjunction between face and mask, between being and playing a role. All that remain are the fragments: personae, interpretations and memories.

* * *

David Savran: How did you come up with the idea of projecting the slide onto Libby?

Elizabeth LeCompte: We had these slides that Spalding brought in and

one day when we looked at that one picture Ron tried it on Libby. Libby's face, of course, was perfect for it. It was large and very flat and broad. Her face could be a projection screen.
David Savran: Any reason why you chose that particular moment in the piece, the only time Libby spoke?
Elizabeth LeCompte: I think that was one of my blocking things. A lot of these details came after the fact, because they worked to make the piece travel, so to speak. The reason Libby spoke there was because it was the only time we had a text of Spalding's mother, the letter. But I had Spalding speak on top of hers because I didn't really like Libby's voice and I wanted to obliterate it with Spalding's. But the performance makes it look like Spalding's reading the letter and he's hearing the voice.
David Savran: And then, at the end of the letter, Spalding slugs her?
Elizabeth LeCompte: They upset the chair. It's not really a blow . . . he pushes her. It was one of the hardest things we worked on in that piece, because Spalding doesn't like to do things like that. And he couldn't "slug" her so that it looked hard enough.
Spalding Gray: I had to hit her right.
Elizabeth LeCompte: So that she could pretend to go flying against the wall. But that was all my thing, it had nothing to do with Spalding or his mother, initially. I did it really as a final "beat" to that scene, to end it musically. I think of those things musically because I don't like to think of them psychologically. I just work for music and then the psychology comes. She would upset the chair with her foot, so that it would look a lot more violent. It was dark and a strobe light flashed. It was a filmic trick.

In *Rumstick Road,* the parallelism between the position of the performer and that of Bette Gray is most powerfully demonstrated in Part III, in the "Letter from Mom." During the "Slide Show" seven slides from Spalding Gray's youth are projected onto a silver screen in the stage right portion of the space. A prerecorded discussion between Spalding and Gram Gray plays over the speakers as they view the same photographs of the house and members of the family. In the live performance, the Man operates the slide projector while Spud and the Woman look on in silence. Shortly after the eighth slide is flashed on the screen, of Bette Gray with two young boys in her arms, the Woman takes a seat in the chair next to Spud while the Man moves the projector back. Carefully he focuses the slide onto the Woman so that her features correspond exactly with those of the dead woman. For one moment Bette Gray suddenly appears "live," her expression frozen in an eerie smile, while she and Spud declaim in unison the "Letter from Mom," in tones that rise to a scream:

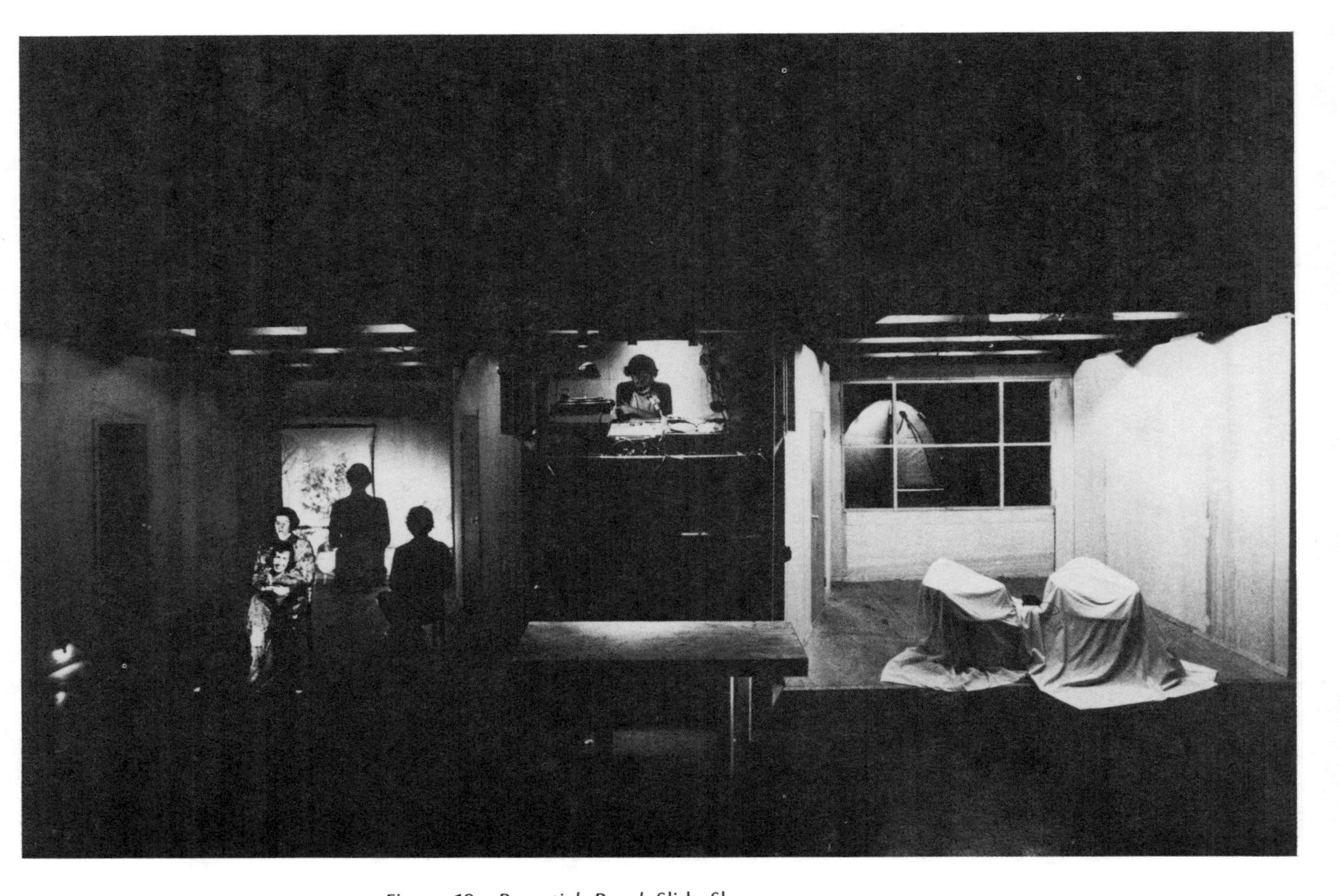

Figure 19. *Rumstick Road,* Slide Show
Libby Howes, Spalding Gray, Bruce Porter.
(Ken Kobland)

> Hi Darling! I'm home and all well and deliriously happy to be here! . . . I feel as though I had been reborn. They call me the miracle patient at Fuller Sanitorium. The Doctor said he had never had anyone get well as fast as I did. The other patients there couldn't understand it. They kept asking me what I had that they didn't have. Love ya, Mom.[25]

The final cry of anger and pain ends when Spud appears to slug the Woman in the jaw and overturn the chair in his fury.

As the slide is focused on the Woman's face, her features disappear behind the smiling countenance, the frozen mask of the dead woman. As if to confirm a new identity, she now speaks the words that Bette Gray once wrote to her son. The "magic" of theatrical conjuration brings her back to life but then immediately destroys the illusion that supports her re-animation: as soon as she moves her lips, the death mask cracks and the two faces disjoin. The force of illusion that has aligned the mask and the face is shattered and the theatrical and the literal are set at odds against each other. Rather than watching Bette Gray, the spectator studies the face of the Woman, now grotesquely distorted by the projected image. He looks from one to the other and, in the glare of misrepresentation, recognizes Bette Gray, too, as the victim of a defacement. In the momentary conjunction, the Woman does not become Bette Gray but rather becomes, like her, deformed by a role that is imposed upon her. Her image remains, no longer the corpse to be dissected, only a pattern of colored light which reflects the various images projected onto her by others: wife, daughter, mother, madwoman, suicide.

* * *

Elizabeth LeCompte: Spalding's right when he says that the Trilogy isn't his autobiography. He is a device to focus the material. The same basic process continues in the other pieces, although he no longer serves that function. And oddly enough it doesn't feel to be much of a change because even then I used different ways of focusing, separating, pulling out material. At first Spalding was bringing in most of it. In Rumstick *he brought in tapes and we worked with the people who had ended up with us. Ron brought the slide projector and put the slide over Libby's face. Ron improvised his part about the doctor during a rehearsal. Libby brought in her costume and made her dance. Everyone brought in things.*

For all but two brief sections of *Rumstick Road* the examination table center stage remains empty, its only specimen an absent corpse. It is used

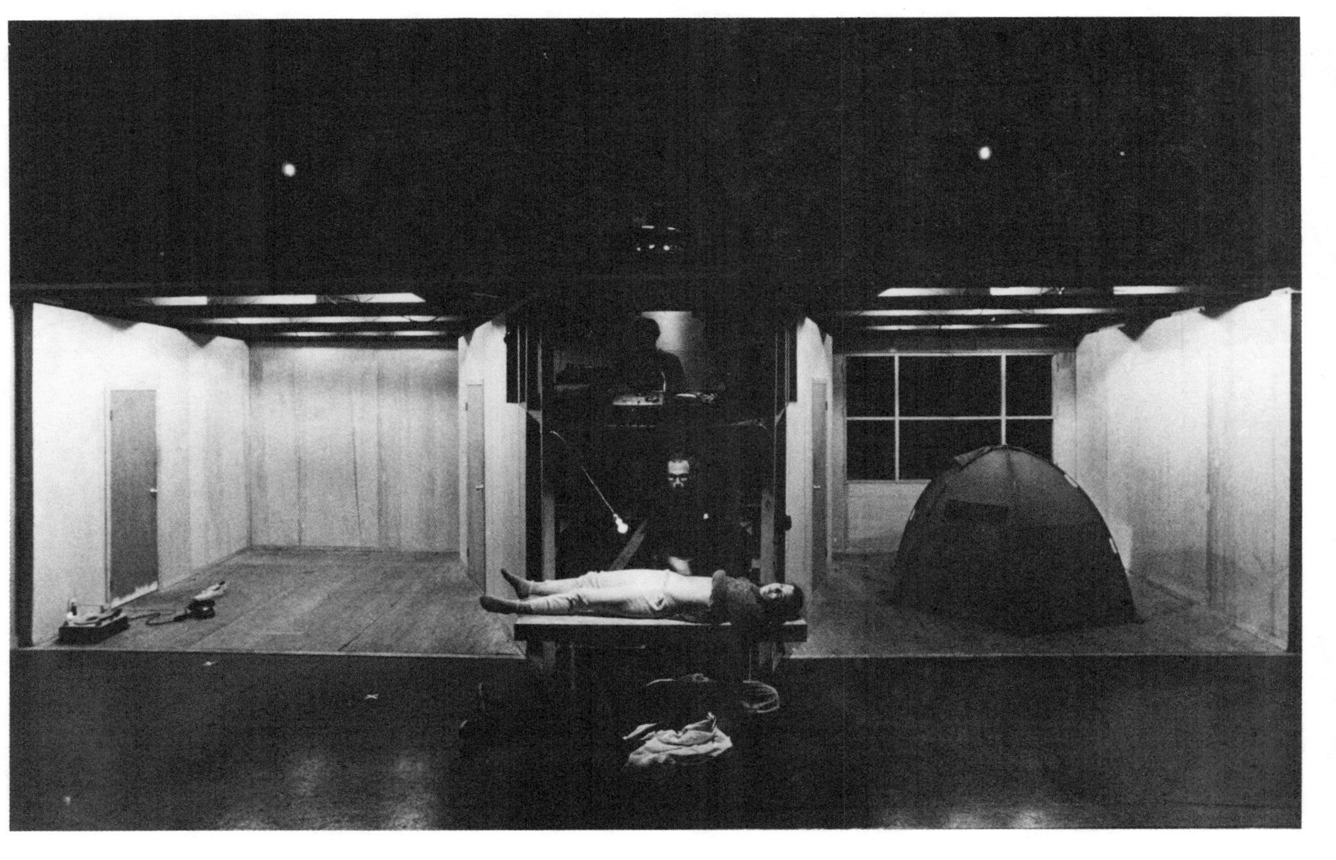

Figure 20. *Rumstick Road,* The First Examination
Bruce Porter, Ron Vawter, Libby Howes, Spalding Gray.
(Ken Kobland)

Figure 21. *Rumstick Road*, House Dance
Libby Howes, Spalding Gray, Bruce Porter.
(Ken Kobland)

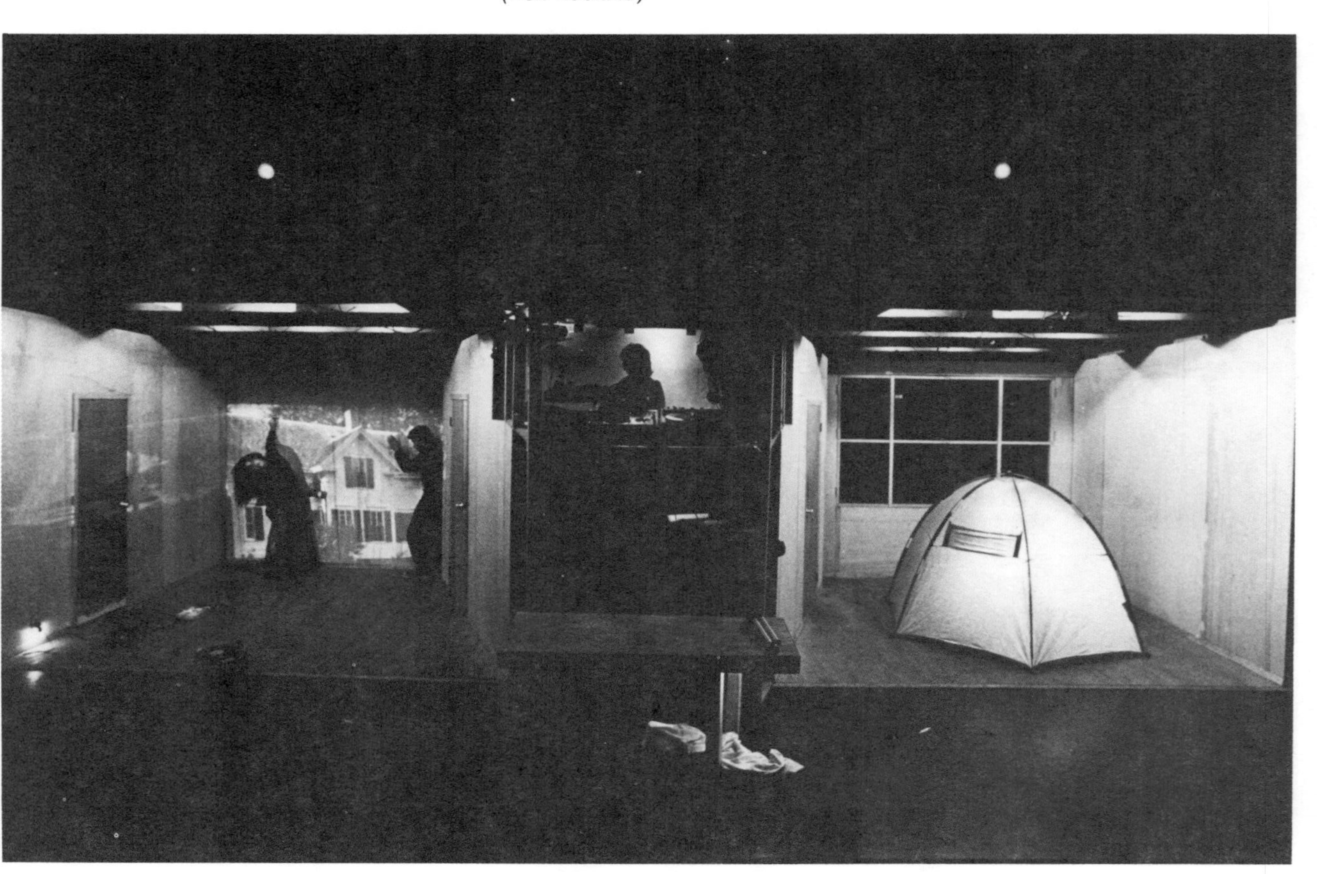

for the first time at the end of Part I when "The First Examination" is conducted upon it, a demonstration of a "process for the effective elimination of excess tension and energies from the midsection—the central torso region of the anatomy." The Man procures the Woman stage right, rolls her inert body onto his own and carries her to the examination table. He places her upon the slab and meticulously rolls her clothes away to expose her abdomen. Turning to the audience, he explains that he is about to demonstrate a form of massage "employing the mouth and the lips" in order to release negative energies from "the central torso region." Using a moveable gooseneck lamp for emphasis, he explains the musculature of the region and begins his demonstration, running his mouth up and down her belly "in much the same way one might work an ear of corn." He turns her violently as he "works" her and finally tests to see if the energy has been displaced by inserting the tip of his tongue "into the ear canal for relative moisture readings."[26] All the while, an instrumental version of "Volare" has been playing, growing progressively louder and more abrasive as the demonstration continues. The Woman, meanwhile, completely passive during the entire sequence, only laughs, with a hysteria that rises wildly as the music crests, her laughter finally protracting into a scream. During this sequence Spud has been sitting under the table, covered in a white sheet—the "Ghost" listening to the examination, the child listening in the next room. As the demonstration and the music reach their climax, he throws the sheet over the two figures and turns calmly to the audience to begin the next part of the piece.

The "First Examination" is the only text in *Rumstick Road* not based on Spalding Gray's family documents. In a way both frightening and sardonic (it is very funny in performance), it shows how an individual, prone to "bodily malfunctions,"[27] is objectified by those who attempt to help her—the sexual specificity of the victim is crucial here. In appearance closer to rape than therapy, the scene demonstrates less a method of promoting health than the dehumanizing experience that therapy becomes when masked by a "scientific" detachment and the patronizing (and patriarchal) belief that discomfort and disgrace must be endured because they are all for the patient's good. It modifies clinical procedure, displacing the patient and examining the examination itself, to suggest that pathology is less conspicuous in the body on the table than in the process—both medical and theatrical—which erects that slab and places the patient upon it.

In the "First Examination" the difference between the sexes appears most clearly in the distinction between two different kinds of action. The Man is constantly engaged in *transitive* activity; he has a direct impact on persons and things, moving through the space freely. He "flies" the tent, moving it into the window upstage left. He manipulates the slide projector so that the image of Bette Gray effaces the Woman. His physical mobility is redoubled by a characterological mobility that allows him to put on and take off the several roles he is given. In the "First Examination" he plays the part of the masseur; later, he mouths the words of Rock Gray, Sr. and, near the end of the piece, he puts on the old woman mask and conducts the "Second Examination," now placing Spud on the examination table.

The Woman, in contrast, remains passive and silent. She seems to be less a subjectivity than a screen upon which the images of others are projected. She never initiates any contact with the other performers. Except during the "Letter from Mom," her action is contained, inward-looking or repetitive. In the "House Dance" in Part II, accompanied by a Bach *Partita* for solo violin, she beats her long hair wildly against a slide of the Gray house at 66 Rumstick Road, stopping her flailing only to let tremors rack her stooped body. For several minutes she persists in this beautiful, formal dance that suggests a kind of corporeal wail or keening. (At this point interpretation is heard in its masculine voice, aligned with he who violates, objectifies, justifies, pins down.) All the while, a taped interview is being played of Gram Gray speaking of her late daughter-in-law:

> It's a real mystery to me how she could have done it . . . or what condition the mind gets in. 'Course we have no conception of what the mind can do. And how could it could've turned that . . . light-hearted, full of pep . . . woman . . . into what she turned out to be was just unbelievable. 'Course there was no question in my mind she was suffering. 'Course I can remember now, in sixty-six when she was having that first upset . . . and we were going into the play room with her one night . . . in the evening and she stood in there in the dark and she said "Gram! Gram, what is the matter with me? Why do I feel that way? What can—what can you do for me? What is the matter with me?" So she was just terribly upset. . . . I just couldn't say anything to it. Oh, you'll be all right now, just never mind. Just quiet down and. . . . [28]

Neither good will nor pity is able to assuage the Woman's distress because the others are unable to understand what the Woman is unable to speak. In a culture that values the speaking voice above any other means of communication, the Woman's silence becomes a mark of powerlessness because it shifts the focus to her body, now an object in the space. Whether being "worked" by the Man, beating her hair against the house, or sitting in the red tent, she does not explain herself and continues in isolation until the end of the piece. Even in reading the "Letter from Mom," she is unable to utter the one word that designates the quintessential woman's role in bourgeois society: her voice cuts off after "Love ya," leaving Spud alone to scream, "Mom."

Unlike the Man's, the Woman's part involves no pretense. She never actively takes on a role but stands passively while one is projected upon her. She is denied control over the roles she plays and can choose only silence and passivity. After the "Letter from Mom" she sits in the alcove

Elizabeth LeCompte: Libby was the dancer through the Trilogy.
Spalding Gray: She was the romantic, idealized mid-Western figure. . . .
Elizabeth LeCompte: The muse, so to speak.

stage right and focuses the slide on the door and then on her hand, making shadows in the pool of light. During the last part of the piece, she crawls into the red tent, spreads a white sheet and makes a bed for herself. She then takes off her clothes and lies down, covering herself with a second sheet, in preparation for sleep and dreams. Refusing to assume a role, she turns in, both literally and figuratively. The quiet end to which her isolation and passivity lead stands in contrast to another end, less gentle and less peaceful. As the voice of Rock Gray, Sr. explains at the end of Part II:

> when I awoke . . . and realized she wasn't in the room and . . . ah . . . and then I suddenly could hear a motor running. . . . I jumped up and uh . . . went out and I realized what was happening . . . and then rushed out into the garage and tried to open the doors and . . . she was in the car and . . . I called the rescue department and they came up and . . . it was too late.[29]

* * *

Elizabeth LeCompte: When Spalding first conceived Rumstick, *he thought of sitting with the tape recorder playing, sitting and looking at the audience, listening to it. Period. That was to be the piece. Then, we all sat around and listened to it. And of course we began to stage the action. Very simply. We staged things for Spalding, and they remained that way, as a staged reading, so to speak, in line with his original intention. The piece was so delicate, the material so private, that I always felt a little embarrassed that I came in and took it over, that I objectified it.*

* * *

By providing a structure for personal material, *Rumstick Road* transforms a private experience into a public theatre piece. Elizabeth LeCompte's equivocal attitude toward the transformation is in part the result of her realization that the *mise en scène* submits the raw material to the same process that the piece is examining. It uses the tapes as the basis for the construction of associations, images and roles. It objectifies them, dividing Spalding's dead mother (in LeCompte's interpretation) into a spiritual female component and a material male one or (in my interpretation) into a passive one and an active one. Rather than attempting, however, to cover up this objectification, the *mise en scène* underscores it by placing the recorded voices in an environment which baldly exposes them to examination, under white lights as glaring as those used in an operating room theatre. (Unlike *Sakonnet Point,* there are no dark corners here.)

In its examination, *Rumstick Road* aligns theatre with medicine, signaling the similarity between the gaze of the physician and that of the spectator. In both cases, vision is used to objectify, to distance the viewer from the object of scrutiny. For the physician, this separation allows him to observe the results of pathology, physical and emotional, from a scientific perspective, a relatively disengaged point of view, an elevated position (he always looks down on the patient, just like the lecturer in Kethan's engraving). For the spectator (who in *Rumstick Road* is also raised above the action) the distance authorizes an observation of character and plot, psychology and action, with the aim of understanding why events occurred as they did. In both cases, the analytical and objectifying gaze attempts to penetrate the "skin" of the object: the physician's hopes to discover the causes of pathology, while the spectator's hopes to uncover the causes of action.

In the "First Examination" Gray and LeCompte undermine the privileged position accorded the gaze of the subject—whether physician or spectator—by exposing the invasive nature of that gaze. The latter always transforms what it studies into an object to be dismembered in the diagnostic process, separated into parts corresponding to the different medical specializations (into heart and brain, for example, or body and mind). The method is problematic, particularly when the condition being examined is experienced by the patient as an objectification of the self (as is suggested regarding Bette Gray). The physician may intervene, with the best intentions, to heal a disorder, little knowing that his own intervention has become a part of the disease.

The gaze of the spectator, meanwhile, aligned with that of the physician, is reduced to its voyeuristic essence, overseeing the reaction of members of the Gray family to a deeply disturbing and traumatic event. Watching the "Interview with Dad in Chairs" and hearing Spalding Gray question his father, the spectator will scrutinize the meticulously choreographed scene, hardly able to determine whether it is being performed live or in lip-sync. At the same time, he cannot fail to note Rockwell Gray, Sr.'s hesitancy and embarrassment when asked, near the scene's end, about his wife's death: "It's the sort of thing I don't like to talk about . . . I . . . I don't like it to be recorded you know."[30] As if aware of its invasive nature, the *mise en scène* accedes to his request. At that very moment "Volare" swells over the dialogue and drowns out his protest, along with the scant information he offers. The music covers up the conversation in embarrassment, as a sheet wrapped round a figure covers up his nakedness.

* * *

David Savran: I find such a sense of violation in Rumstick Road, *when you turn to the audience and tell them that your grandmother asked you not play the tape of her reciting the Scientific Statement of Being, and then you go ahead and do it.*
Spalding Gray: Those were not choices I would have made. They were Liz's choices . . . a kind of Brechtian device, to be provocative. I'm sure that's part of what upset Michael Feingold and put me on a bad track with the Voice. *But I stand by it.*

David Savran: Spalding told me that the line, "My Grandmother asked me not to play this tape at this performance," was your idea. You're the one who's pointing out the violation.
Elizabeth LeCompte: That's a tactic I often take. I needed to state the facts. Like in Dragnet. *Just the facts. Not so much to confront the audience but to confront the material. Sometimes it's hard to tell from the way I work whether it's a confrontation of the audience or the material. It can be both. That's why I'm labelled . . . that's why it's aggressive. It's an aggressive attack on the material. Spalding tends to circle around it, while I go all the way into the middle and try to explode it. Yes, I think he was uncomfortable with that. It's not his way. And he wouldn't have done that. He would have been more politic with the critics. But then I knew that he would also play the piece in front of his grandmother—he invited her to see it but she declined. I wanted to be true to the facts, to the relationships, and I think explaining her view and then watching Spalding countermand it showed important things about Spalding, the character, and our way of making theatre.*

In *Rumstick Road* Gray and LeCompte twice clearly violate the wishes or rights of the people interviewed. At the beginning of Part III, Spud introduces a tape of his maternal grandmother reading from Mary Baker Eddy by telling the audience that she had asked him not to play the tape in the performance. Near the end of Part III, Spud recreates a telephone conversation with a psychiatrist who treated his mother. He performs his half of the interview "live" while the doctor's responses are played from a tape recording of the call made without the doctor's knowledge (the program uses a pseudonym, Dr. Henry Bradford, to identify him). The psychiatrist discusses Mrs. Gray's condition with her son in a not unkind, if perfunctory way, trying to explain her disorder and the choice of therapy. In particular, he defends the electric shock therapy: "Well, if she got that, that's the treatment, that's the—that's the treatment that she should have gotten."[31] Finally, he attempts a dubious reassurance: "And don't be frightened by a hereditary disposition.... You may not necessarily get it."[32]

Undeniably, Gray and LeCompte have violated the rights of at least two people by stealing their words and presenting them in a public forum. With the exception of "The First Examination" and Spud's direct addresses, all of the texts have been pirated and juxtaposed against a *mise en scène* that subjects them to an incisive, if ultimately ambiguous, examination. For LeCompte, this theft of language is far more than a convenient way of obtaining texts; it is a necessary step toward a radical confrontation of the canons of art and society.

The act of theft questions the ownership of a text once it has been spoken, once it has issued from the speaker and "disappeared," either into a tape recorder or into a book. The Group appropriates this stolen language, not as an act of protest or civil disobedience, but because the theft opens up an expansive field of irony. It marks the text as property to be transgressed: spoken and denied, appropriated and torn apart.

> *Elizabeth LeCompte: As the theatre dies, it is being protected by a clique of people who are narrowing it back to the writer. And because we don't work that way, we trespass everywhere. We plagiarize. We steal. We are outlaws.*

Roland Barthes explains: "The revolutionary task . . . is not to supplant but to transgress. Now, to transgress is both to recognize and to reverse; the object . . . must be presented and denied *at the same time*."[33] Further, he notes that this transgression must operate as subversion from within; it must take place within the confines of the culture in question, "within a play of structures and writings." In contradistinction, any critique that

Figure 22. *Rumstick Road,* Interview with Dad in Chairs
Libby Howes, Bruce Porter, Ron Vawter, Spalding Gray.
(Ken Kobland)

attempts to establish an independent mythology will be doomed because bourgeois society will always co-opt the mythology for its own purposes. Given modern culture's endless capacity for recuperation, "there is only one thing a writer has the power to wrest from this society: its language; but before this language can be destroyed, it must be 'stolen.' ..."[34] It must be violently wrenched from its context; it must be seized from the cultural continuum. Only then can it be turned against the voice that uttered it, can it be used as an instrument to dissect the society that produced it.

Furthermore, the use of personal tapes in *Rumstick Road* is considered exploitative because it makes public that which is deemed private. By violating the speaker's trust, it objectifies him, turning him into a case in point, an emblem, an actor in a generic social process.

> *Spalding Gray:* Rumstick Road *was incredible for me. To hear that material, to ritualize your relatives like that. Toward the end of the piece, I used to hear my grandmother as sheer poetry.*

Ironically, however, this destruction of subjectivity will also initiate the disentanglement of the subject, by providing a new perspective. For Spalding Gray, the publicization of his personal history is a necessary part of the process that allows him to come to terms with his mother's suicide: "At last I was able to put my fears of, and identification with, my mother's madness into a theatrical structure. I was able to give it some therapeutic distance,...some perspective."[35] The master irony of *Rumstick Road* becomes evident to the spectator when he realizes that the forces that comprise the collective pathology, that institute the process of dehumanization, are the same ones that allow the theatre to exist.

* * *

Elizabeth LeCompte: What was most interesting about Rumstick *for me, in the long run, was the confrontation, the moral issue of the material. Because that's something which has never been.... As with* Route 1 & 9, *I still don't understand its ramifications.*

The moral questions raised by the use of private documents led to the first public controversy over the Wooster Group's work. According to an article in the *Village Voice,* the taped conversation with Mrs. Gray's psychiatrist disturbed several of the Obie Award judges and they refused to consider it for the Award in 1977: "The conversation was bugged without the 'beeper' required by law. Some members of the Obie Award panel argued that *Rumstick* should be withdrawn from their deliberations when they discovered this violation of the physician's right to privacy."[36] In 1980, the controversy again reached the pages of the *Village Voice,* in Michael Feingold's review of performances of *Rumstick Road* given at the American Place Theatre. Feingold wrote:

> I'd like to register a vehement protest about the morality of using private documents and tapes in this kind of public performance. Prefacing one tape with the announcement that his grandmother has specifically asked him not to use it in the performance, Gray obviously thinks he's found a terrific way to rivet the audience's attention. So, obviously he has. But I feel cheapened by having been made to participate in this violation of a stranger's privacy.
>
> It's all very well for Gray to want to create a work of art out of a traumatic event in his life,... but to make a point of including dishonorable transactions like this in it is to brutalize the audience, implicating them in the artist's pain instead of offering them a share in its transcendence.[37]

The week after Feingold's review was printed, Spalding Gray wrote a letter to the *Voice* in response:

> Michael Feingold protests "brutal exploitation" in *Rumstick Road.* Of my mother's psychiatrist, I admit it. It was a brutal act. So was the shock treatment he gave her before her suicide. If I am guilty, it is of being part of that chain of brutality, but I know of no pain this theatre piece has caused him. We changed his name to protect his "innocence."
>
> The tape of my grandmother's voice was a gift. She asked me to keep it as something personal. I chose to give it away. A brutal act perhaps.... We live in a brutal time that demands immediate expression. By using private words and documents, *Rumstick* employs the painful and "exploitative" mode common to modern autobiography.
>
> I have been working from a pain that often bleeds through. Feingold longs for transcendence without having to feel that pain. In *Rumstick,* pain is a point of departure that needs to be shared with the audience.[38]

In *Rumstick Road* Gray and LeCompte dramatize their recognition that an act of dehumanization cannot be contained and isolated. Gray realizes that it is always part of a "chain of brutality," manifest, in *Rumstick Road,* in countless discrete moments: in his father's inability to deal with his mother's illness, in the psychiatrist's treatment of Bette Gray and his discomforting reassurance given her son, in the taping of private conversations and in the public presentation of those tapes. The chain of brutality, moreover, cannot be stemmed. It reaches into every system of representation, producing both language and theatre. It allows repetition; it permits actions and characters (both alphabetical and theatrical) to be figured forth. It ensures that the act of reproduction will always be an act of violation.

Gray and LeCompte realize that the transcendence of this lineage of brutality is impossible, that one can never rise above these relationships, or above metaphysics—they are ingrained in thought and language, and in the operation of theatre. As a result, they do not aim for an impossible transcendence but rather a deconstruction of the chain of brutality. To institute this deconstruction, *Rumstick Road* draws attention to the invasion of privacy, not for sensational ends, but to make the passive and silent spectator aware of his complicity with the act of violation, to implicate him in an exploitative and voyeuristic act.

Feingold understands that this brutalization immerses the audience "in the artist's pain" and yet he still longs for a "share in its transcendence." He fails to recognize that there can be no transcendence here, no break in the chain whose brutality Gray exposes by revealing his own involvement. This revelation necessitates the betrayal of trust and ensures that the transactions between Gray and both those he interviews and those for whom he performs will be, in Feingold's word, "dishonorable." Given the choice of subject matter, the only alternative to this dishonorable transaction would be a dishonest one: the creation of a cathartic fiction, like *The Cocktail Party,* that appears to rid the play-world of disease only because it has disguised and naturalized the real pathology. Gray and LeCompte refuse this act in the knowledge that it always creates a dramatic (i.e., cathartic) experience in which transcendence and absolution will be always only dramatic (i.e., fictive). They refuse renunciation because they realize that there is no position outside the chain of brutality, no way beyond theatre.

David Savran: I don't think Michael Feingold ever tried to understand why Rumstick Road *is brutal.*
Elizabeth LeCompte: But who can answer to taste? Maybe Michael Feingold doesn't want to see real brutality on the stage.
David Savran: He wants to see it transcended.
Elizabeth LeCompte: Exactly. And his experience of what transcending brutality is . . . is his experience. It's a matter of taste, finally. You're stuck with that: taste.
David Savran: But his idea of transcendence lets him off the hook. It doesn't implicate him.
Elizabeth LeCompte: No, but I don't think he goes to the theatre to be made guilty. I mean, who does? I don't either. If it happens, I'm surprised. But again, it's a matter of taste. How real, how direct do you want your theatre? In that piece Spalding was talking very directly. I was making

metaphors. It's interesting to me that Feingold took it the way he did. That disturbs me less than the people who said, "Thank you, Spalding, for being so wonderful bringing your life into our living room." And of course, some people may not even have thought that that was Spalding up there. I'm still fascinated by that. What did they think he was doing? It's very important for me that Rumstick *is performed by us, even though we gave the rights to somebody else to do a version of it. (I don't want to stop anybody from doing anything. I'd like to set a good example for people like Arthur Miller.) The important thing about* Rumstick *was that Spalding was actually up there, the person that it happened to. With anyone else playing it, it becomes something that Michael Feingold would like. It becomes a play, like [Emily Mann's]* Still Life.

* * *

Spalding Gray: The pieces are about the place names for me. They are and they're not. When I look back on it, the idea was, first of all, the Charles Ives piece I like very much, Three Places in New England. *And I like the title. When you listen to the piece, it evokes . . . it's evocative but it's not like movie music. It's not that concrete. And because I had left to come to an art community, an art ghetto, I wanted to remember it and sanctify it by giving it a name, the way you would name a child after your grandmother. And in each case, the piece was close to the name for me in what it evoked. But I wasn't trying to re-enact the past. I wasn't trying to run in* Sakonnet Point *like I ran as a kid. I was trying to run like Spalding Gray in hiking boots would run then. But somehow, when I thought about naming that piece, I thought about those summers in Sakonnet Point. And so I thought we'd name it* Sakonnet Point *because that's a way of giving it a double resonance. A meditation on the actual place the way you'd meditate on someone's name. And because it was personal, it would become a strange kind of name for someone else. It's not a New York title. It's not a New York place. It's an Indian name.*

And Rumstick Road *was clearly named for Rumstick Road although that's not where my mother committed suicide. But that's not important. It's really poetic license. The name of the road, the history of the house . . . who knows? it may never have occurred had she stayed in that house. The suicide happened in a house that was not grounded in her history, her town. Her father, I guess, built the house next to the one she lived in on Rumstick Road. The whole thing was very close. That was the first time leaving Barrington, when they moved across the bay. It's funny to think of that as a big displacement in this day and age, but for her I think it was. Again, we talk about exploring points of view. That's what we try to do with* Rumstick Road, *to ask the question.*

Rumstick Road inserts itself into a chain of brutal events in order to demonstrate the articulation of that chain. Similarly, it anatomizes the means of theatrical production to expose the ubiquity of psychic fragmentation, role-playing, and representation. By virtue of the breadth of these projects, the Wooster Group would seem to suggest that the individual is trapped in these configurations—doomed, as it were, to theatre, madness and brutality. There is, however, another aspect of this anatomization of self and society which unsettles these fatalistic intimations.

Throughout *Rumstick Road* there runs a sense of a power of illusion far more disruptive and dangerous than that associated with the simple act of impersonation. Many times, the piece provides access to a sense of the *magic* of re-presentation: when the slide of Bette Gray is projected onto Libby Howes, when Ron Vawter and Spalding Gray perform the "Interview with Dad in Chairs" in lip-sync so accurately that Vawter appears to some spectators really to be speaking. In an almost

> *Spalding Gray: One night I looked across at Ron and heard my father's voice coming out of his chest. I thought Ron was actually talking. I did a double take. It was a perfect illusion. He had learned how just to slur his lips so it didn't look like he was over-articulating. And he had the breathing down exactly.*

shamanistic way, these activities call up spirits, animating the inanimate. They induce a sense of wonder at the power of theatre to perpetrate illusion, a wonder that is the other side of the disquietude induced by the contemplation of the destructive and dehumanizing effects of the theatrical. In *Rumstick Road* this intimation of the magic of performance is not, however, an appeal to an idealist vision that values the transcendent over the concrete. Its function in the piece is strategic: it disrupts the voices of certitude and authority, it questions the privileged position accorded reason and the disciplines that lay claim to scientific truth.

Near the end of the piece, the status of non-rational experience is confronted in "The Second Examination" and the "Letter from Dad." In the former, Spalding Gray asks his grandmother a question about his mother on tape while the "live" Spud questions the Man, now wearing the old woman mask and sitting in a wheelchair:

> She told me once when she was younger . . . when she used to go to the symphony alone . . . that she . . . was sitting in her chair . . . and next thing she knew she was floating up . . . to the ceiling . . . looking back at her body . . . sitting in the chair. She got very high.[39]

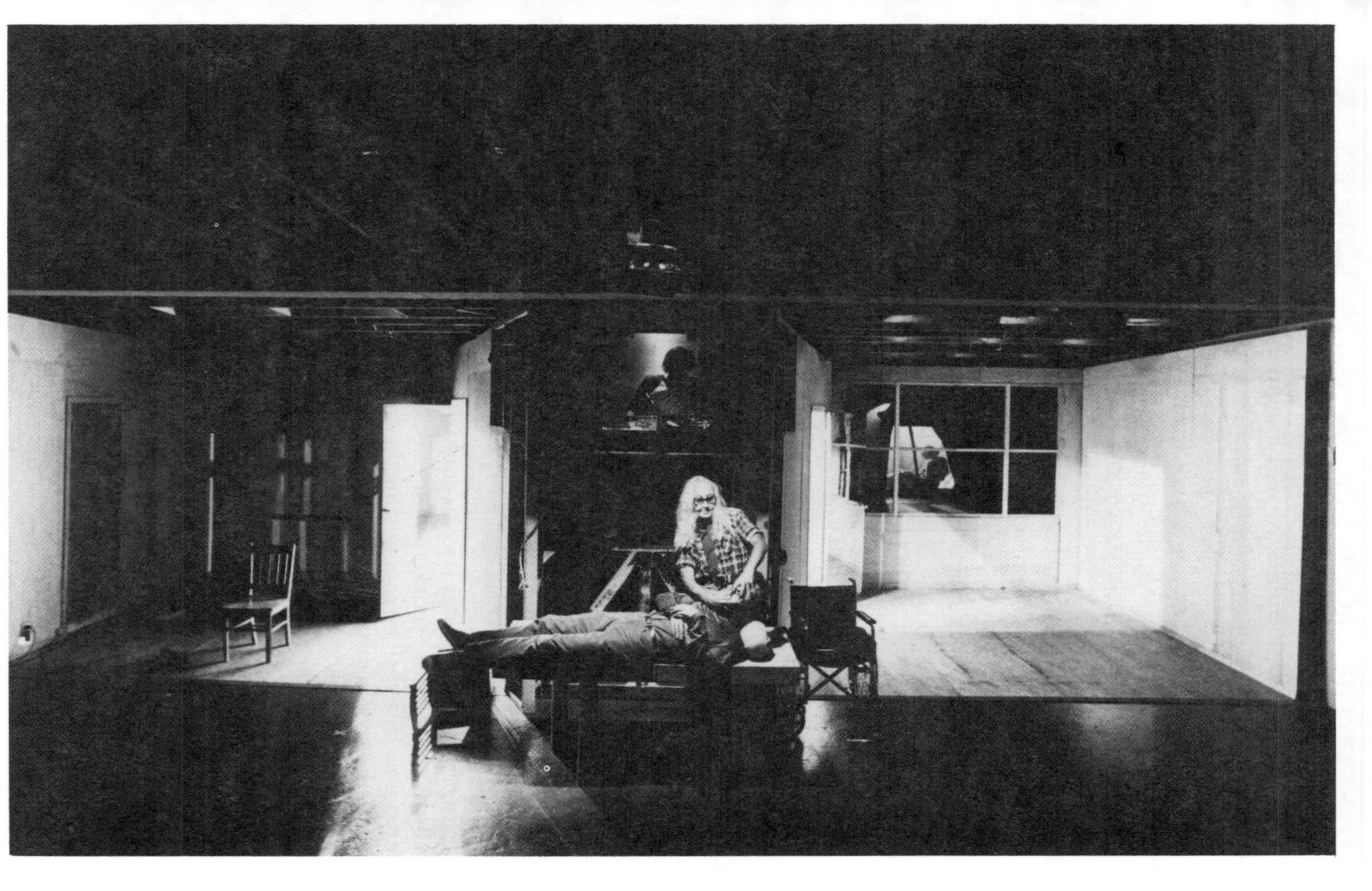

Figure 23. *Rumstick Road,* The Second Examination
Bruce Porter, Ron Vawter, Spalding Gray, Libby Howes.
(Ken Kobland)

In reply, Gram Gray ascribes Bette Gray's visions to her "fl--l--lighty imagination" and Christian Science: "I had no patience with visions . . . at all . . . I thought it was all in her warped imagination."[40]

The confrontation between the spiritual and the material is crucial not because it forces a choice between the two but because it undermines the distinction between reality and illusion, truth and falsehood, sanity and madness. *Rumstick Road* questions these concepts and modes of experience, using one form of knowledge to play off of and disrupt a second; it does not aim at the production of a discourse of truth or a master perspective (with all the latter implies regarding the gender of a discourse). At the end of the piece, Spalding Gray reads a letter from his father that he received in February 1966, more than a year before his mother's death. Spud prefaces it by noting that "After reading it and re-reading it I was forced to re-examine all the material I had collected so far."

> Mother is not doing well at all. I had high hopes that she might get better at Tenacre, but, if anything, I think she is worse. . . . I did talk with her last Tuesday, but it was very discouraging—she is now certain that she is insane and that she can never recover. This is a very difficult frame of mind to recover from. While I keep avoiding the thought, I find myself more and more wondering if maybe this is so—it does happen to people—but I can't believe it is really happening to us. . . .
>
> Friday night when I came home I went into the bedroom and found glass all over the floor—then discovered that the storm window and one 8 by 10 pane next to mother's little shelf corner in the front had been smashed. I was about to call the police and looked around for the stone or other object, but found nothing—then discovered feathers and after looking further found a partridge, dead on my bedside table. It's hard to believe that a bird which weighed one and a quarter pounds could go through two windows, brush through the curtain, knock over the TV aerial and, without losing any altitude, zoom across the room hitting the corner and dropping dead on the table without even disturbing the lampshade. It took me about two hours to clean up the mess and, I might add, dress the bird for the ice box. Gram Gray came for the weekend and we had a delicious partridge dinner Saturday night.[41]

Rock Gray's story of the partridge and the broken window throws a very different perspective on Gram Gray's dismissal of her daughter-in-law's out-of-body experience. Now her son describes an incident that is just as inexplicable and whose strangeness will be redoubled by the associations that the bird summons up. Both Bette Gray's experience and the "Letter from Dad" concern a principle actor who disrupts the routine of others by a real or imagined flight. The mysterious nature of both incidents is heightened by the bird's traditional association with the sacred (in Christian mythology it is an emblem for the Holy Ghost) as well as its wide use as a symbol, from Homer to Ibsen. Perhaps the most striking aspect of Rock Gray's narrative, however, is the final destination of the dead partridge: Saturday night dinner. If we accept its Christian symbolic value, daring to eat it becomes a wild and reckless profanation of the sacred (an act of *hubris,* or tragic pride). At the same time, however, the matter-of-fact disposal of the bird would seem to mock the very interpretive process that would turn it into a symbol, including my own discourse.

In consuming and destroying the symbol, *Rumstick Road* refuses both catharsis and dialectical synthesis. It does not encourage an audience's experience of transcendence to provide resolution, but presents transcendence itself (both Bette Gray's "floating" and the flight of the partridge) as a dubious and bizarre experience. At the end of the

Spalding Gray: The days of composing and performing the Trilogy were very, very high times for me, bordering on the religious. I felt like I'd entered a monastery.

piece, this questioning of the act of rising above substitutes for closure, providing the spectator not with certitude, but with a sense of intoxication, of the mysterious that obviates the search for truth. Watching the performance, he too may get "very high," floating above his seat, looking down at the traces of violence that far overreach the bounds of the performance space.

Ron Vawter: I don't know if Spalding's father was trying to be metaphorical in the letter. But it was so astonishing to us. Life's ability to come up with such amazing, not metaphors, but events that are so revealing, in such idiotic and amusing ways... amusing us with the tragedy of life, which is blameless and without victimization, which shows sensitivity and insensitivity. Why did he put that anecdote in the letter? Is it because he thought it was something Spalding would like to hear? What did it mean to him? What if it didn't mean anything to him? What if it didn't occur to him that there might be a connection? It hit the note of the piece, that place between being able to perceive and being totally unable to perceive a situation.

* * *

Nayatt School

Elizabeth LeCompte: In the Trilogy I kept Spalding at the center of the story, because that's where he's strongest and most comfortable. He's telling the story, or apparently telling the story. But there's no story to tell, so to speak. He's hunting for the story.
David Savran: A pretext.
Elizabeth LeCompte: Yes. And in Nayatt *Spalding remained at the center even though he was no longer telling his own story. If people saw* Rumstick, *then they would attach . . . they would see this was the same character. But if they hadn't seen* Rumstick, *it was a whole different piece.*

Spalding Gray: Nayatt School *was dreamy, fleeting . . . and a very beautiful piece. With* Rumstick Road, *I was always a little outside of it because I felt like I was laying out the family underwear, in the sense that my job was to open the drawers and say, "look: this and this and this and this," like a scientist almost, a researcher. In* Nayatt *I was able to lose myself in the celebration of the madness.* Rumstick Road *was the documentation of the madness. And in hindsight, I have a lot of feelings about how these were religious, shamanistic . . . very, very important rituals for me, for Liz, for everyone . . . that celebration after the mourning. 'Cause I never went through the mourning for my mother's death.* Rumstick Road *was the working out of the facts and* Nayatt *was the celebration.*

Ken Kobland: In Nayatt, *my first film collaboration with the Group, I think Liz wanted to expand the media spectrum of the work, the size of the work—to involve film as memory. The main film was projected over the space, the black-and-white one of the children in* The Cocktail Party, *the children who have now grown up, one, in fact, now dead. The idea was that the piece would be, with the film involvement, a piece of contradiction, of time passing in different ways. There was the story of Celia Coplestone, the martyr, and there was the story of* Nayatt School*—of making* The Cocktail Party.

Nayatt School (1978) is an explosion of texts, performers, images, props and media. It is a celebration that is unique among the Wooster Group's work, embodying the thrill of discovery, of coming upon a world alternately sublime and horrific. It is the first Wooster Group piece to use a wild assortment of texts and the first to incorporate excerpts from a

Figure 24. *Nayatt School*, Part V, *The Cocktail Party*
Ursula Easton, Ron Vawter, Tena Cohen, Libby Howes, Michael Rivkin.
(Bob Van Dantzig)

classic play. In Part III the Group performs two comedy–horror sequences from the record *Drop Dead* by Arch Oboler ("A Day at the Dentist" and "The Chicken Heart") as well as a scene written by Jim Strahs, "The Breast Examination." Framing these three scenes are two excerpts from *The Cocktail Party* by T.S. Eliot. In the first Spalding Gray and Joan Jonas (later, Willem Dafoe) read an excerpt from Act II of the play. In the second, Spalding, the Man (Ron Vawter) and the Woman (Libby Howes, later Kate Valk) are joined by four children for a dramatization of selections from Act III. In addition to these live performances, Spalding and the sound operator (Bruce Porter, later Jim Clayburgh) play a total of fifteen records, ranging from disco music to the Berlioz *Requiem* to the theme from "Peter Gunn." The non-musical selections include, prominently, a 1950s recording of *The Cocktail Party* with Alec Guinness and a Folkways instructional record, "The Understanding and Self Examination of Breast Cancer." The piece is divided into six parts, each one labelled an "Examination of the Text."

*   *   *

Schema of Nayatt School

Part I — *The First Examination of the Text: In Which Spalding Tells About Himself and Introduces a Record* (The Cocktail Party)

Part II — *The Second Examination of the Text: In Which Spalding Plays the Part of the Doctor and Introduces a Woman Who Plays the Part of Celia, and They Enact a Reading of the Text* (The Cocktail Party, *Act II)*

Part III — *The Third Examination of the Text: In Which Spalding, The Woman and The Man Play Doctor in Three Scenes ("A Day at the Dentist," "The Breast Examination" and "The Chicken Heart")*

Part IV — *The Fourth Examination of the Text: In Which Spalding Introduces a Record and the Stage is Set for a Cocktail Party*

Part V — *The Fifth Examination of the Text: In Which Spalding Introduces the Children in Their Parts and The Man, The Woman and Spalding Play a Scene With Them* (The Cocktail Party, *Act III)*

Part VI — *The Sixth Examination of the Text: In Which Spalding, The Woman and The Man Destroy the Records and The Man and The Woman Depart*

*   *   *

In completing the Trilogy, *Nayatt School* returns to innocence to dramatize its loss. It juxtaposes children against adult performers in *The Cocktail Party* to contrast a capricious and lawless innocence with the restraints of the reputedly cultured adult world. It celebrates madness, both the madness of Bette Gray and the passion of Celia Coplestone. It analyzes the experience of dehumanization and examines what Gray calls "the victimization of women in male-dominated social structures."[42] It dramatizes this victimization by playing two kinds of texts off each other, the "soap operas" and "horror stories" that Gray talks about in his opening monologue.[43] In reading a scene from Act II of *The Cocktail Party,* the piece points out the sentimentality of the play's vision of a mystical pathway to illumination. Later, in performing excerpts from Eliot's Act III, it casts light upon the shadows of that pathway and dramatizes the madness and destruction to which it can lead. Between these scenes, it performs two comedy–horror sequences and a breast examination that present another perspective on the victimization by forces beyond the individual's control.

Although *The Cocktail Party* is the ostensible subject of *Nayatt School's* six "Examinations of the Text," the act of examination insistently deflects the analytical gaze of the spectator off the play and onto various contingent texts and social processes, onto the theatrical and ideological forces underpinning Eliot's "comedy"[44] of adultery and crucifixion among the English "smart set."[45] *Nayatt School* institutes a critique by using the play as a foil that it imitates and undermines at the same time. It provides an analogue to the play's depiction of social trauma and personal crisis by presenting a spectacle of mad and obsessive expansion. Everything grows and multiplies wildly and unrestrainedly, as if the teacher had just stepped out of the classroom. Characters, media and props proliferate and commandeer the space: the live performers play a multiplicity of roles; the live action is doubled by a film of a previous performance; maraschino cherries, plastic glasses and old record players multiply maniacally. At the end of *The Cocktail Party,* Eliot restores order and checks the crisis. *Nayatt School,* in contrast, does not lead to the restoration of any social order but rather celebrates the triumph of disorder and the descent, literally, into chaos. The teacher never returns. The records, which Spalding Gray has wiped clean and played carefully at the beginning of the piece, and which have accumulated so many associations, are destroyed at its end: the performers climb up onto the table, scratch the records with knives and scissors, cut them up and finally set them on fire.

October 10, 1977 [First rehearsal]—
Looking at pornography, films, books & shows.
Lizzie wants to do classical Mr. Roger science experiments
Libby: Inabilities of teachers to explain different realms of cognizance
Spalding's outline:
Institutions
forms: ways of relating to the world
religion, psychology, politics, astrology, chance
Performance: the presentation of self through roles
Apocalypse: end of the world phenomenon
He said (and Liz) that we'd be working with two groups of children.

October 11—themes: spiritual vs. material
slow start, building layers of information
theatre theme mixed in
4 Quartets
"We shall not cease from exploration and the end of all our exploring will be to arrive where we started and know the place for the first time."
Kennedy [assassination] continually playing underneath—the disaster emerges from the commodities
Ronnie: cancer, mortality, disease
Lizzie: away from condemnation of society
Spalding: loss of innocence
A child's perception of reality
Kennedy A.= first loss for our generation
No attempt to go back but to use children to observe their ways of relating, to try to have their views—one metaphor is theatre—what it is to perform, to act

Excerpts from Libby Howe's record of rehearsals,
the *Nayatt School Notebook*

* * *

Jim Clayburgh: I've seen the pieces... as groundplans moving through the space, vertically and horizontally. Nayatt *is basically just* Rumstick *dropped through the floor. It's the exact same groundplan. The booth became the open space and the room, left, was taped on the floor. It's as if the* Rumstick *floor collapsed and certain things just happened to fall a little bit farther. And* Point Judith *also. And* Route 1 & 9. *And* L.S.D., *believe it or not.*

Ken Kobland: Liz's conception of the space for Nayatt School *is so dynamic, detailed, activated. The performers penetrating, going down into that giant arena. And with the film, going back into another time because some of the people are no longer there. The film was a constant next to the variables, the people who aren't there, which is also a part of* The Cocktail Party. *Of the monologues. Of the past. Of the Wooster Group.*

When the spectators enter the Performing Garage for *Nayatt School,* they climb up a set of stairs to a steeply raked seating area raised eight feet above the floor, opening onto a large space stretching both above and below them. At the edge of the platform runs a long narrow table on which are placed three record players (fanolas). Below, lies the groundplan from *Rumstick Road,* as if "dropped through the floor." A trapezoidal wooden house sits stage right, with a large front window and a plexiglass roof. Opposite, its mirror image is taped onto the black floor. Another long narrow table runs diagonally across the floor, disappearing into what appears to be the gaping mouth of the red tent from *Sakonnet* and *Rumstick.* The house itself is designed in reverse forced-perspective, with severely raked walls and floor. Directly behind its front window runs a trough in which performers sometimes pass on their knees, appearing as midgets next to the others further upstage on the raked floor.

The *trompe l'oeil* space within the house and the discontinuity between the house and the rest of the setting produce a fragmented environment and a number of distinct spatial scales. For the spectator, the collision between the scales induces a sense of disorientation which is redoubled by his vertiginous perspective on the action, placed far above

> *Bruce: tiered audience, scaffolding seating, office and room exposed and tilted toward audience, anti-gravity room*
>
> Nayatt School Notebook

the floor, overlooking an eight-foot precipice. He stares out at the open space (like a giant squash court, or an operating room theatre) unable to see the floor area directly in front of the platform. As if in compensation, the house has had its roof removed but it presents only a skewed perspective, like a Cubist fun-house. Unlike the setting for *Rumstick Road,* this one mocks any attempt to discern a single vanishing point. It offers only multiple perspectives.

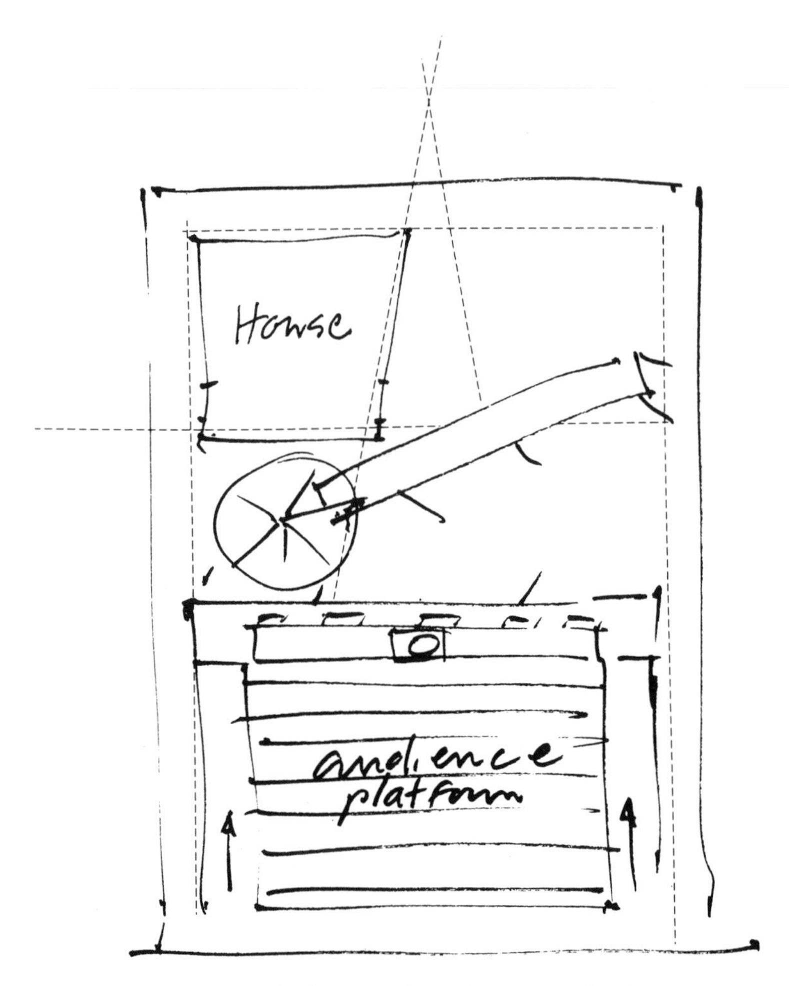

Figure 25. Performance Space for *Nayatt School*
(Elizabeth LeCompte)

Spalding Gray: The real seeds of the monologue were in Rumstick Road, *in the first direct address to the audience, saying "My name is Spalding Gray," and talking about the house. But the monologues never would have come into being had not the Group been my first supportive audience, at the table, in* Nayatt. *And then it was a matter of shrinking the table down to a desk.*
Elizabeth LeCompte: As I am expanding it.
Spalding Gray: Although the seeds of the monologue were in Rumstick, *the realization of it was something else.*

Elizabeth LeCompte: In Nayatt, *I was picking up on something I knew he wanted to do. Because that was my structural thing, to have him face out. But it was something he was doing all along. I remember for years before that, he would...*
Spalding Gray: In Tooth of Crime *I would tire of looking at Joan [Mackintosh] and look at the audience instead, for a relief.*
Elizabeth LeCompte: And beyond that, the storytelling...at home, personally.
Spalding Gray: Oh yeah, sure, of course.
Elizabeth LeCompte: He'd constantly come back to me and tell me stories as though they'd been previously constructed. And he'd demonstrate things. Remember, you'd bring a record and say, "Now listen, I want you to hear this part."
Spalding Gray: Right.
Elizabeth LeCompte: And they would be, like, performed—personal performances. I was just the audience, I wasn't Liz. He wasn't talking to me as his good friend, or his lover, or anything. He was talking to me as the audience.

Spalding Gray: The more I get comfortable with writing, the more I'm able to be alone with it and not feel that I'm dying and disappearing because I'm not being seen by the eyes of the audience. For whatever reason, whatever my particular matrix of neuroses is about, it's about being seen. I've been upstate for almost three weeks and no one knows me, no one recognizes me, and I begin to disappear, and get shaky about my identity. Walking on a dirt road I go by this woman, she comes by, she says, "Hello." Then she goes down and picks some flowers and she comes back and we cross, again, on the same dirt road. And she goes, "Well, hello again." And everything changes in me. There's a history there. She sees me as this recognizable person that she's seen for a second time. And that changed the whole evening. It's as though it made my body fill up and gave me outlines. Up until then, I didn't...in a way, it was an ambiguity between me and the landscape.

The First Examination which begins *Nayatt School* is a gently ironic monologue delivered by a clever and ingratiating performer. Spalding Gray recounts his personal associations and experiences with *The Cocktail Party* and introduces a recording of the play. He addresses the spectators in a manner both formal and intimate, earnest and ironic, attempting to draw them into the play and to explain his perspective on it. At times he seems almost to be mocking the play; at other moments he seems genuinely engrossed in and excited by the characters, situations and poetry. In any case, his fascination is infectious; he gains the audience's confidence and evokes a warmly empathic response. After reading a description of the play's action, he speaks about his college experiences as an actor and his involvement with another production of *The Cocktail Party,* directed by John Wynne-Evans, in which he played the part of Alex. He remembers performing the play at a nunnery in Albany to an audience that was very receptive and "entirely black—a sea of habits."[46]

Spalding Gray then introduces a recording of *The Cocktail Party* featuring Alec Guinness as the doctor, Sir Henry Harcourt-Reilly. Gray announces that in "this version" about to be performed he will play the role that Guinness played.[47] He explains, however, that having been raised by his mother as a Christian Scientist, he has had little experience with doctors. For those unfamiliar with the play, he provides a summary of the action and plays excerpts from the records, talking through them as they play.

In this monologue, the first extended one of his career, Spalding Gray finds his place and identity within the Trilogy. Coming out on stage alone and engaging the audience, he *is* the piece for all of Part I. For the first time in the Trilogy, he emerges as a whole being. His body is filled in, given outlines. He is an adult, speaking in his own voice, no longer dependent, as he was in *Rumstick Road,* on the taped voices of others. He is a person communicating, a character named Spalding. He speaks to others, he is recognized by others, he has a vocation: he is an actor. The opening also establishes Spalding Gray's place and identity within the development of his career. For the first time, he addresses the audience directly and at length. He need no longer pretend that he is simply allowing the latter to oversee and overhear him in his interactions with another performer. He has a vocation: he is a speaker, an autobiographer, a story-teller.

January 20, 1978—
Spalding begins with improv to explain play plot enough so that the C[ocktail] P[arty] I scene makes sense
Object/Subject quote most exciting to Spald
autopsy—to see with one's own eyes
At CP I the machine "breaks down" and Joan plays just *reading but builds to personal involvement*
Spald cutting back and forth as Psych[iatrist] and commentator

January 25—
Liz wants more, a lot *more introduction*
name books, record players—all things, tapes

February 8—
The intro scene
Liz: What is the Cocktail Party? What are you doing with the Cocktail Party? "I don't know. I really don't know."—Spald
Liz: I want something very grounded in what you're doing, or what you think you might be doing. Start with the record, how you found it, listening to it . . .
Liz: Leave it on and talk through it.
Sp: I can't act it. I can't manufacture.
Liz: It works when you keep talking.
Sp: I can't play it.
Liz: At least 10 minutes about play leading up to office encounter, Celia and Reilly.
Ron: Just your relation, wild and random associations
Liz: A brief description in first minute.
Sp: Written out.
Liz: You write it out, then riff.
R: Nothing to do with structure, but how you're getting off on the play.
Liz: Where it works is where you have associations. The piece isn't about the record, it's about your relationship to the record & Celia's circumstance—record, images, idea that Celia is going to a psych[iatrist]—what was it about, why chosen for R[umstick] R[oad] and why not able to use in RR?
Sp: Every time I listen, I end up listening.
Liz: Yes but be active not passive, move through it rapidly.
Sp: Draws me in the plot, strong driven magnetic.
Liz: Return to following record jacket & comment.
Sp: Never know what the needle will do, must hear record to be able to riff but then sucked into listening.
Liz: Set up a record of free association—parallel to floor movement w/ kids.

Nayatt School Notebook

In its focus on Spalding Gray's experiences as a performer, his coming to maturity both within the Trilogy and within his career, *Nayatt School* emerges as a meditation on performance and the phenomenology of the subject. It examines how the speaking, feeling subject reacts to a world which is constantly impacting upon and threatening him. As such, it contrasts with *Rumstick Road* which is, rather, a meditation on the status of the object and the relentlessness with which theatre produces objects. The earlier piece immerses performers and spectators in an endless process of objectification; it denies the victim a voice. *Nayatt School,* on the other hand, begins with the experience of the performer and provides a subjective account of the same process. It explores the mechanism that transforms the speaking and feeling subject into an object, not by showing his complaisance (as in *Rumstick Road*), but by allowing the subject to articulate his response to this process, his sense of position. It provides the subject with highiy individualized and

> *Celia is connection to text for audience. Underline* her *story and its relation to the texts.*
>
> Nayatt School Notebook

expressive speech, appropriating the words of one of the most articulate victims in twentieth-century drama, Celia Coplestone. It amplifies the voice of the violated one, of the sacrificial victim just before it is torn apart.

In its examination of subjectivity, *Nayatt School* elaborates on an important speech from the first act of *The Cocktail Party.* In his introduction, Spalding draws our attention to this "favorite passage" of his in which Sir Henry Harcourt-Reilly analyzes Edward Chamberlayne's sense of alienation and panic when he discovers that his wife has left him:

> Yes, it's unfinished...
> But there's more to it than that. There's a loss of personality;
> Or rather, you've lost touch with the person
> You thought you were. You no longer feel quite human.
> You're suddenly reduced to the status of an object—
> A living object, but no longer a person.
> It's always happening, because one is an object
> As well as a person. But we forget about it
> As quickly as we can.
> ....
> Or, take a surgical operation.
> In consultation with the doctor and the surgeon,
> In going to bed in the nursing home,
> In talking to the matron, you are still the subject,
> The centre of reality. But stretched on the table,
> You are a piece of furniture in a repair shop
> For those who surround you, the masked actors;
> All there is of you is your body
> And the 'you' is withdrawn.[48]

In explaining the experience of alienation, Reilly defines the subject as the "centre of reality," the fixed point, the essence which is always being objectified. *Nayatt School* both expands and undermines this notion of objectification by accepting the centrality of the speaking subject only to question it, to show that it is an illusion, a ruse. Spalding Gray's engagement of the spectator in the opening monologue is the beginning of a process that leads to the speaker's fragmentation and the audience's estrangement, as "Spalding" is gradually subsumed by a host of other parts. By the end of the piece, after he has played an assortment of variously pathological roles, it becomes clear that his charm and charisma have been used to make him a pretext, a false center. *Nayatt School* suggests that rather than being a fixed point of reference, a stable personality, Gray's appearance as "Spalding" is only one role among many. It questions his status as a primary three-dimensional subject in the midst of various two-dimensional characters. It may well be that he is simply the collection of the roles he plays: Sir Henry, teacher, mad scientist, dentist, doctor, son.

* * *

Elizabeth LeCompte: Nayatt *is very difficult to mount.*
Willem Dafoe: Do you really think I want to recreate my role of the chicken heart?
Elizabeth LeCompte: He was great.
Willem Dafoe: I wore a pink t-shirt.
Elizabeth LeCompte: It was an essential role in Nayatt, *and it sounds stupid but...*
Michael Stumm: The flopping tent.
Elizabeth LeCompte: It was very hard to do, physically. And Willie was about the only one who could do it.
Willem Dafoe: It was very funny, if you can imagine, prime time rehearsals and there are many, many things to do. And Liz is drilling people on how to be the chicken heart. And they're failing left and right. She's getting angry. And their acting careers are going down the drain. Their self-esteem is going down the drain. They're gonna kill themselves because they can't do the chicken heart. It was really extreme.
Peyton Smith: Get inside the red tent! Inside!
Elizabeth LeCompte: You know, it starts to go bum-bum inside. Bum-bum, bum-bum.
Willem Dafoe: It starts to go and then it runs around and then it starts to eat the Woman and chew her up.
Kate Valk: Who did it last time?
Willem Dafoe: I did.
Kate Valk: Were you in the chicken heart?
Elizabeth LeCompte: Yeah, he would run down from Celia Coplestone.
Kate Valk: Would I run in there with you and scream?

Willem Dafoe: Yeah, yeah.
Kate Valk: That was you in there??
[Laughter.]
Elizabeth LeCompte: That's the thanklessness of the role.

Ron Vawter: In the Trilogy I took a lot of pleasure from performing in a new way. I saw myself as a stand-in, or surrogate, not playing a role so much as standing in for people that Spalding wanted to have in the same room, in the scene.
David Savran: Like, in Rumstick Road, *his father or grandmother.*
Ron Vawter: Yes. But I never tried to act older, or like I thought his father would be. I always saw myself as a surrogate who, in the absence of anyone else, would stand in for him. And even now, when I'm in front of an audience and I feel good, I hearken back to that feeling, that I'm standing in for them. Anybody might as easily be up there, but I'm the one who happens to be there at the moment. That's the feeling I have about any character I play, that I'm there in place of the real thing or of anyone who's watching it. And that makes me feel very generous, very energized. This feeling came out of the Trilogy because I behaved in those pieces in place of people who were important in Spalding's life, or members of his family. So I always had the feeling, not so much of inhabiting an imaginative or fictional world of my own, but of being a theatrical "stand-in."

In performance as it has been traditionally conceived, the performer must surrender his identity to that of the character he plays. He must allow himself to be usurped, to be violated by another, just as, in *Rumstick Road,* Libby Howes is violated by the image of Bette Gray. In all its work the Wooster Group breaks with this pattern by asking the performer not to sacrifice his subjectivity, but to retain it and simply stand in for someone else. The performer will make no attempt to impersonate, to portray a character with any fullness or psychological depth. He just goes through the motions.

In *Nayatt School* the performers work from an instrumental rather than a psychological basis. They never become the characters they play, remaining simply the medium used to produce them. Like Willem Dafoe animating the red tent, the performer and his activity remain clearly separated, and the former can disappear into the latter only because the two are qualitatively, unmistakably different. The red tent only *becomes* the chicken heart because it is so obviously *not* a chicken heart. The performance retains its identity as work, as a product of human labor, by clearly separating performer and character as two stages in a process of production. Both performer and character thereby resist reduction to a psychological essence, remaining simply figures among a series of surrogates, dancers in the choreography of displacement.

As a result of the gulf between actor and role, the possibility of meaning is always being disseminated across a wild proliferation, across a series of doubles. This play of substitutes ensures that none of the objects (as well as none of the performers) can be used as conventional symbols. Instead, they seem to mock any attempt to read them symbolically. The red tent, for example, may appear to be a symbol for woman from the accumulated weight of the earlier pieces. It is kept at a distance from the main performing areas in *Sakonnet* and most of *Rumstick,* and is used as a haven for women in both pieces, a place of music and rest. Although it is, in shape and coloration, suggestive of breast or womb, it never becomes a symbol for woman (or the Woman). To become one, it would have to lose its original identity, its literality, and become filled with a second, invasive identity. Rather than surrender its specificity, this non-symbol offers in *Nayatt School* a parody of the process whereby it would become a symbol for the Woman: it chews her up. It thereby suggests that this process, like the character-making process, necessitates a destruction of identity, that it can only produce a secondary meaning by evacuating the old. *Nayatt School* refuses to empty object or performer. Instead, it exposes the "femininity" of all symbols, the fact that, in order to mean, they will have had to be emptied, violated, transgressed.

* * *

Kate Valk: Nayatt *was the hardest piece to learn. Because I was so much shorter than Libby, Liz made me wear platform shoes. And Libby's so fluid, the way she moves. It was really hard to do. I had to sync my movements on the floor with the film. Liz used to scream and scream and scream at me. I would go back and cry in the tunnel. I thought she hated me. But it . . . got the job done. [Laughs.] By the time we got it up, it was the most metaphysical experience I'd ever had . . . performing that . . . where you start and where you end.*

David Savran: Would you describe yourself as an autocratic director?
Elizabeth LeCompte: I think I have an autocratic style. I don't think that the way I work is autocratic. I like to run a tight ship. I like to have the final say, not so much because I want the power of it, but because otherwise, I lose my way. These workers bring this material to me, and I sift and siphon through it. It isn't that some material is "better" than other material. I use it when it links up to something very particular with me, when it extends

my vision slightly. Then I can encompass the material. It's a slow process and it's not democratic in any way. But autocratic is the wrong word for it.
David Savran: What I'm trying to get at here is the question of exploitation. It was said Spalding exploited his family... accusations could be leveled against you for exploiting the children in Nayatt School.
Elizabeth LeCompte: They were.
David Savran: But I've always noticed that the performers seem fulfilled, both personally and artistically.
Elizabeth LeCompte: They wouldn't be here if they weren't. But I am exploiting them, and myself, in another way by not paying them enough to make a living. As a director, I'm so keyed now to finding where people are and bringing them out. Because... I'm a voyeur and I know that what excites me are real feelings and real interests in people. When they're pretending an interest, or a way of performing, I'm not interested.
David Savran: Like Richard Schechner.
Elizabeth LeCompte: Of course, yes. Very much. And I've found a balance so that I only work now with people who understand what this "exploitation" means. It really has to do with my contract with the performers, the unspoken contract. All of us, all of the Group members understand the contract and we trust each other. We want what the other can give. And there's no confusion about it.

Willem Dafoe: In performing, you have these transcendent moments that give you a terrific kind of personal pleasure. It's almost spiritual. It's interesting because the way that most people in the theatre find pleasure is through different masks, different characters. With us, you're placed in a structure that makes you see, not really yourself, but feel something that you don't normally get to feel. And it's totally your own, it's not filtered through a character.

Elizabeth LeCompte does not pretend that she can bypass the chain of brutality described by *Rumstick Road* and the rest of her work. In working, she has consistently pushed performers to limits, to the point where they are forced to confront something in themselves and their activity, to recognize their position in the work and in the world. (In the same way, she pushes material to a limit, to the point where its inner contradictions become evident.) The moral tone of this process is consistently and deeply ambiguous, and depends, in large part, upon the spectator's expectations and desires, his "taste." For many in her audience, her work becomes (like Brecht's) a powerful force in demystifying the culture at large. Her exploitation of performers and material is thereby recognized as necessary, if never wholly benign. For others (including many critics) her work merely reflects and perpetuates the violence circulating in the society-at-large.

Perhaps the most accurate way of describing LeCompte's position is to note that her work takes place both within and without a network of exploitative relations. She depends upon them and disrupts them at the same time. All of the people involved in the Group's activities are aware of their contract with her and with each other. All submit in the

> *Elizabeth LeCompte: I have to be very careful about the performers. I have to trust their instincts, trust their ability to give themselves pleasure—something I learned from Spalding. I have a lot of trouble working with an actor who does not know how to tap that pleasure.*

knowledge that their "exploitation" leads not to enslavement, but to an understanding of self and community, and to pleasure. Rather than being hidden, these power relationships are dramatized in the work itself, in the exposure of the mechanics of performance, the forces of control. All of the pieces feature a figure who, by virtue of his position in the performance, controls it. All feature a director who reflects the real director, seated at the back of the theatre at every performance. At the beginning of *Nayatt School* Spalding Gray coaches Joan Jonas innocently in a scene from *The Cocktail Party.* By the piece's end, however, his petty tyranny has been exposed as part of the dehumanizing process, as an example of the manipulative relationship between director and performer and between artist and audience.

Because of the Wooster Group's exposure of exploitation, its work is well-suited to examine realistic drama's practice of taking the process of objectification for granted—the same process, after all, that realism uses to create characters and symbols. In presenting *The Cocktail Party, Nayatt School* points out the play's internal contradictions, its deeply equivocal (and equivocating) attitude toward the loss of control over one's body and one's life. It sees that *The Cocktail Party* demonstrates the destructive power of objectification and the end to which it leads. Yet, at the same time, it realizes that the play accepts and sanctifies the process by framing it as part of a transcendent, theological design. The Wooster Group uses the horror-comedies to show that loss of control is a terrifying experience. Next to the horror of the ever-growing chicken heart that finally devours the world, the death of Celia Coplestone may appear trifling (just as the skit's sensationalism may appear trifling next to Eliot's elevated drama). But *Nayatt School* demonstrates that the process of

Figure 26. *Nayatt School*, Part III, The Breast Examination
Spalding Gray, Willem Dafoe, Ron Vawter, Libby Howes.
(Nancy Campbell)

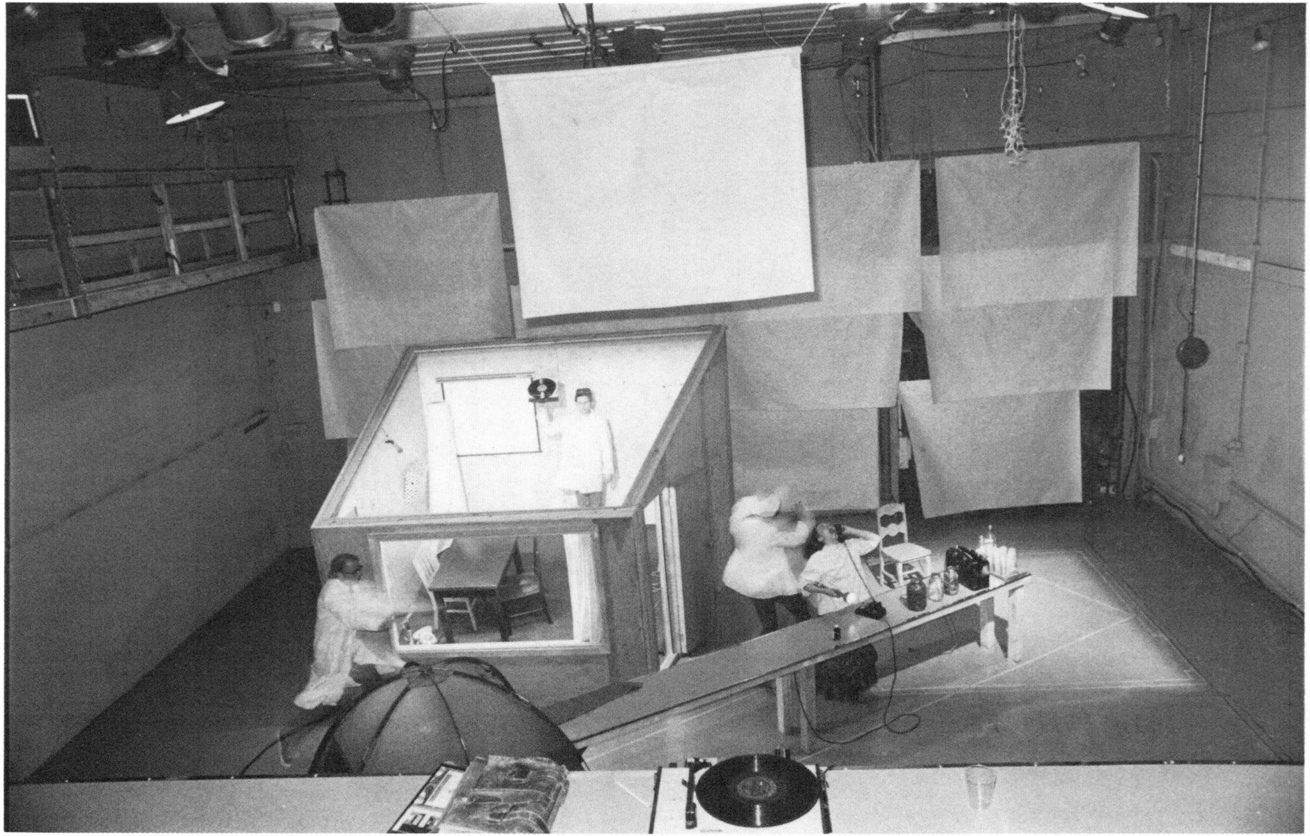

Figure 27. *Nayatt School,* Part III, The Breast Examination
Spalding Gray, Libby Howes, Ron Vawter.
(Bob Van Dantzig)

destruction in each is the same, that the mad scientist in "The Chicken Heart" and the mad doctor in "The Breast Examination" are just the other side of Sir Henry Harcourt-Reilly. The piece suggests that the latter's methods are as reckless and dangerous as the obscene doctor and the transvestite nurse who assure their patient that her breast examination will be painless and then ignore her screams:

> L: It's like fish hooks tearing, ripping open the flesh. I'm sorry. I'm sorry. I just can't stand it.
> R: There, there, Mrs. Stanley. Don't be foolish.[49]

October 29—
Liz—body, music and words all equal elements
Warm up. breast examination and lung cancer movies
cells take on personalities, traffic.
tie it into the horror films and chicken heart
Breast examination very close to pornography. Alienation of the body.
lewd attendant smiles.
de-eroticize the body in a situation with doctor.
tie together sex, death, horror
horror: fear of looking at it
fear of living with cancer
our own bodies
room=science lab, doctor's office, principal's office
no talk of whole bodies
the wisdom of the body/the cancer/like the body is working from the inside=suicide

Nayatt School Notebook

* * *

Reading The Cocktail Party

Ron Vawter: Once we were performing Nayatt School *in Philadelphia and I fell off the back of the high platform. During the last section, the destruction of the records, my chair went over and I fell over backwards. And there was a wild moment when I was in midair. It was dark, black, so I couldn't even tell how I was going to land. And as I was flipping in the air I saw Spalding up on top of his record player. It looked like he was shitting on it. And that was a very vivid moment of knowing what we were doing, and the nature of records and recording and memory. When I landed, I broke my arm, and Liz stood right up and said, "Obviously the play is over now." Spalding didn't even stop performing. He told me later that he looked around and he couldn't believe that his eyes were giving him the correct information. 'Cause that's not how it was supposed to happen. And it turned out there was a doctor in the house. And he brought me to the hospital.*

The action of *The Cocktail Party* is a paradigm of cathartic drama, moving from social and personal disorder to a final restoration of equilibrium. The play begins in crisis, in the throes of the Chamberlaynes' marital discord. It uses the semi-aborted cocktail party to dramatize the disorder and reveal the Chamberlaynes' manipulative relationships with each other and with their lovers, Celia and Peter. It begins as a comedy of manners, thick with small talk and gossip, only to turn into a theological drama. Sir Henry Harcourt-Reilly, the psychiatrist (identified mysteriously and pregnantly as the Unidentified Guest in Act I) has come to the cocktail party to uncover the truth. In collusion with Julia and Alex, he plans to interview Edward and find out "What you [Edward] really are. What you really feel. What you really are among other people."[50]

For the duration of the play, Eliot uses Reilly to expose the characters' concealed emotions and motives. Following Reilly's lead, *The Cocktail Party* (like psychological drama generally) moves from outer deception to inner truth. It dramatizes the destruction of illusion, in the belief that when people recognize and confront the truth they will be in a position to solve their problems. At the beginning of Act II, Reilly initiates the cure of Edward and Lavinia by exposing their hidden desires and fears, thereby paving the way for reconciliation. In the last half of Act II, he interviews Celia Coplestone, Edward's spurned mistress, diagnosing her spiritual complaint and setting her on a different road, on a mystical pathway to salvation.

In Part II of *Nayatt School* the scene between Reilly and Celia is read by Spalding Gray and Joan Jonas. Celia there unburdens herself to the man she's described as "a very great doctor."[51] She speaks of her feeling of "solitude" and the realization that she's "always been alone. That one is always alone."[52] She continues, describing a sense of sin which "is more

> *Joan Jonas—metaphor of non-actress for role of Celia, disenchantment and disconnection, playing scene well but not necessarily "acting style thing"*
>
> Nayatt School Notebook

real" than anything she's ever experienced and yet remains unrelated to anything she's "ever *done*": a feeling "of emptiness, of failure/ Towards someone, or something, outside of myself."[53] Celia believes that she must "atone" for this condition, this ontological sickness—the result of

Figure 28. *Nayatt School,* Part II, A Reading of a Scene from *The Cocktail Party*
Ron Vawter, Spalding Gray, Joan Jonas.
(Bob Van Dantzig)

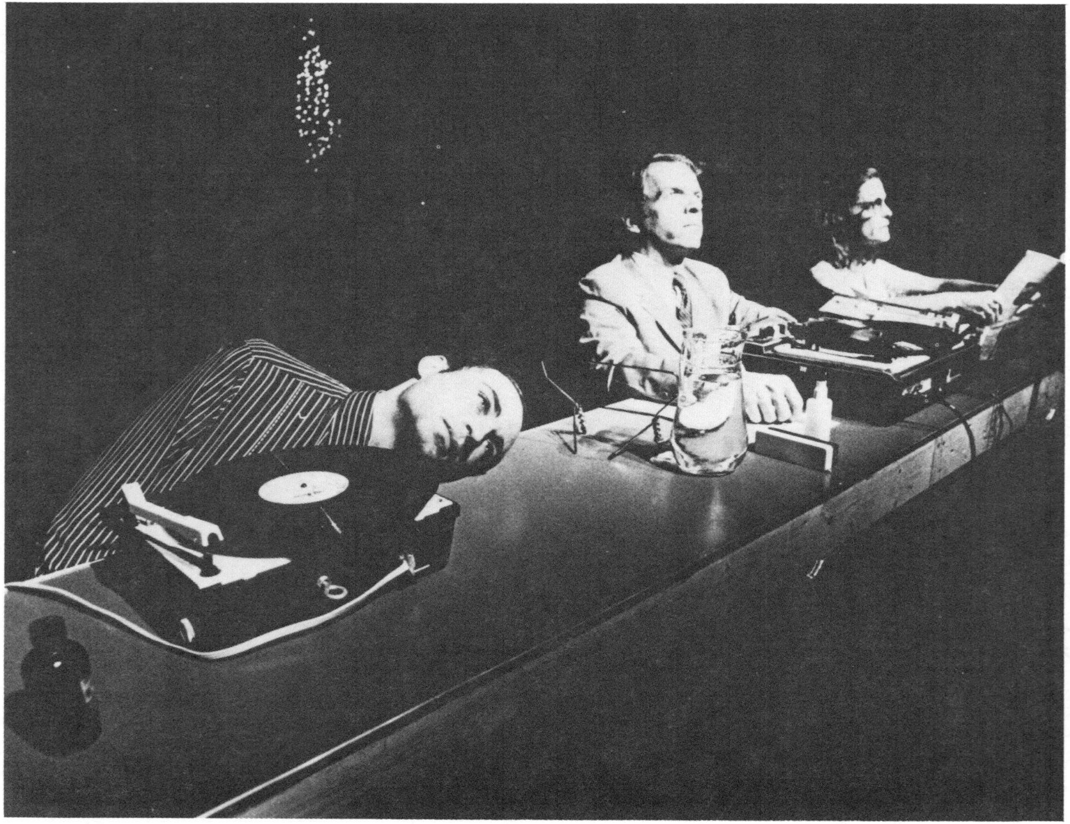

merely being alive. She longs to recover a pre-lapsarian sense of wholeness and reality which would transcend the falseness of secular

> *Spald—unimpassioned, more involved in the relationship of Spald and the text*
> *Joan—concerned in emotional, impassioned action, carried away*
> Nayatt School Notebook

love. As she speaks, Ron Vawter puts sweet, soothing music on the fanola and glycerine in eyes. He places his head down on the table and begins to weep softly as Celia tells Reilly how she longs for a perfect fulfillment, a Divine ecstasy "In which one is exalted by intensity of loving/ In the spirit, a vibration of delight/ Without desire."[54]

Spalding Gray then throws his script over his shoulder (dropping all pretense of simply reading the scene) and tells Celia that he can either "reconcile her to the human condition,"[55] so that she may return to the world, or else direct her in a way of

faith—
The kind of faith that issues from despair.
The destination cannot be described;
You will know very little until you get there;
You will journey blind. But the way leads toward possession
Of what you have sought for in the wrong place.[56]

The music changes to disco ("Love in C Minor"), at first played very softly. Celia tells Reilly she will choose the second way, the mystical path, and he offers to "send a car" for her that evening to take her to his sanitorium.

> *Liz: Go beyond comic.*
> *Sp: Sincerely interested, but won't it look like psych is mad, not patient?*
> *Liz: Both MAD but slow in coming.*
> Nayatt School Notebook

The reading of the scene becomes more and more frenetic as the music grows louder and louder. As it crests, Reilly screams at her: "Go in peace, my daughter. Work out your salvation with diligence."[57]

January 6, 1978—
CP I improvisations—Joan, Ron, Spald
J: Celia feels strange trying to communicate the problems to a stranger, what she can't even describe to her friends.

S: Reilly is poker-faced but flipped out about definition of delusion, can't remember Webster's so describes delusion as a country resort.
J: Celia thinks she is ill. Reilly keeps licking his lips, it makes Celia sick to her stomach.
Themes: Libby & Joan embody Bette
women going to doctors
Fantasy of Doc controlling a woman
" of Spald counselling his mother:
something that can never be realized
Ronnie should play Edward
Ronnie completes "the good life" of Rumstick
Chicken Heart=alienation of body, total panic, paranoia

Nayatt School Notebook

* * *

Spalding Gray: In Nayatt School *I wanted to have an image of anarchy, and it was going to be fifteen ten-year-old boys running beserk, doing anything that they wanted to do. So we worked with them for a whole winter in a free workshop. It was very disappointing when we didn't use them. Disappointing for them, too, but they would have destroyed the set.*

In Part V of *Nayatt School,* the Wooster Group turns to the last act of *The Cocktail Party,* picking up the story of Celia, two years later. In Eliot's final scene Alex explains that Celia had joined a "very austere" nursing order and had gone off to Kinkanja only to meet death by crucifixion at the hands of some natives, "very near an ant hill."[58] The other characters react to this revelation with surprise and a shiver of horror but are soon comforted by Reilly's explanation of the process of which Celia's death was a part. In its presentation of this scene, the Wooster Group casts the

CP II—things "going wrong" during improvs
clarity *of scripts vs.* insanity *of party*
Ed and Julia dancing—Big & little—little are dolls and used as dolls
Develop all to increasing violence

Nayatt School Notebook

roles of Julia, Alex, Peter and Lavinia with 10-year-old children, costuming them in oversized adult clothes, wigs, sunglasses, etc., as if they'd just raided their parents' closets. The *mise en scène* fragments Eliot's last act by breaking up the action with a series of brief and frenzied improvisations by the adults and the children (accompanied by "Love in C Minor," the Berlioz *Requiem* and the breast cancer record). For example, just before the sequence in which Alex describes Celia's death, the three adults (playing Edward, Reilly and the Maid) perform appropriate cocktail party business while the children improvise as follows:

> JULIA—Have a toast with Sir Henry. Talk loudly with Henry and give three high screams.
> ALEX—Pour water and miss second glass. Refill glass. Ram cups on table. Talk about "how I was a cheerleader." Scream 1 or 2 times.
> LAVINIA—Put on mask. Talk and scream loudly.
> PETER—Talk about salaries. Take a phone call from the Maid.[59]

As the play reaches its climax, the improvisations become increasingly frenetic and wild. Julia picks up the phone and shrieks "hello, hello, hello." Edward shoots Peter who staggers and dies. One by one, each of the children "dies," either by collapsing in his or her "dead circle" drawn on the floor, or by being carried and placed there by one of the adults.

At the end of *The Cocktail Party* (as opposed to *Nayatt School*) the fabric of society is made whole. Order and decorum triumph over the irrational. Conjugal values are reaffirmed. Celia has fulfilled her "destiny";[60] she has been martyred and her martyrdom, in turn, elucidated. To dramatize this process, Eliot uses psychoanalysis as a model for social development. According to his scheme, the opposition between conscious and unconscious is echoed on a cultural level by the opposition between particular social relations and their mythical and mystical base. Eliot suggests that all social dynamics, even the most banal, are ultimately determined by action taking place on that basal level, in society's "unconscious." Because of Celia's acceptance of the will of the "Guardians," she is sacrificed and the social order is restored, both at "home" and abroad.

In the Wooster Group's version of *The Cocktail Party,* Eliot's play is torn apart and disorder triumphs. Instead of being purged, the madness grows; cancerous cells replicate; the chicken heart devours everything. The action builds to chaos, in echo of the fragmentary phrases that accompany the improvisations, from "The Understanding and Self-Examination of Breast Cancer": "Some medical scientists feel that cancer cells appear to represent anarchy. They seem to go beserk or run wild in the body. . . . Here science is in trouble."[61]

At the end of the piece, the madness of the second *Cocktail Party* leads to the final sacrifice, the destruction of the records—all of them,

Figure 29. *Nayatt School*, Part V, *The Cocktail Party*
Erik Moskowitz, Ursula Easton, Ron Vawter, Tena Cohen, Spalding Gray.
(Nancy Campbell)

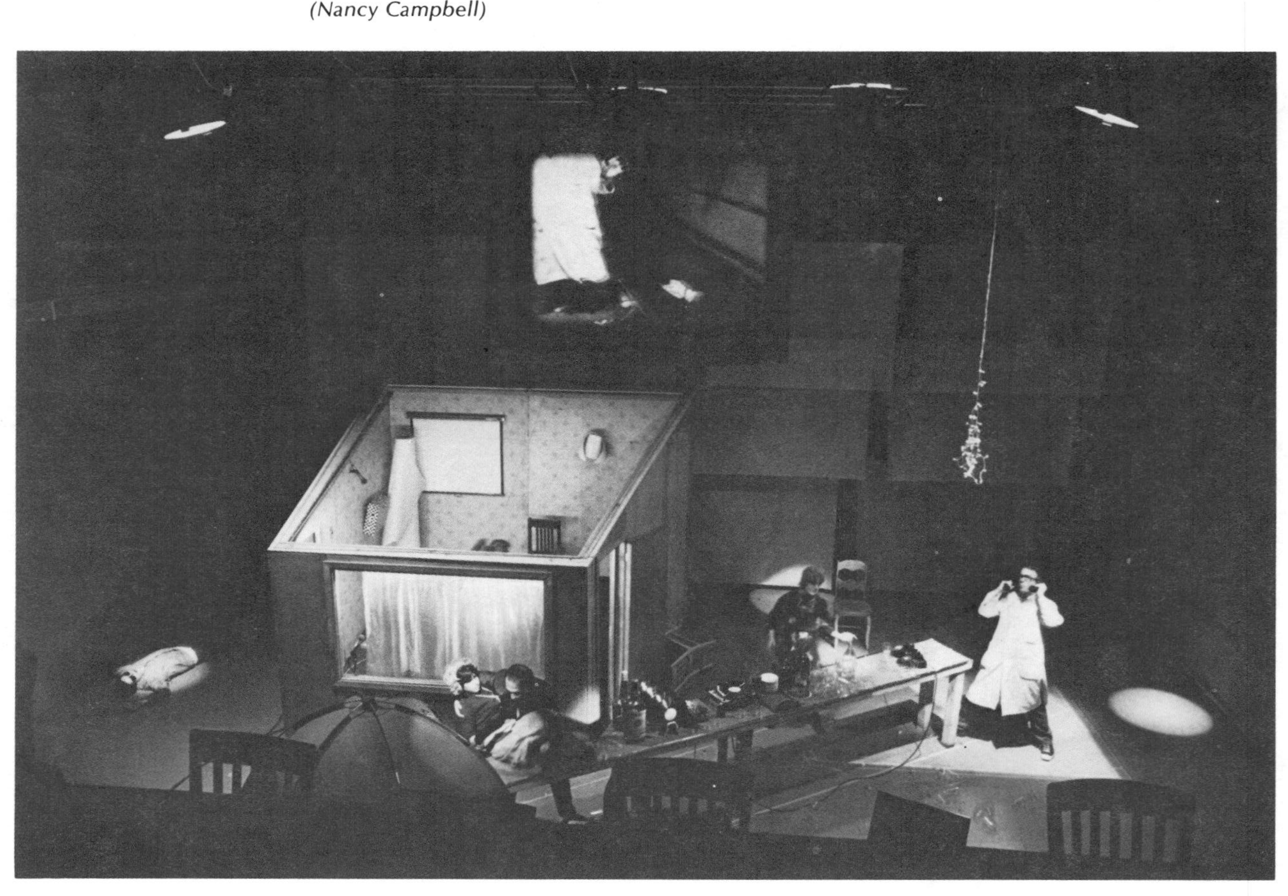

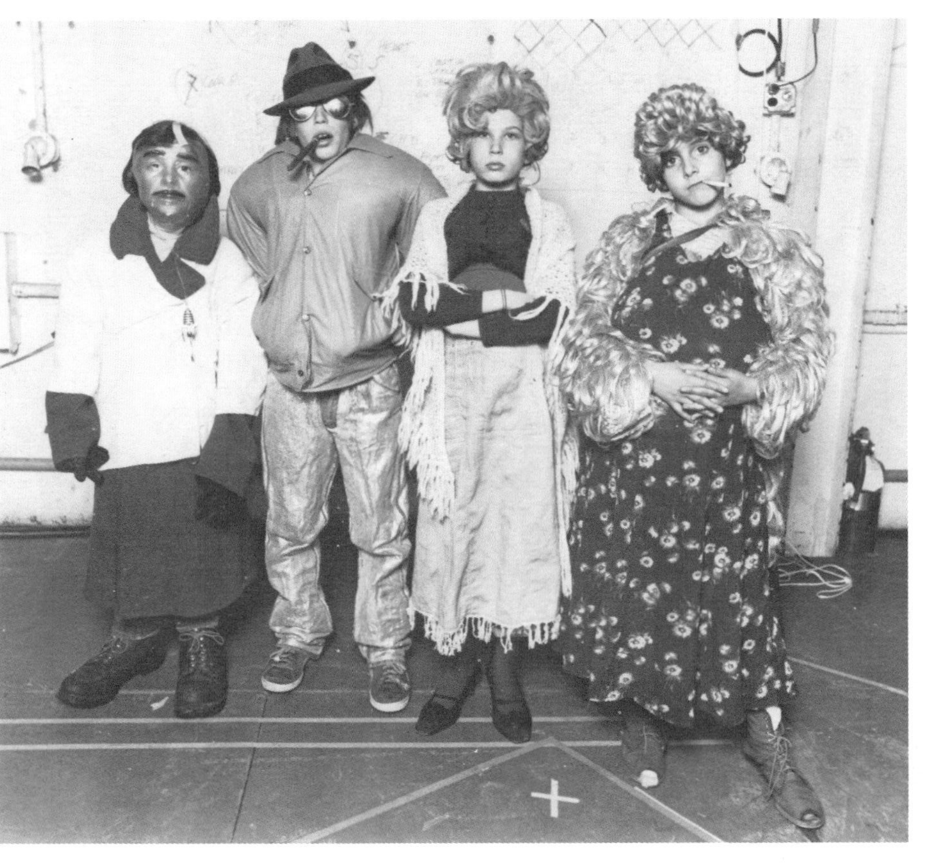

Figure 30. *Nayatt School,* The Children
Michael Rivkin, Erik Moskowitz, Ursula Easton, Tena Cohen.
(Clem Fiori)

including, through a punning equivalence, the records of Bette Gray's treatment (Dr. Henry Bradford in *Rumstick Road*: "the record has been disposed of, burned..."[62]). The performers climb up to the table and wildly destroy the black vinyl, attacking it with knives, scissors and an electric drill, accompanied by "A Mighty Fortress is Our God." The spectator, formerly at a safe distance from the action, is now assaulted with the madness. No longer addressed by an ingratiating lecturer, he is now confronted by three crazed and semi-naked performers squatting over the fanolas in front of him, in simulated masturbation, destroying the records. His privileged position is mocked by the psychotic transaction to which he has no choice but accede. After the incineration, the Man and the Woman flee across a narrow ledge, high above the floor, to the other side of the performance space, while Spalding descends to the house once more, to listen to the Bach *Partita*. Although the flight of the Man and Woman may provide the spectators with a sense of relief—they're no longer voyeurs being assaulted—it offers no safety or security for the performers. Instead, it further threatens their welfare by placing them in an extremely precarious position, the most dangerous in the piece. In a vision of great power and beauty, the Man and Woman flee from Eden, naked and innocent, the abyss surrounding them. At any moment they could lose their balance and fall into the chaos below. Anything could happen.

* * *

Ron Vawter: When I first went into the military, I was released from active duty to go into a Franciscan seminary. 'Cause more than anything else I wanted to be a chaplain, a green beret chaplain. My idea was to drop in behind enemy lines... parachute in and dispense spiritual gifts to the men behind the lines. That was my idea of the highest thing I could do.
David Savran: To Americans?
Ron Vawter: To Americans, yeah. The special forces would be dropped into Cambodia or the Dominican Republic, during the revolution there. And I was very idealistic at the time. I had a very pro-military idealism. And I thought that if I could parachute in and dispense spiritual gifts and then be airovac'ed out, that that really was it. So I went into the seminary. And one year we produced a passion play, on Good Friday. We were staging the crucifixion and we had put this one seminarian up on the cross as the Christ figure. We put the cross in cement blocks with two wire supports off to the side. Then we strapped his hands down. I was a centurian, looking up. The crucifixion was going along as planned and Mary Magdalene came in and Mary Mother, all weeping and crying.

Those were the locals from the College of Saint Rose. And all of a sudden, I heard "pling, pling" as the wire supports snapped and the cross... teetered a little bit. Everyone on the stage froze because the cross does not fall in the crucifixion. That's not how the story goes. Then it tipped all the way forward and he fell. You could see his fingers coming forward a little bit as he imagined... and it was CRASH!! You could hear the unmistakable sound of bone being crunched. And there was silence on the stage. No one moved a muscle. The audience was quiet. And finally, from under this bloody mass came a nasal voice that said, "Holy shit!" And with that, as if on cue, someone from the side pulled the curtains closed, in a very slow tempo. And the audience very quietly got up, very solemnly got up and filed out of the auditorium, without a word being spoken. That theatre experience has always impressed me as an odd and wonderful rendering of the Passion. And I've always sought to repeat experiences like that in the theatre.

In *The Cocktail Party* Celia's pathway to illumination leads to what was doubtlessly an agonizing and hideous death, crucifixion near an anthill. Eliot, however, mitigates the horror by presenting it as a sacrifice, a martyrdom. He makes it clear that Celia has willingly given her life, not only "for a handful of plague-stricken natives"[63] but also for those left in London, those in a position to recoup her loss. In the last act, the news of her death is an indispensable dramatic catalyst, providing the characters with the kind of illumination so familiar from cathartic drama. It effects the play's psychoanalytical cure, bringing renewed health and life to those left behind.

For Spalding Gray, the story of Celia Coplestone was the primary factor which drew him to *The Cocktail Party.* As he has explained, Celia "was a fantasy of what my mother might have been had she the intellectual distance to articulate her nervous breakdown."[64] For Reilly,

> *Ken Kobland: In the small room, the Woman projected a super-8 film that was a play on Celia's martyrdom. She simply gets up and walks around the chair and, in a moment of silence, a bright yellow halo drifts in from the corner. The film repeats the phrase, "I should really like to think there's something wrong with me—because if there isn't, then there's something wrong with the world, and that's much more frightening."*

however, Celia's crisis is less psychological than religious and he deals with her more as father-confessor than psychiatrist, directing her toward a patently theological salvation. The play dramatizes Celia's submission to Reilly and her acceptance of a mystical pathway, of suffering "On the way of illumination."[65]

Like *The Cocktail Party, Nayatt School* uses a woman's death to create an affirmation of life, a means of liberation, a ground, even, for the "celebration after the mourning." Unlike Eliot's drama, however, it does not valorize the brutalizing process. Instead, it subverts the "comedy," exposing the madness that has been repressed, the chaos that lurks behind the restraint of Eliot's play-world (and the adult world generally) and which is always threatening its decorum, like a bunch of rowdy children. In Part V, *Nayatt School* gives these children free rein. It uses them to play members of the "smart set," not to parody Eliot, but to work the same kind of psychoanalysis that he attempts in the play, to reveal the *real* cruelty concealed beneath the veneer of civilization. It dramatizes the experience of chaos, the indescribable which, as Reilly explains, "can only be hinted at/ In myths and images. To speak about it/ We talk of darkness, labyrinths, Minotaur terrors."[66]

Nayatt School unleashes the monsters: Eliot's "python" and "octopus,"[67] as well as the less classical (but equally mythic) cancer. It explodes in wild insanity, a release of all that has been repressed and stigmatized. It does not aim at the representation of pain, knowing that real pain will always transcend representation. Instead, it studies the forces that produce pain, the disease whose symptoms are crucifixion and suicide. It unleashes a passion play, celebrated on the edge of a precipice.

February 26—
Porn—working with records and record player
work on records   with props
school machine disintegrates
destructive open decay
a little queasy on the edge
same machines turn into lazy susans
cutting records burning playing smashed records
the adults going crazy during last cocktail party while kids are normal
the records as plates for dinner
Ronnie slowing record with penis
Libby with breasts
Liz: "downright pornographic . . . too much."
the breakdown
to chaotic play
finally crazy
"The next scene is pornographic. If you have any objection, please leave."

Sp wants kids and *the pornographic scenes*
"the Lenny Bruce in me"
Ron: You can't get out of it. You can't go back. Once
you're out of a state of innocence, you can't go back.
So we can't expose these kids because you can't go back.
It's just a sick perverse world.

March 5—
porno destruction of records
pornographic christianity—A Mighty Fortress
during frenzy
just holding flame: Ronnie; drill: Spald; scissors: Lib
Beginning of play, great care w/ records, perfect handling
towards end with destruction
Ron: 3 faces of Shiva Sak=Creation RR=Protection
NS=Destruction

Nayatt School Notebook

The end of *Nayatt School* is an epiphany that celebrates the God of a malignant universe, the One whose icon is cancer, whose priests are madmen and whose hymn is "Love in C Minor." In *Nayatt School* this malevolent God is abetted by men who fashion themselves His agents and who delight in the willful manipulation and destruction of subjectivity. They include most of the characters played by Spalding Gray. In the last act of *The Cocktail Party* (in a sequence dramatized in Part V), after the guests are told of Celia's death, Lavinia turns to Reilly and tells him that she noticed his face "showed no surprise or horror/ At the way in which she died.... I thought your expression was one of... satisfaction!"[68] He does not deny it and explains that when he first met Celia, it was "obvious" to him "That here was woman under sentence of death./ That was her destiny. The only question/ Then was, what sort of death? *I* could not know./ ... All I could do/ Was to direct her in the way of preparation."[69] He acknowledges that "she suffered more ... than the rest of us" but explains that it was all a "part of the design."[70]

In deconstructing *The Cocktail Party, Nayatt School* questions the center—the speaking subject, empathic performer, infallible physician, dentist, scientist and psychiatrist—to expose the circulation of power. It places this authoritarian subjectivity opposite a more weak and passive subject, a succession of victims—Celia, Mr. Houseman, Mrs. Stanley. It shows that all of them are scapegoats, substitutes sacrificed lest those who manipulate them be found guilty. In *The Cocktail Party* Reilly is deemed innocent because his victim is shown to be guilty. Eliot blames

Celia by insisting that her actions were foolhardy and suicidal: she knew of the insurrection, "but would not leave the dying natives."[71]

Nayatt School demonstrates that the chain of authority which passes by fiat from God to his many ministers is a chain of brutality. It points up Reilly's paternalistic attitude ("Go in peace, my daughter") and questions his status as a *raisonneur*, speaking with the voice of the poet of the *Four Quartets*. It questions the treatment given Bette Gray by her psychiatrist. It questions the malpractice of the doctor who arrogantly exercises his prerogative by examining a patient as if she were a piece of meat. It questions the authority of the playwright and the singularity of his text ("Spalding: Did you miss that? Joan: It's not in my text").[72] Quibbling over the two printed versions, the performers demonstrate that every reading is a misreading and every reenactment a projection. It questions Eliot's theology and its attempt to displace moral responsibility. It looks at martyrdom and sacrifice and sees not the workings of divine grace, but of porno-theology, the knowledge of an obscene God, celebrated in the destruction of the records (accompanied by "A Mighty Fortress is Our God"). For the Wooster Group this porno-theology is the pathway toward recuperation and peace, toward re-possession, as in the sentence: "*Nayatt School*... is about Spalding's love for the image of his mother, and his attempt to re-possess her through his art."[73]

David Savran: What did you feel at the end of Nayatt, *as you scurried across the wall?*
Ron Vawter: I always had a sense that the picture was of exceptional beauty. There was a feeling of escape and flight from the chaos and the confusion that had been constructed on the floor... from the destruction. I often thought of Adam and Eve's flight, in the Masaccio painting, half-clad and covering up their genitals and that moment, that lyrical moment of the loss of innocence and the realization of what that meant. It's hard to say actually what I was feeling then... those are all pat answers. But it was a great thrill, in part because it was a dangerous thing to do. We only had the width of a 2-by-4, thirty feet up in the air. I was swinging across those things which were nailed into the wall quite loosely. And they had been there for a long time. I would experience a thrill in the knowledge of what that did to the rest of the piece, the clear, strong motion across the back wall, above Spalding in the house listening to the Bach from Rumstick Road, *by himself, isolated, man-in-the-glass-booth-type. And knowing that it was Libby and I—Libby who played... who stood in for his mother, often, and I who stood in for his father, among other people—knowing that we were passing above him and escaping, going off, at the very end of the Trilogy.*

* * *

Point Judith

Spalding Gray: In Rumstick Road, *Liz took me as the sensitive, searching young man. And then my character got more and more perverse. In* Nayatt School, *an older, kind of crazy doctor, the searching doctor. Then on to* Point Judith *and a downright obscene character. So there are lots of different aspects. It's not really different from acting, in that way.*

Elizabeth LeCompte: In Nayatt *it was a long struggle to find the form of Spalding's monologue. But as he began to realize its power, he loved it. That was what he was looking for. And he didn't need the Group anymore. I think he needed us emotionally to support him offstage. But he no longer needed the Group to work out his material. So it was a natural break. He went off into the work on the monologues. By that time, I had already established a way of working, using other material, so it wasn't a big break for me. I tried to make* Point Judith *a gentle good-bye for the character, Spalding, to let him exit within the piece, so that the pieces could segue. One of the characters had just gone out of them. I left a remnant of him in* Route 1 & 9, *but only his voice. In* L.S.D. *he comes back as a performer. And it's completed. That persona ended in* Route 1 & 9. *The piece is about death and it really is an end, very clearly. And of course that parallels a lot of personal parts of our lives. But that's kind of boring because everything is said in the pieces about the personal lives. If you look, it's all there. Jim Strahs came in and took over in "Rig" to make the transition because I was not going to use Spalding's voice. So instead Spalding says, "I'm going to perform a play," and he performs another male's words.*

Spalding Gray: There are two crucial things about Point Judith *for me. One is that I'm returning in the way that I came in, as an actor, because I'm playing the role of Tyrone and he was an actor. He was an actor who played only one role, and that has a lot of ramifications. And the other essential thing, physical thing, was the farewell.*

Point Judith (1980) is the most symmetrical, the most balanced of all the Wooster Group pieces. After the madness of *Nayatt School*, it restores an equilibrium; it completes the movement from performance, from pure self-presentation, to drama. It brings Spalding Gray to vocational maturity, placing him in a theatrical setting in which he not only speaks with his own voice, as a master of ceremonies, but also plays three clearly defined and distinct parts. Although all have autobiographical implications, they now play more conspicuously off his position in the Wooster Group than events in his past. In Part I, "Rig," he plays Stew, one among a "cast of characters" featured in a "play" (the first time a Wooster Group piece is so described!) written by Jim Strahs.[74] In Part II, "Stew's Party Piece," (a thirteen-minute version of O'Neill's *Long Day's Journey into Night* performed at break-neck speed) he plays James Tyrone. In Part III he plays Mother Elizabeth in Ken Kobland's "By the Sea," a film that follows the daily rituals of a group of four nuns.

Point Judith was composed as the epilogue to the Rhode Island Trilogy and marks the farewell of Spalding, the character that Gray and LeCompte had developed over the five-year period. Like the first piece, *Sakonnet Point, Point Judith* (note the symmetry of the juxtaposed names) uses a single boy among a group of adult performers and hearkens again to innocence, and beginnings. Unlike *Sakonnet,* however, it surrounds Spalding with a group of predominantly male, not female, performers, and focuses on the dynamics among men isolated from women. (It was originally to be titled *Fathers and Sons.*) Far from being a nonverbal dance piece like *Sakonnet,* its first part, "Rig," is the most conventionally dramatic segment of the first four pieces, overflowing with a kind of logorrhea, with extravagant and tortuously obscene language.

* * *

Schema of Point Judith *(An Epilogue)*

Part I *RIG*

Stew, the foreman, and his crew on an oil rig in the Gulf of Mexico

Part II *STEW'S PARTY PIECE*

Long Day's Journey into Night *with Stew as the father and his crew as the rest of the family*

Part III *THE CONVENT*

The men leave the rig
Film: "By the Sea": Stew Plays the Mother Superior and his crew play the nuns

* * *

Figure 31. Giotto, "Annunciation to St. Anne"
Arena Chapel, Padua.

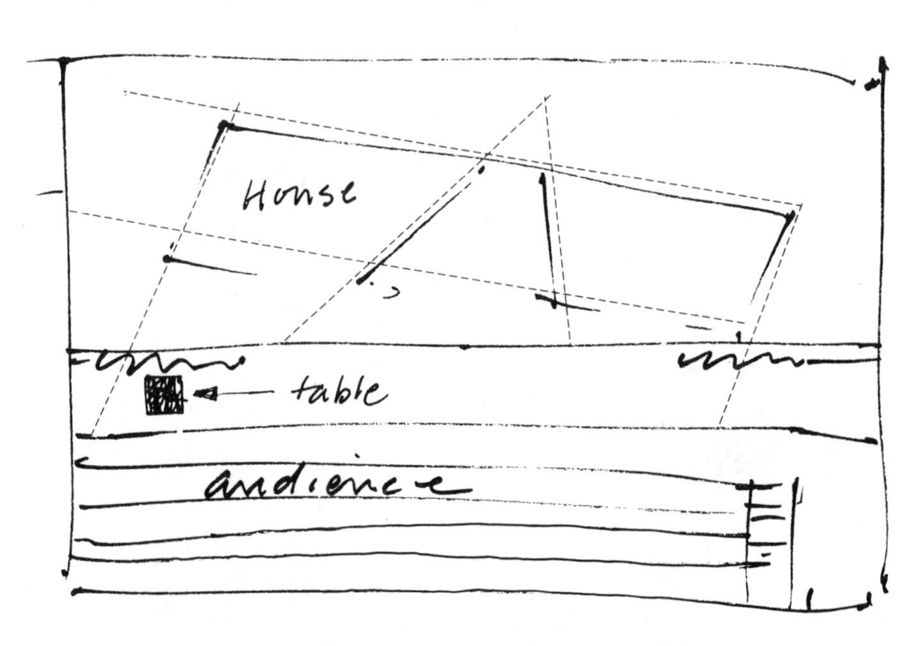

Figure 32. Performance Space for *Point Judith* (*Elizabeth LeCompte*)

Figure 33. *Point Judith,* The Convent
Libby Howes.
(Nancy Campbell)

Point Judith uses *Long Day's Journey* as a hinge, around which swing two myths, two dreams (or nightmares) of isolation, one male and the other female. LeCompte writes that the relationship between "Rig" and "By the Sea" opposes "a man's mythic fantasy of 'male isolation'" on an oil rig against her own "mythic fantasy" of women in a convent.[75] "Rig" plays off the scenes of male bonding in *Long Day's Journey*, expanding on the aggression and rivalry between father and son, and between brothers. It substitutes for James Tyrone's Connecticut summer house, shrouded in fog, an oil rig in the Gulf of Mexico. It trades in Baudelaire, Dowson and Wilde for Elvis Presley and Jan and Dean. It exchanges Fat Violet for Tammy the Pox. And it transforms Edmund's songs of "Love and desire and hate,"[76] his dreams of Romantic isolation, into an obscenity.

Part III of *Point Judith*, "By the Sea," elaborates on Mary Tyrone's experiences as a girl, her education in a convent and her dream of becoming a nun.[77] The film follows the nuns in their daily rituals, in and around their plywood house that sits above the water of Long Island Sound. It realizes Mary's dream in a medium that is itself phantasmal. When the spectator realizes, however, that all except one of the nuns are being played by men in drag, that this so-called woman's fantasy has been literally engineered and figured forth by men, he is led to recall that Mary's dream is also a vision of a male playwright.

* * *

David Savran: In Point Judith, *didn't "Rig" start as an improv?*
Elizabeth LeCompte: No.
Spalding Gray: Yes, it did, in the sense that we would stage that poker game... and Jim would listen.
Elizabeth LeCompte: Yeah, but that was after we knew we were going to hire Jim to write it.
Spalding Gray: Yeah, but he would listen to the improvs. And then he would go and write the improvs.
Elizabeth LeCompte: [Laughs] Yes.
Ron Vawter: We actually did have some wonderful improvs. I just now saw Spalding as Cathleen. Remember one day we dressed you up, Spalding, in a dress, with a wig from The Marilyn Project?
Elizabeth LeCompte: He was so sad, yeah.
Ron Vawter: You were like a little big, dumpy sister, or something. I remember that's the time when Matthew or Mike was trying to molest you, or something.
Spalding Gray: I don't remember it.
Elizabeth LeCompte: I don't believe you can't remember that. He was trying to seduce you, or something.

Ron Vawter: Yes, he was trying to seduce you.
Elizabeth LeCompte: What was it about? Were we working on Long Day's Journey*?*
Ron Vawter: Improvs on Long Day's Journey *and talking dirty. And Strahs would sit around and listen to it and bring in three pages.*
Elizabeth LeCompte: We used to play cards with this guy...
Ron Vawter: Sid.
Elizabeth LeCompte: ...who was a real poker player. They were very funny too.
Spalding Gray: So there were improvs going on.
Elizabeth LeCompte: But we knew Strahs was going to write it. I don't think we realized it would be quite as raunchy as it was.
Spalding Gray: A lot of that came off the boys' improvs. I think Jim was blown away by that, that kids that age should be talking like that, that they would articulate those kinds of images.

Matthew Hansell: I remember very well the first month or so that we worked together. I was twelve then. Spalding, Ron, Michael Rifkin and I all sat down at the brown table. Liz and everyone else went away. We had big, huge wine jugs filled with water and cards and poker chips and cigarettes and cigars and all this stuff laid out on the table. And we were playing that we were, like, old men and we were swearing and telling dirty jokes and talking about sex and everything else. I thought that was really fun. I'd never done anything like that before.

Elizabeth LeCompte: I'd sit in Point Judith *and watch women walk out as Spalding said some horrible obscenity for the fourth time. I would think, "Don't they know this is a woman's vision?!? That a woman had commissioned the writing, directed and staged it?" I think many people believed it was Spalding. Does that make a difference? It goes back to the questions about* Rumstick*. What do you know about the circumstances, the making of the piece? How did Michael Feingold know we were telling the truth about Spalding's grandmother? Maybe we made that up. Maybe Spalding's mother never died. Does that make a difference? Those questions are so much more interesting to me—you know, life and the theatre, my fantasy life and my real life, where they meet.*

For *Point Judith* the audience sits across the length of the Performing Garage facing a long black curtain that runs parallel to the rows of seats, like a conventional theatre curtain. Between the audience and the curtain, at extreme stage left, stands a table on wheels on which sits a record player. Around it the men in "Rig" will gather. In Part I of this most linear of Wooster Group pieces, the table is moved three times across the space, along a line parallel to the seating, until it occupies the extreme stage right position. For Parts II and III, the curtain is drawn back and the performers move into the depth of the space (as in *Nayatt School*). There a plywood house sits on four legs, much like the one from *Nayatt School*, but with neither plexiglass roof nor raked floor. It contains a bed, gold-colored radiator, a red box used for prop storage, a vacuum cleaner and a picture of Jesus with a flock of lambs at sunset. It is, in fact, modeled after the house in a fresco by Giotto, "Annunciation to St. Anne," where it provides the woman's chamber, the site of the epiphany. It is bisected by a white curtain, turning it into miniature stage on which a drama less conventionally religious than Giotto's is enacted. The house occupies the stage right half of the space and becomes, in Part II, the Tyrone estate, Mary's house that "was never a home,"[78] and the screen on which are projected out-takes of "By the Sea."

"Rig," of course, denotes the oil rig on which the men are working, but it also means both a penis and a wanton woman, the subjects of most of the conversation. As a verb it means to dress, or to manipulate or to romp lewdly, all of which the piece does. At the beginning, Spalding Gray introduces the performers and describes the characters that they are about to play. Gray plays Stew, the foreman and master of ceremonies. Vawter and Dafoe play Dan and B.B., respectively, two "hotheads." And Hansell plays the youngest of the men, Kid, an orphan and a drifter.[79] In "Rig," these four pass their time on a floating oil rig off the Louisiana coast, playing cards, drinking, looking at "girlie" magazines and talking about sex.

"Rig" is filled with an intense and visceral antagonism, vividly dramatizing the rivalry between men who are always on edge, always ready to explode. In fact, however, no such explosion occurs. The deep

> *Willem Dafoe: Spalding, specifically Spalding, but also Liz, one day came up to me to ask me to work on a new piece. When I started, what we were doing was mirroring what was happening in the personal Group relationships, in some ways. By the end, Spalding's input was different and his stake was very different. So that truly was his exit.*

and pervasive tension (that was present in the improvisations, and which Strahs picked up) is disruptive rather than apocalyptic. It fragments the dramatic action so that it never attains the momentum necessary to lead to disaster. In fact, the dramatic culmination toward which the antagonism points is not presented in "Rig" at all, but in "Stew's Party Piece," in the frenzied and violent *Long Day's Journey*, at the end of which Stew as Tyrone shoots the other performers dead.

Figure 34. *Point Judith,* Rig
Willem Dafoe, Spalding Gray, Matthew Hansell, Ron Vawter.
(Nancy Campbell)

Figure 35. *Point Judith*, Rig, B.B.'s Party Piece
Willem Dafoe.
(Bob Van Dantzig)

The real violence in "Rig" is not in the action, but in Strahs's dialogue. The men use extravagantly graphic and suggestive metaphors, piling image upon image in a series of virtuosic riffs. They describe assorted sexual acts and rhapsodize over whores, venereal disease and female genitalia. In a kind of strange euphemistic ritual, the latter are always given figurative names: biscuits, muffins, honey buns, broilers, gravy, oyster, meat pie, crust, cheese, etc. The men refer less to male genitalia and so their range of names is somewhat more limited, if no less colorful: pretzel sticks, pork swords, chipped beef. The persistent use of food metaphors suggests, of course, that sex is simply the gratification of appetite and women—and men—the objects to be devoured.

What is remarkable about the language of "Rig" is not that it is so obscene, but that it is strangely beautiful. Strahs's metaphors are so flamboyant that they stretch referential language to its breaking point. As they become more and more baroque only Kid, who has not learned the intricacies of figurative speech ("All this talk about food, I'm hungry"),[80] becomes confused by them:

> DAN: What went sour?
> STEW: On the rig? You mean you never heard of her, the Watson 887 deep-water-driller out of Port Arthur? Well, she had a woman on board. That's what.
> KID: You were on her?
> STEW: Was I on her. I'll tell you. Ante. Storms were blowing up around her skirts; what a gale. She was a twelve-legger with the big mud-sucker slung off her fan tail. . . . That was the jinx. We all knew where her room was. Every man-jack rubbing up against her door on the way to anywhere, mess hall, crapper, the chain room . . . Wasn't long before she began to bubble up.
> KID: The rig?
> STEW: No, nink, her. . . .
> B.B.: I heard she was a nympho.
> DAN: You heard nothing of the kind. That's the worst thing you can say about a woman. The worst.[81]

Kid misunderstands Stew because of the ambiguity of the pronoun "she," used to refer to woman, rig, Nature. For the men, this ubiquity of the feminine signals less the eroticization of their environment than their desire for control over the animate and the inanimate. Everything becomes feminized for them, objects to be penetrated, subjugated, enrapt in the flow of power.

* * *

Reading Long Day's Journey into Night

Ron Vawter: One of the great memories I have of Point Judith *is "Stew's Party Piece," with Willem. We were mother and son of the family, of the*

Figure 36. *Point Judith*, Stew's Party Piece
Ron Vawter, Libby Howes, Matthew Hansell, Willem Dafoe, Spalding Gray.
(Nancy Campbell)

O'Neill family, thrashing about the inside of the house. And I can't remember a performance when one or the other of us, or both of us, weren't bleeding. Because we were moving so fast and it was such a crazy collision. And even now, if you look at the inside of the Point Judith *house, you'll see that it's all spattered with blood. There were moments in there when I would get these wild rushes of sibling rivalry and male aggression and hysteria. And, of course, the frenetic tempo. I would get these waves of recognition about brothers and sisters and family. And the blood, too. I'd see my blood on Willem and it would become more than a representation.*

In its treatment by LeCompte, *Long Day's Journey into Night* is pared down to its famous lines, accompanied by non-stop action. In *Point Judith,* it provides both another perspective on Spalding Gray's history and a vision of the Wooster Group at a crucial moment in its history. (It is the only play the Group has used which is explicitly autobiographical.) Finished in 1940, it dramatizes an August day in 1912 in a house very much like O'Neill's father's house in Connecticut and brings onto the stage characters very much like his parents, his brother and himself. The play portrays vividly the self-destructive tendencies of all the protagonists and their individual problems: Mary's drug addiction, James Tyrone's stinginess and sense of personal failure, Jamie's obsession with alcohol and whores, and Edmund's tuberculosis and attempts to become a poet. From the beginning, O'Neill builds a powerful sense of the characters' entrapment—in house, in family and in society. They are all both victims and victimizers, trapped in a network which encourages mutual recriminations and waves of self-destructive guilt: "The man was dead and so he had to kill the thing he loved."[82] Throughout *Long Day's*

> *Matthew Hansell: In* Point Judith, *I played, like, the family dog. I was tied up to the house. One day it was really wild, with everyone screaming at each other. And Liz wanted to put me in a dog harness and tie me, like, three feet from the house, which I wasn't too happy with. I got pissed off and she got pissed off and everyone was yelling and I just sort of screamed at her and walked out. But I came back the next day.*

Journey (and more ambiguously in the Rhode Island Trilogy) the network of violence and guilt is shown to be boundless and self-perpetuating. The men, in their attempt to shield Mary from unpleasant truths, simply increase her sense of isolation. Her loneliness, in turn, leads her back inexorably to the narcotics that isolate her all the more conclusively from the men.

The ubiquity of self-destructive behavior is reinforced by a powerful sense of inheritance in the play. Its portrait of the family suggests that the individual has only limited control over his life because so much has already been determined, both by genes and environment (this theme certainly hearkens back to Spalding's telephone conversation with the psychiatrist in *Rumstick Road*). As Mary explains to Edmund about Jamie: "He can't help being what the past has made him. Any more than your father can. Or you. Or I."[83] Thus, Edmund was "born afraid" because his mother "was so afraid to bring [him] into the world."[84] Once, in despair, Mary attempted to throw herself "off the dock,"[85] and in the last act, we learn that Edmund, too, has tried to commit suicide.[86]

In *Long Day's Journey into Night,* O'Neill attempts to come to terms with his family some thirty years after—in a project which has obvious similarities to that of Spalding Gray. For O'Neill the composition of the play is conceived of as a kind of exorcism. In his dedication he announces to his wife that her love has "enabled [him] to face [his] dead at last," and that he has written the play "with deep pity and understanding and forgiveness for *all* the four haunted Tyrones."[87] Although none of the characters is liberated in the course of *Long Day's Journey* including O'Neill's surrogate, Edmund, the play is clearly intended to attest to the playwright's deliverance. As the Wooster Group deconstructs the play, it examines the quality of that deliverance by questioning its definition of sex roles.

* * *

Kate Valk: Trying to fill in Libby's part in Point Judith *and* Nayatt School *was very difficult. Liz put me into rigorous training because Libby has terrific upper body strength. And in* Point Judith, *there's the dance with the sheet. So they made me do calisthenics and play volleyball every day and lift weights. I was already working on the blackface for* Route 1 & 9 *and that's why Liz made me . . . why I was in blackface for* Point Judith. *My hands were white. And actually there's a painting that inspired Liz for Willem's character, for Mary. Manet's* Olympia. *The naked white woman and behind her, the black maid. That's why she had me stand back there, as the maid.*

Ron Vawter: In our work, politics operate on a deep, deep level. We are not overtly, or I should say, superficially political. None of us. We don't belong to political parties or feminist organizations. But I think we don't need to, because what we put into these works is so much of how we really feel politically. And I don't mean the politics of persuasion. If these

works are not about the ascendency of women, then they're about nothing. If they're not about the problems of sexuality, then they're about nothing. About the sexes relating, to each other, and among themselves. Male to male.
David Savran: As in Point Judith.
Ron Vawter: Yes. The politics are really a foregone conclusion.

In *Point Judith* the Wooster Group questions O'Neill's project by pointing out, in "Rig" and "By the Sea," what the playwright has taken for granted. In *Long Day's Journey* the Tyrone men conceive of woman as either whore or nun, trollop or saint. *Point Judith* questions this opposition by showing that the sheltering of Mary and her sanctification (like St. Anne's in "The Annunciation") are a necessary part of the process that makes all other women whores. It recognizes the interdependence of adoration and denigration, the fact that both processes lead to the same end, turning woman into an object, a fetish:

> Woman—Nun——Whore
> Woman content in her role as non-rational, spiritual
> person. INTUITION AS A PRISON. AVOIDING THE RESPONSIBILITY OF "MAKING HISTORY"
> MARY=hiding in the convent
> hiding in the whorehouse/in marriage
> In both cases she is chattel for men.[88]

Whether considered whore or nun, a woman is robbed of her subjectivity; she is put off to the side, excluded from an active life. Like Mary Tyrone, she is isolated, forced into a psychic prison, by the men around her. "Woman as outsider/no voice."[89]

Although women are isolated in *Point Judith,* they are not unique in that regard. The men are equally alone, and equally dehumanized. As an epilogue that, in certain ways, breaks with the Trilogy, the piece no longer presents the relationship between men and women as being, in essence, one of victimization. As Cathleen, Libby Howes is not the helpless sufferer she was in *Rumstick* and *Nayatt.* She is as isolated in her own sphere of action as all the other performers in "Stew's Party Piece," but neither she nor Willem Dafoe as Mary is ever singled out as a victim, as both were in *Nayatt School.* Instead, *Point Judith* studies the self-destruction of the victimizers, the men (like the Tyrones) who are as crippled as the women they abuse. It focuses on the social dynamics that create the precondition for victimization. Like *Long Day's Journey,* it does not conclude that any one man is to blame. It diffuses responsibility (unlike *The Cocktail Party*) and demonstrates that the process of dehumanization will turn on those who practice it. Willem Dafoe may be the only one to speak Mary's lines, but, as LeCompte explains, "All of them play the mother role."[90]

As in *Rumstick Road,* the one real woman in *Point Judith* maintains a silence, but one that leads to an end completely different from her long sleep at the end of the earlier piece. She plays Cathleen, the outsider, relegated to the background, to tending the house. Unlike the other characters in *Long Day's Journey,* O'Neill treats her contemptuously, the servant whose "stupid, good-humored face wears a pleased and flattered simper."[91] In reconceiving Cathleen, *Point Judith* gives Libby Howes (and later, Kate Valk) a part totally different from the series of victims she played in the earlier pieces. In doing so, the Wooster Group undermines O'Neill's hierarchical distinctions between class and gender and dramatizes the constructive nature of the work that O'Neill gives his "stupid" serving-girl. In "Stew's Party Piece," she runs the house. She turns on the vacuum cleaner from which the fog pours. She arranges the furniture outside the house. She billows the white sheet and, at the end, throws it over the house. After the chaos, when the other performers have left, she cleans the house and straightens it up. She is the one character in *Point Judith* who performs useful, instrumental activity. In contrast to the men in "Rig," who appear only on their time off, and the family in *Long Day's Journey*—the leisured few who simply pass the time—she works.

Point Judith does not cast Libby Howes as a victim, and thus does not produce the same Woman of the earlier work. Instead, it reexamines the social process that the other pieces had studied, but introduces a third term that disrupts the opposition between victimizer and victim. This transfigured role marks a new beginning for the Wooster Group and is the strongest attestation to its break with the obsessions of the Trilogy. In *Point Judith* the Woman is the one who works, who arranges, who puts things where they belong (in what is a development of a traditional function ascribed both to woman and to the theatre director). She plays the same part that Cathleen does but produces a totally different effect. The smallest, most peripheral part in *Long Day's Journey* becomes prominent and vital in *Point Judith.* The very activity that makes her contemptible to O'Neill becomes the source of her deliverance. For the first time in the Wooster Group's work, a performer executes a series of tasks methodically and at a normal tempo. For the first time, she is connected, clearly and simply, to the concrete reality of everyday life and to the mechanics of performance. In her activity, she discovers a new energy; she develops strength and direction, like the Biblical Judith (whose story Cathleen reads in Part III) who approaches her conquerer, Holofernes, as a maidservant. In that guise, she gains his confidence and after he has fallen asleep drunk, decapitates him with his own sword.

* * *

In the following excerpts from interviews, Spalding Gray and Elizabeth LeCompte look back on their period of collaboration. Although the arrangement is intended to suggest a dialogue, the quotations were all extracted from separate interviews conducted over several weeks. The conclusions are provisional and, like all memories, highly colored by the present.

Spalding Gray: I think that Liz and I . . . It's impossible to speculate. I don't know that we would have stayed together if it wasn't for The Performance Group, because we plugged into a larger organism and we were able to gratify things we couldn't in our relationship. So it became almost religious, in a ritual way, as, in the old days, a healthy community would deal with mourning, or certain holidays.
David Savran: And now your position in the Group has changed.
Spalding Gray: Yes, what's difficult for me at this point is trying to be supportive of the Group and lend my whole being, which I can't do anymore. For whatever reason, my need was to be centrifugal, to be the major subject matter and the focal point in the Trilogy.
David Savran: Do you miss those days?
Spalding Gray: Absolutely. But I knew it had to come to an end. I was getting curious about the outside world. It was as though I'd entered a religious order for a while. And I wanted to know more about myself in relationship to other people, outside of the Group. I was talking about the ritualized, theatricalized ways of relating to Liz. Our relationship became primarily worked out in the performance space, rather than the bedroom, or the loft or therapy sessions. So, every night, waving good-bye in Point Judith *was an actualization and a preparation for saying good-bye to Liz and to the company for a while. So every night, when I'd go through that spotlight, it was an actual exit. And then I'd come back and do it again. And I probably could have done it over and over and over, just like Jimmy Durante. It's just a wonderful . . . because we're always saying good-bye to every experience. So I miss it enormously. And of course I use it as a measuring stick by which I'm looking for other experiences that can give me some of that, and it's very difficult.*

Elizabeth LeCompte: Point Judith was the big transition for me because I'd always used Spalding as the pretext, the storyteller, so that people could easily identify with his character.
David Savran: Because Spalding is so empathic on stage.
Elizabeth LeCompte: Yes.
David Savran: And he thereby provides a center.
Elizabeth LeCompte: And the center became more and more prominent as the pieces went on because people identified all the elements as his. And that was very difficult for me. But I don't regret it, because it was wonderful. I think that it was a double leaving of each other, in a way, a healthy, good one. Because Spalding was too sympathetic a character. He couldn't inhabit my anger. He came the closest in Nayatt, but it was uncomfortable for him. Ron is the personification of that for me. Willem also. And now, I've been able to work with more of my personality: in Kate, a humor that I could never really bring forward because Spalding usurped it, in a funny way, as a storyteller. Spalding's persona was very dominant, very needy. Now the pieces are structured so that one strong personality does not absorb so much of the attention.

Spalding Gray: When Liz and I are collaborating at our best, we would both be struck by the power of the same image. It would evoke things in us that were, maybe, different, but it was evocative all the same. So I miss the collaboration with Liz. I hadn't spent a lot of time trying to figure out where the collaboration went awry, but I think, when we originally came together in a relationship, we were both very insecure. That's what we had in common when we came to New York City. And we both grew under the aegis and direction of Richard Schechner and were given our wings. And I think that we were running very balanced all the way. Maybe toward the end of Nayatt and into Point Judith, I probably became jealous of her position, not that I wanted to be a director, but her overview, the fact that she was outside of the experience. And at the same time, to say that I was jealous of it is strange, because I didn't go out and do that. What I did do was go out and do something that I wanted to do. Because I knew that she was doing something she wanted to do and was very turned on by it. And I think that the competitiveness and the jealousy came about through my realizing that I wasn't turned on by the performance. Or I got more desirous to be... it was beginning to get... the collaboration was beginning to get... I don't know. I think I ran my course. I couldn't see doing anything beyond.... I ran out of juice. I couldn't see... there was nothing vital for me, thematically, beyond. I really felt that we'd run a very full course in these works. And I felt complete. And I thought, I hope I can move on to something else and feel that same completeness, a similar completeness. And it isn't... it's *there but it doesn't have that transcendent, quasi-religious aspect, that intensity of living together and making those works together . . . it never can. Because I'm working with people now, I'm relating to people in the outside world that are in a very banal situation in their lives. They don't do an hour of exercises every day. But I had to have the courage just to walk out the door.*

David Savran: So as the Trilogy progressed, there was more of a need on your part to deflect the attention off Spalding.
Elizabeth LeCompte: Yes. And I think that it was hard on Spalding, because he was giving up his centrality. He's always afraid of loss. And I think he gets a little nostalgic about stuff that he would be perfectly happy to get rid of. It was very healthy for both of us. He's right, it was a wonderful working situation, during those times. But it's always the memories of those. . . . It was wonderful for him also because he got a lot of credit sometimes for things that other people did. And he had a very, very supportive family. As he drifted off into his own work, I began to receive more of the support, as the artistic center. He was receiving sole credit for the ensemble work for many, many years, and still does.
David Savran: Yes, I know.
Elizabeth LeCompte: And now the other performers are getting a lot more attention, finally. Spalding was so dominant that nobody else was seen. Also, I've come around to another voice. In L.S.D. *I've come back again to the voice of the storyteller, with Nancy Reilly, or Ann Rower, the babysitter. But it's a female voice now. And it's much less . . . needy. Spalding's a very wonderfully needy performer. He needs his audience to love him very much. And he performs wonderfully under that, he blooms. But for me, because of my particular political bent and because of, as you call it, my anger . . . I don't like to play with that stuff too much, it's like playing with fire.*

Spalding Gray: Although I knew about the sixties and all that, when I got outside of the Group, I wasn't ready for the realization of how fragmented our culture is, how broken down. I used to have problems during Rumstick Road, *when I was wheeling Ron around in the chair I would think, "I could actually be in the nursing home wheeling my grandmother now, whose voice we're using." And I'd go through a lot of guilt, as I still do with art, with art versus what I call service. My guilt is that I keep thinking, one day I will stop my self-production and go to work as a therapist for disturbed children, or some social work. I keep thinking that would be more gratifying but it's a fantasy. . . . Teaching helps a little, at Columbia, but, you know, it's not exactly the needy. I think that Liz is in less conflict about . . . I mean when we were at the TCG convention, someone stood up and said, "I would like to know what* Our Town *means to you, Miss LeCompte. I would like to know, Robert Wilson, what you think about* Einstein." *And Wilson said, "I just don't think art has any, should have any, connection with politics, morality, grinding social axes. It may or may not. I don't know what I've done until after I do it." Liz was up in the balcony and she was the only one that clapped. And no one followed her.*

David Savran: I'm always surprised when I hear that because, to me, the Group's work is so political.

Spalding Gray: Yes, I think that Liz has a very integrated political personality, that it's deeply rooted in her. She doesn't have to think about it. She was a social worker in Harlem when we first came to the City. That's what she did for a living. And she's very well read, she's very well educated. She reads the paper. She keeps up with current events. I was talking with Ken Kobland last night and he said, "Listen, I don't think that art should have to answer to any kind of political or moral issues." I think the artist should, at other times, when they're not working. But that falls into a kind of personal thing: you answer to your family, you make your choice about voting, you work or you don't work for a nuclear freeze. But I don't think it means that the artist's work should necessarily reflect that. And that's where I agree with Liz. Because it's the old story, as soon as you start doing art about it, you can't encompass it, you can't . . . It's not art. Art is about the inarticulatable.

David Savran: Spalding was telling me about the incident at the TCG convention, about Robert Wilson's comment on the politics of his art, and your response. Initially, I could hardly believe that you didn't conceive the work in political terms. But I'm beginning to understand that the politics is a residue . . .

Elizabeth LeCompte: Yes, which I accept.

David Savran: And that the choices you make are intuitive, gut choices that happen to be political because you're a political person.

Elizabeth LeCompte: Yes. And because I am angry, it oftentimes appears to people that the work is willful. But I'm not angry when I work. It's only when I have to face people, who I don't know, who are challenging me, that I get angry. There's a misinterpretation that I sit down with that anger and say, "OK, today we're going to . . ." I've been cast in the role of an iconoclast and I've been called someone who enjoys that, who does it for the sake of doing it. But I think that's a misapprehension. Any iconoclasm is a result of the working process that I enjoy so much. Whenever you're dealing with things that you don't fully understand, that you have some confusion about, you're bound to step on people's toes.

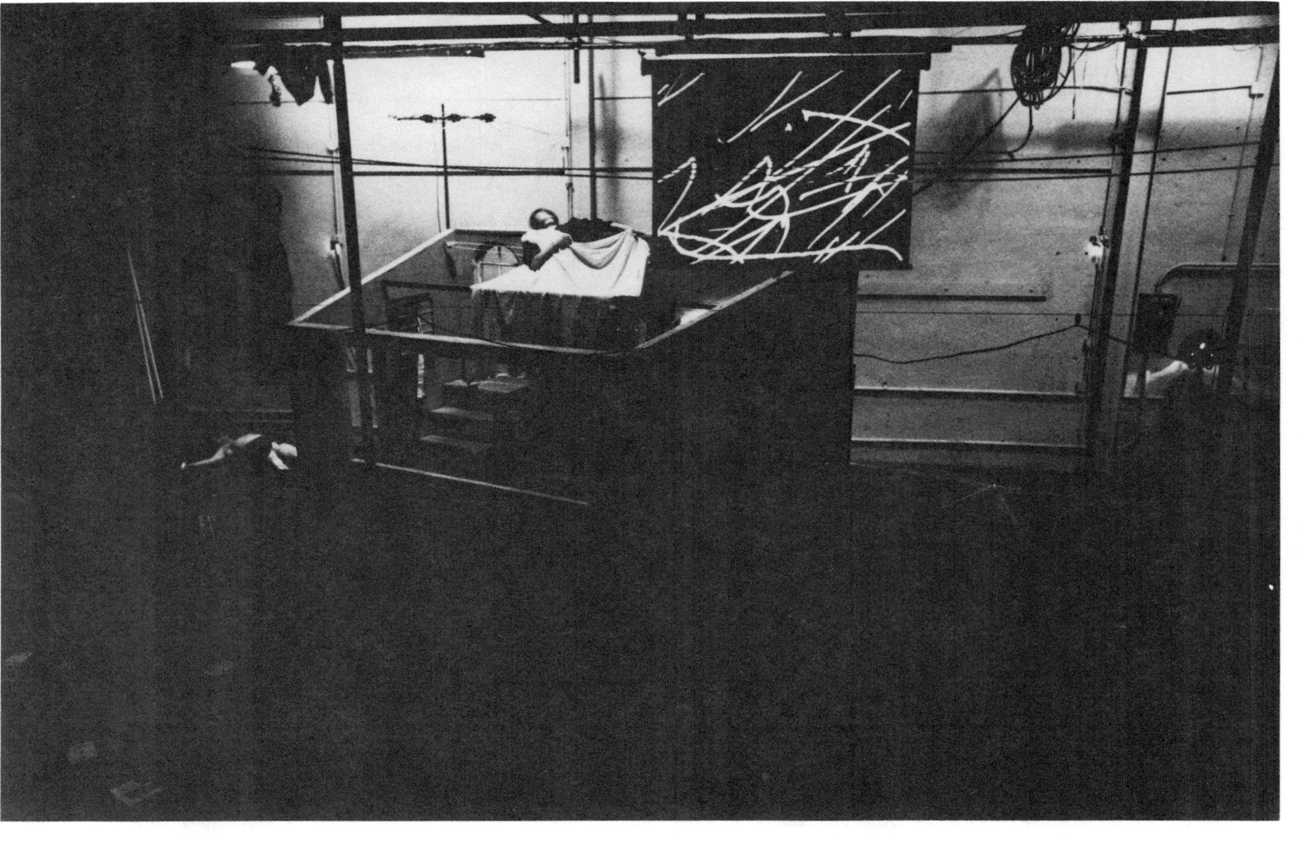

Figure 37. *Point Judith,* The Convent
Willem Dafoe, Libby Howes.
(Nancy Campbell)

Figure 38. *Point Judith,* The Convent, Home Movie
Libby Howes; Ron Vawter and Spalding Gray in movie.
(Nancy Campbell)

* * *

Ken Kobland: In Point Judith *the idea of the film was to recreate—it's a memory piece, too—Mary's days in the convent. Another uni-sexual grouping, the convent as opposed to the oil rig. It's based visually on the Book of Hours, a book of daily activities, cyclical life, small actions and small acts. The idyllic times.*

As a dramatic structure, *Point Judith* is the most linear piece by the Wooster Group, remaining, until the final film, a single dramatic movement interrupted by four "Party Pieces." Although the longest, Stew's presentation of *Long Day's Journey into Night*, shatters the already loose theatrical conventions established in "Rig," it does not disrupt the narrative thread. On the contrary, its status as a-play-within-a-play reinforces the tension of the underlying story. The narrative line does not break until the men finish their work and Dan says, "Forget it, B.B.,it's all over."[92] Then they head out to other ports, Stew to Rhode Island, to Point Judith. The men take the front curtain down and gather their tools. Then all four wave good-bye and exit out onto Wooster Street. This farewell is the climactic moment, the turning point of the piece and of a phase in the Wooster Group's work. It leaves Cathleen alone in the performance space, in the house, cleaning up the mess, while the final color film runs, the woman's fantasy, the dream of communal, religious life, of dedication to service and a higher goal.

"By the Sea" is a beautiful and meditative film, a gentle postscript, silently underscoring the farewell, bringing together (although not synthesizing) a number of images from the Trilogy. The camera constantly pans the seashore, "mimicking the motion of a lighthouse beacon, arbitrarily 'illuminating' the landcape,"[93] overseeing the four nuns in their activities in and around the house. The film begins with scratches on black which, Ken Kobland explains, "come out of (and return into) the physical action of the play; its cataclysmic destruction of the text and its chaos."[94] The first shot is of the *Point Judith* house sitting on the rocks at low tide (later it is surrounded by water). Then the nuns are seen in the water, at work. Sister Muriel (Willem Dafoe) proudly holds a big piece of seaweed. The Postulate (Libby Howes), in a white habit unlike the others, is making the bed. The nuns go out in their rowboat and catch a big fish. There is a shot of a nuclear power plant in the distance. The Postulate cleans. Evening falls. A sick nun is seen in bed, being cared for by Sister Margaret (Ron Vawter). The frames of this dark image (the only night scene) have also been scratched so that rays of light appear to be shooting from the house.

While this film is being shown, the "live" Cathleen comes out of the house and holds up a small screen on which is projected a short 8 millimeter black-and-white film, "conceived as a 'home movie,' both ours and theirs (the nuns)."[95] It starts with a close-up of the fish (the final echo of the metaphors in "Rig") and moves to a medium shot of Sister Muriel examining it. The latter then takes a photograph of the three other nuns: Sister Elizabeth (Spalding Gray) sitting in the middle, flanked by Sister Margaret and the Postulate, in echo of the final image of *Rumstick Road.* In the next shot, the nuns frolic in the water, diving and swimming. They wave good-bye and come up out of the water. The film ends with a freeze on the Postulate's face. "Live" Cathleen then replaces the portable screen. Above, "By the Sea" concludes with a medium shot of the Postulate next to the picture of Jesus, getting ready to leave, as the "live" Cathleen prepares to do exactly the same. Cathleen departs.

Point Judith is structured so that the farewell is its focal point. The waving good-bye of Spalding Gray and the other men is echoed as the nuns wave in the "home movie," as the Postulate prepares to leave and as Cathleen finally exits. Outside the piece, Spalding Gray's departure from collaborative work is redoubled by Libby Howes's farewell. (Except for the *Route 1 & 9* porn film, this was her last work with the Group.) With Howes's departure a particular persona is ended: the silent woman, the dancer, the passive one, the victim. No single female performer picks up Howes's specific energy in the later pieces. Kate Valk and Peyton Smith bring to the subsequent work a much more active and verbal female presence. Even when Valk plays Cathleen in a later run she performs the part in blackface and makes no attempt to imitate Howes's qualities as a performer.

For Spalding Gray, the waving good-bye marks the end of a phase of his career, an end point (as opposed to *the* end) in a process of coming to terms with the past: his relationship with his mother and the other members of his family; his relationship with Elizabeth LeCompte and the other members of the Wooster Group. The route through the Trilogy and its epilogue takes him from silence to language, from self-presentation to theatre, along a path that begins in innocence and ends (in the piece that takes him out of the Group's collaborative pieces) in the adult world. He takes his position both within and without a chain of fathers and sons, both within and without the Wooster Group. In the epilogue, he stands *epi-logos*: beside, among, after, above the word: in the same position relative to his history that O'Neill adopts, in his dedication, relative to the action of *Long Day's Journey.* He breaks with O'Neill, however, at a crucial juncture by refusing the latter's "pity" for the members of his family. Rather than seeking an impossible transcendence, he articulates the feelings of the subject in response to the violence around him. He always remains a part, a speaker who, in his solo monologues, examines and undermines the linkage of a chain of brutality from his own highly vulnerable position.

The relationship between the male and female fantasies in *Point Judith* is essentially an adversarial one. LeCompte sets "Rig" and "By the Sea" in opposition to each other and both in confrontation with a series of patriarchal formations: *Long Day's Journey into Night*, male authority, dramatic tradition, the power of the written text, the nuclear family, psychiatry, and, additionally, both Spalding Gray's centrality to the work and Richard Schechner's leadership of The Performance Group. In setting herself against these various formations, she does not attempt a systematic critique, knowing that it would make her the mirror image of that which she is seeking to dismantle. Instead, she works by discontinuous attack, a kind of aesthetic guerilla warfare, subverting the received meaning of texts and other cultural artifacts. She builds through deconstruction, producing pieces that spill over into each other and remain always provisional, always incomplete.

Although *Point Judith* is focused toward Spalding Gray's farewell, it also dramatizes Elizabeth LeCompte's emergence from behind Gray's shadow. Like Cathleen, she had remained behind the scenes, performing "woman's work." As he departs, however, she becomes the publicly acknowledged artistic center of the Group's activity and develops theatrical action which valorizes the practical task of putting things in

> *Elizabeth LeCompte: When I first walked into the Garage, I wanted it. And I stayed past the time when, I think, a man would have left, because I had nested there, in a sense. I slowly ate away from within, until Richard was left with just the shell. And I had all the core working for me, invisibly, in the middle.*

order. At the same time, LeCompte conceives another kind of work associated more with male than female activity. Originally, *Point Judith* was to end with the sequence that begins the "live" portion of *Route 1 & 9*, the building of the skeletal house (a process of construction that provides yet another metaphor for her own work). In that "original" ending, with Cathleen set against the workmen, LeCompte fashions herself both domestic and constructer, the keeper and the builder of a house: both the house that undergoes a series of transformations from *Sakonnet Point* to *L.S.D.* and the Performing Garage itself, the house "bequeathed" to her by Richard Schechner when he left The Performance Group and it changed its name to the Wooster Group.

Figure 39. *Point Judith,* Construction of Set for Film "By the Sea" *(Nancy Campbell)*

* * *

Hula

Elizabeth LeCompte: Always before you people go down to a show, I find I say the same thing. And I wondered why. Then I remembered that it was the one thing that John Wynne-Evans said to me when I did my first performance with him in a two-person play called The Constant Lover. *I played a coquette with a parasol opposite him. And every night I was so afraid that my lines choked in my throat. I just couldn't play. I couldn't do anything. In fact, I was so nervous that oftentimes, when I was supposed to tap him lightly with the parasol, I would beat him with it, because I didn't know what to do with my energy. And he would say to me, "Liz, just have a good time." I always think, before a show, what's the core of what I want to say to you? And it comes down to: have a good time.*

* * *

Ron Vawter: We were all stuck in New York the summer of '81. And Liz's father was dying and she couldn't leave. None of us had any money to take a proper vacation. It was very hot. It was a disgusting August. And we were all depressed. We were all broke. We had talked about making a little dance piece and we wanted to pretend that we were on vacation, physically and emotionally (Liz and Willem were very involved in Frank's dying). So, what we made was this take on Hawaiian entertainment, what you might see if you were in Hawaii and went to the local Holiday Inn for a Hawaiian show. At the same time, we wanted to make a good dance piece, but make it a little gaudy, a little tacky. So Kate found the Hula *album. We made little stories up for each one, taken more or less from the album descriptions. One night, we had this hula woman come, a woman who teaches hula, who said that we were OK—and we had only the most clichéd idea of what hula was; we'd never even gone to see one.*

* * *

In *Hula* Willem Dafoe, Kate Valk and Ron Vawter impersonate Ray Witfield and the Johnsons, performing a sequence of hulas to tacky Westernized Hawaiian music. Before each of the songs, Peyton Smith reads the record liner notes that the Group has used as cues for constructing little stories dramatized in dance and pantomime. Clad only in grass skirts and adorned with leis around their necks and ankles, the three performers hula energetically and mellifluously.

Figure 40. *Hula*
Kate Valk, Willem Dafoe, Ron Vawter.
(Nancy Campbell)

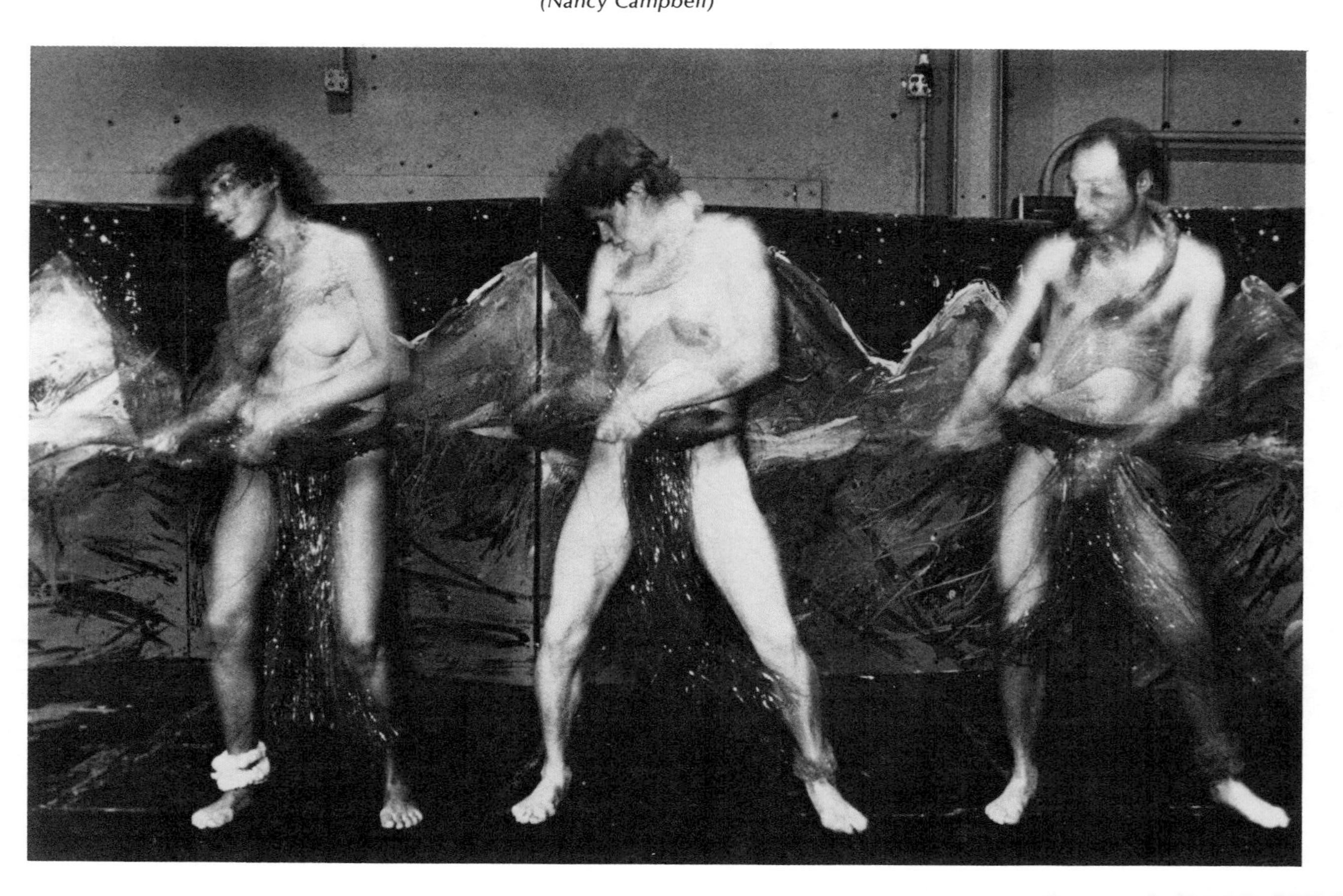

* * *

The Text:
Tonight the Wooster Group presents Ray Witfield and the Johnsons who will be performing Hula *by the Waikiki Hula Boys. I will be reading the introduction to each song off the back of the record.*

From the liner notes to Hula *by the Waikiki Hula Boys, Columbia CL 565, circa 1960:*

"King Kamehameha" tells the story of the famous King's conquest of Oahu. Coming with his warriors from Hawaii, he "pushed his enemies over the Pali." This song describes how he drove his foes to the top of the mountains and drove them over the sides of the famous pass, called the Pali.

"Ua Like No A-Like," another favorite song of Hawaii, is a very old melody, here arranged by Danny Stewart. A love song, its point is that each person has the same likes, insuring a happy romance.

"The Hukilau Song" reflects the world-famous Hawaiian community fishing expeditions. This song tells how the giant net is taken off-shore, then slowly drawn in as it catches all the fish in its path. The entire village joins in the sport, since they share in the catch and celebrate with a big feast, complete with songs and hulas.

"Beyond the Reef" is an example of fine Hawaiian music by a composer from the mainland. Jack Pitman, a New York pianist, went to Hawaii on a visit and liked [it] so much that he settled there, writing this song about the idyllic life he found.

"Lovely Hula Girl" was written by Jack Pitman and Randy Oness, in tribute to the grateful hula dancer who spins out stories with her supple hands.

* * *

David Savran: What about Hula*?*
Elizabeth LeCompte: [Laughs.]
David Savran: What was the genesis of Hula*?*
Michael Stumm: Listen, Hula *is a dead issue only because if they never ever... I mean, think of it now... you made the decision to urinate on stage. And now everyone will say the back is broken... the integrity of the piece is lost if you never urinate on stage again.*
Willem Dafoe: I wanted to do it so badly.
Elizabeth LeCompte: We'll do it at the Bessie awards.
[Laughter.]
Norman Frisch: It will be in the press across the entire country.
[Laughter.]

Willem Dafoe: We did it in rehearsals and it was beautiful. We were singing this song, we were hula-ing along, and we pissed! And it was beautiful. Ron and I had these big pools around us, like we were horses, and Kate had this feminine, cute little delicate little puddle.
[Laughter.]
Elizabeth LeCompte: And I was . . . aghast!!
Jim Clayburgh: I was too. I was shocked.
Michael Stumm: From then on, it was all downhill for Hula.
Elizabeth LeCompte: Even you guys were shocked.
Kate Valk: I know. It was sort of shocking.
Norman Frisch: Peyton, you can be like . . . I remember when Hair came to Boston. I was in junior high school or something. They had these television ads and there was one girl in the cast who didn't take her clothes off. And she used to come on TV and say, "Hi, I'm from the cast of Hair. I'm the nice girl." Something like that. "I'm the one who doesn't take my clothes off. We want you to come see the show. . . ." Peyton could do those ads for Hula. [Laughter.] "I'm the nice girl in Hula. I'm the one who doesn't piss at the end."
Elizabeth LeCompte: Well, the genesis of Hula I think was . . . who bought the hula record?
Kate Valk: I did.
Peyton Smith: A loaded idea.
Kate Valk: I'm trying to remember where I got it. On Sixth Avenue.
Elizabeth LeCompte: And you used to use it for warm-ups.
Kate Valk: No, I went out specifically, you told me to go buy a hula record. It wasn't one of those things where somebody just had a record, like "Echoes of Latin America." There was this exercise that we did with hula. You just go like this. [Demonstrates a hula.]
Elizabeth LeCompte: That's right.
Kate Valk: And you decided we should do, like, an exercise record, stupid dances. And we did.
[Laughter.]
Willem Dafoe: Plus, Kate had shown her proficiency at bogus sign language.
Elizabeth LeCompte: That's where it started. A whole ceremony, that's right.
Peyton Smith: And I wasn't in town. We were working on Route 1 & 9 and I went to Provincetown that summer. And Kate came up to visit and she goes, "Oh, we're doing a great thing, it's so wonderful! We're doing record interpretations to hula. It's so great!" Remember that? You stood out on the little deck and you showed me some steps like this. . . . [Demonstrates a hula. Laughter.] "It's not difficult," she said, "it just looks great!" And I thought, "Oh God, what are they doing?!?"

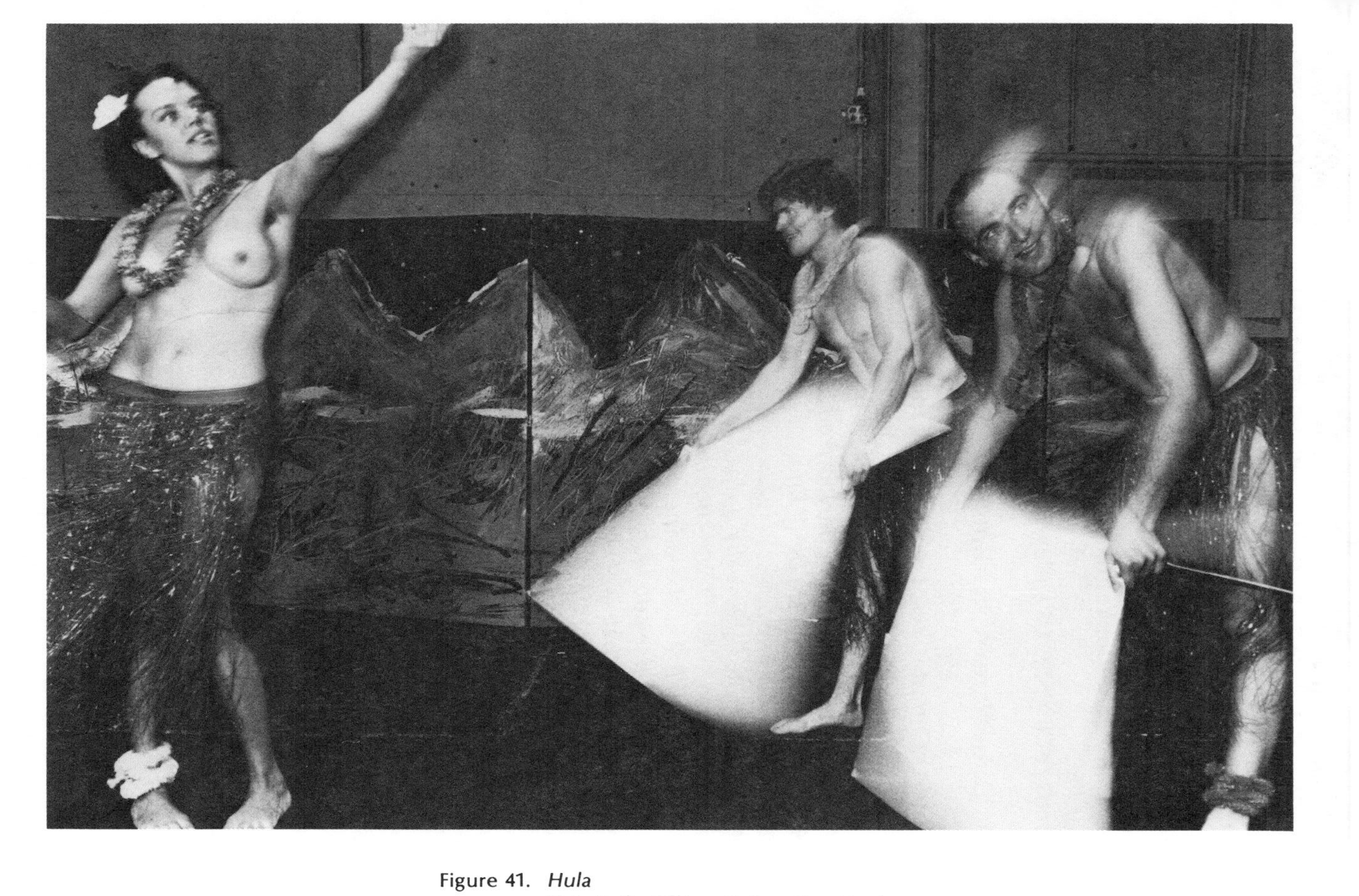

Figure 41. *Hula*
Kate Valk, Willem Dafoe, Ron Vawter.
(Nancy Campbell)

Willem Dafoe: One memorable thing was when we were getting the costumes together. Kate figured out the grass skirts that we would wear. And of course Ronnie and I had these penises... and we painted them green, with make-up. But it was make-up that dried to this kind of chalky....
Kate Valk: They looked like iguanas, hanging down.
[Laughter.]
Willem Dafoe: They looked like the most diseased dicks you've ever seen in your life.
Elizabeth LeCompte: Like they were putrified and were going to drop off.
Willem Dafoe: It really was awful.
[Laughter.]
Elizabeth LeCompte: Yes, I had this idea that they'd be beautiful green dicks, that would look like a frog's, or something.
Jim Clayburgh: Or some kind of tropical fish.
Elizabeth LeCompte: Yes. But they looked... horrible. They looked like the final stages of syphilis. I don't know. I give up on Hula. *We tried...*
Kate Valk: I give up, too.
Elizabeth LeCompte: We really burned out on it.
Michael Stumm: I swear it was the urinating thing.
Kate Valk: I think it was the urine. Somewhere... the urination.
Michael Stumm: Once you realized you couldn't make the leap of doing something new, or that shocking, or that... whatever.
Kate Valk: I tell you, I didn't like the way the boys pissed.
Willem Dafoe: What, with a big smile on our faces?
Kate Valk: I don't know. I didn't like it. I can't tell you.
Peyton Smith: What about the way?
Michael Stumm: Too barnyard, is that what?...
Kate Valk: It turned the whole show.
Willem Dafoe: That's what I liked about it.
Kate Valk: It turned the whole show. Never again could I be, like, innocent.
Peyton Smith: Yes.
Willem Dafoe: I can't be innocent ever since that private party. We went to this party and they thought it was like a total gag, like a strip-o-gram.
Michael Stumm: A strip show, yeah.
Peyton Smith: These two people came to see us, came to see Hula.
Norman Frisch: They hired us....
Peyton Smith: These two downtown, like, yuppie types came to see Hula *and thought it was so clever. And they were going to a birthday party and the theme was beach party. All these people, all these yuppies, go to the Hamptons together.*

Michael Stumm: They weren't yuppies types. They were a little old to be yuppies.
Peyton Smith: They weren't. They were thirty [laughs].
Kate Valk: They were geek-y.
Michael Stumm: They were geeks, not yups.
Peyton Smith: It was awful. But they were like lawyers, and doctor types. The two people who saw the whole show knew what it was, and this was their big present. The birthday girl didn't know. Nobody knew anything about it. We were going to come and do Hula, *right. But the audience thought it was strip-o-gram! So they're yelling, "Take off your skirt, bend over and spread 'em!"*
Willem Dafoe: It was all the ugliest people out of the whole crowd coming right to the front and yelling, "TAKE IT OFF!!"
Peyton Smith: And talking through the whole thing.
Willem Dafoe: And shooting pictures. It was just ugly. Very ugly.
Peyton Smith: And then when we left, that guy came up to me and wanted us to come do it for his sick friend in the hospital!! [Laughter.] And the sick friend was Teri Garr, in the hospital. And I said, "I don't know, I don't think so."
Michael Stumm: It was very ugly shit.
Willem Dafoe: It was pretty bad.
Kate Valk: That . . . I don't know . . . really ruined . . . that whole last run. . . .
Jim Clayburgh: What's so sad is that it was the best it was ever performed, some of those nights. It was the loosest, freest and most expressive. And I found, funniest.
Kate Valk: It was very funny. And everything was clear, the way we did it.
Elizabeth LeCompte: It's a painful show for me because it's so . . . I would smile through the whole thing. And with something that I have had a hand in making, I never do that, I never enjoy it. I can never be far enough away to enjoy a piece. But I always enjoyed Hula *that way. Pure pleasure. So it was always very hard for me when audiences missed the choreographic humor in it. And this last run was so beautifully done.*

* * *

Ron Vawter: In Hula*'s last incarnation, we wanted to piss. We thought it would be a last little thing, a little* frisson *at the end. In the final song we don't really dance so much, we just sing. So we were trying to dress up the end, and Willem and I thought . . . it's one of the parts where we're being very sweet . . . that just out of the excitement of the moment, that we would all unload our bladders. And we tried it a couple of times in rehearsal. And it was really funny. But it was a little repelling too, a little*

Figure 42. *Hula*
Kate Valk, Willem Dafoe, Ron Vawter.
(Nancy Campbell)

repugnant. It was too much. And Kate had some funny feelings about that. You know, this may be a crass thing to say, but I think Hula *is, altogther, a very political piece. But you won't find it on its surface. We're not going to talk about the despoliation of Hawaii, but...*

David Savran: [Laughs.]

Ron Vawter: But it's all there. And it's very troubling, very disturbing, I think, this co-opting and destruction of another culture by Americans. That's self-evident, obvious.

David Savran: Right.

Ron Vawter: There's the militant Living Theatre approach, organizing cells to combat this kind of thing. But, unfortunately, that work does not actually persuade. I'm not sure that Hula *persuades, but for the artist making these things, it's a more interesting, viable way of trying to speak, to articulate disgust and anger, than some sort of political exegesis.*

* * *

Peyton Smith: Do you remember that one night a friend of Ronnie's came to see Hula*?*

Kate Valk: [Laughing.] Oh my God, that was the best night I've ever had.

Elizabeth LeCompte: All the people laughing.

Kate Valk: She was stone drunk. She was stewed to the eyeballs.

Peyton Smith: And she laughed so hard and so long that she gave me the laughs.

Norman Frisch: Peyton couldn't get through two sentences.

Kate Valk: She was so funny.

Peyton Smith: And I was thrown off. There's no way I can imitate it. 'Cause she was completely drunk and laughing so loud and ridiculously. I was trying to read and had to keep putting the record jacket down and say, "I'm sorry, I'm really going to do it now." She was a big fat woman laughing like "AHH-HA-HA-HA!!" And the audience was laughing at her, not at Hula*. [Laughter.] So then Ronnie goes out to have a drink with her afterwards. And he goes, "So, did you like the show?" "Like the show?!?" she says. And she throws her pantyhose down on the table, soaking wet. "Here's how much I liked the show!!—SPLAT!!!"*

Part III

L.S.D. (. . . Just the High Points . . .): History as Hallucination

> *History is the concrete body of development, with its moments of intensity, its lapses, its extended periods of feverish agitation, its fainting spells. . . . The forces operating in history are not controlled by destiny or regulative mechanisms, but respond to haphazard conflicts. They do not manifest the successive forms of a primordial intention and their attraction is not that of a conclusion, for they always appear through the singular randomness of events.*
>
> Michel Foucault, "Nietzsche, Genealogy, History"

The Concrete Body of Development

"I'd just started jogging my memory and so the stuff is still kind of coming up." The woman seated at the end of the table tries to remember, she tries to piece together what happened twenty years before. She tries to recall Timothy Leary from Cambridge in 1961. She provides two titles: "I decided to call it *L.S.D.(. . . Just the High Points . . .)* or *Leery about Leary,* which I was."[1] Then she remembers what the party was like.

L.S.D. begins when nine performers climb onto a large platform and all except two take their seats behind a long table. The lone woman, Nancy Reilly, sits at the stage right end of the table, a Walkman in hand, and, as the rest are getting settled, she holds the headphone up to her ear. She turns it on and listens to an interview that the Wooster Group conducted with Ann Rower in 1983. Rower had been a Harvard graduate student and babysat for Leary when he was living in Cambridge and conducting experiments at Harvard with LSD. She wrote to the Group offering them her recollections when she found out that they were working on a piece about Leary. As Nancy Reilly hears Rower's voice, her own memory is jogged: speaking into a microphone, she remembers her lines—and Ann Rower's recollections.

The nature of Reilly's task and her placement on the rostrum allow her to recreate Rower's own position on the afternoon of the interview. She listens and talks, while next to her the men prepare to read. Jim Clayburgh, meanwhile, has put a Maynard Fergusson record on the record player. Beneath her words, the sad, gentle music rises. She listens and remembers and as she does the words and actions of others—her memories incarnate, as it were—interrupt her narrative, texts by Timothy Leary, Aldous Huxley, Jack Kerouac, William Burroughs, Allen Ginsberg and others. Each of the male performers reads the words of another man, someone who cannot be present, from the pile of books in front of him. Each performs for each is literally on stage, on a platform that isn't quite a conventional stage but that imitates a raised raked stage, complete with curtains hung at either end.

This platform is not the stage of memory on which the past is magically present. Instead, it is a part of a performance space that conjures up the dynamics of memory in the tension between the absent "real thing" and the substitute at hand: between stage and platform, character and performer, Ann Rower and Nancy Reilly, Timothy Leary and Jeff Webster. All of *L.S.D.* is structured around this difference, this gap which, like the downstage trough, the long slot cut out of the platform to accommodate a long lower step, divides imitator from model, present from past, here from there. All of the movement in the piece is movement back and forth across this gap, from the concrete here and now to events that took place elsewhere, in a past from which only phantasmic fragments can be salvaged. These fragments are called up as memories or written words, texts cut off from their now-departed authors, stranded, like the voice of Ann Rower on the cassette tape, or cast adrift, like the lines of a play.

Structurally, *L.S.D.* is the most intricate of the Wooster Group's pieces, the one in which the play of reflections is the most complex and elusive. (It is no wonder that the setting for *L.S.D.* is the reverse of the one for *Nayatt School*.) It is held together by the thread of Ann Rower's recollections and by the two basic performance tasks: reading and dancing. Both of these activities (Nancy Reilly's listening is also, of course, a form of reading) dramatize the gap inherent in the act of reflection, or figuring forth. Reading is made possible by temporal discontinuity, by the persistence of a discourse in time, by the disparity between author's intention and reader's interpretation. Dancing, on the other hand, as

Figure 43 *L.S.D.*, Part II
Jim Clayburgh, Ron Vawter, Michael Kirby,
Nancy Reilly, Peyton Smith.
(*Bob Van Dantzig*)

used in *L.S.D.*, exemplifies spatial discontinuity, the diffusion of images through illusional space. The two formal dances in the piece, ending Parts II and IV, are both built on a visual trick, on a *trompe l'oeil* connection of a pair of men's legs to a woman's body. Every turn of the piece dramatizes the schism that results as continuity in time and space is lost, as one attempts to look back to the past and out toward a different place.

* * *

Schema of L.S.D. (. . . Just the High Points . . .)

Part I *NEWTON CENTER: In Which the Men Read From Great Books and The Babysitter Remembers the Leary Household*

Random reading from the books of authors who might have been at the Leary household, circa 1960
The Babysitter interrupts occasionally
Reenactment: "69" incident with Arthur Koestler

Part II *SALEM: In Which the Men are Joined at The Table by Women in Costume and Excerpts from a Play are Performed*

Excerpts from The Crucible/The Hearing
Poppet Dance

Part III *MILLBROOK: In Which The Reading Continues and a Man in Miami Arranges a Gig in One Of The Local Hotels*

Re-creation of LSD Session
The Babysitter continues
Video: Miami
Reenactment: "Bathroom" incident with Watts's secretary

(Same Scene Five Hours Later)

Ron calls from "Miami"
Band
Blackout
Faint Dance ("Pale Blue Eyes")
Video: Millbrook Woods

Part IV *MIAMI: In Which The Men Debate and a Troupe of Dancers Impersonates Donna Sierra and the Del Fuegos*

Liddy/Leary Debate ("I feel very sad . . .")
Shoe Dance

* * *

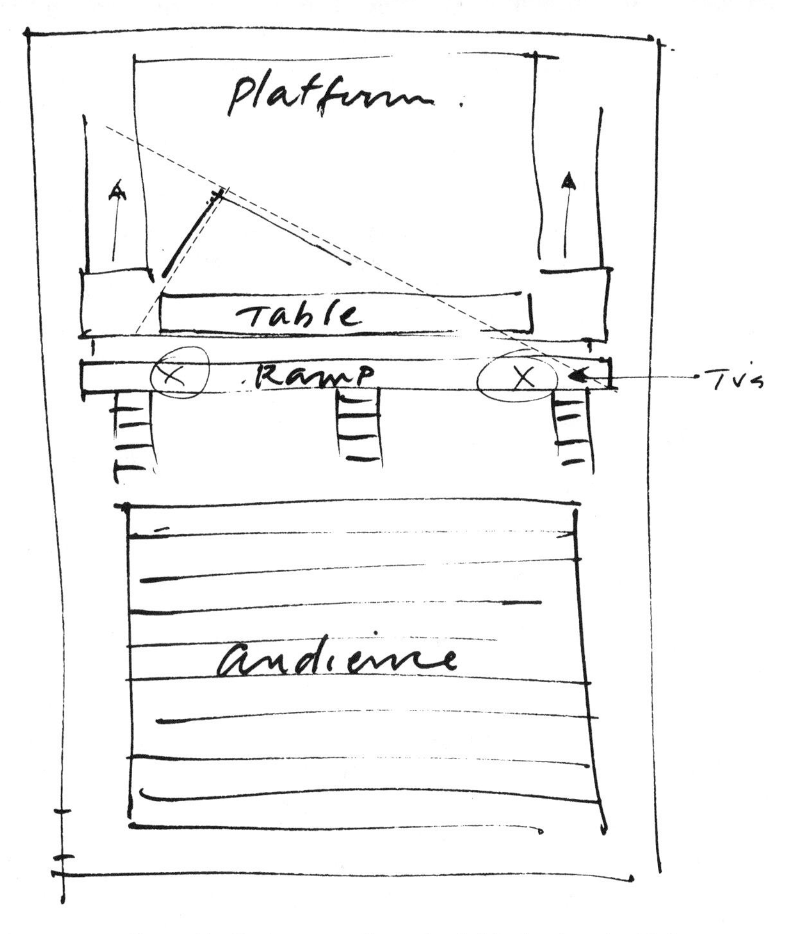

Figure 44. Performance Space for *L.S.D. (...Just the High Points...)*
(Elizabeth LeCompte)

Like the Rhode Island trilogy, *L.S.D.* performs the play of memory, the movement back and forth across the temporal gap. Unlike the earlier work, however, which focuses on personal memory, *L.S.D.* examines cultural memory—that is, history—by interweaving personal memories with a great diversity of texts, by setting Ann Rower's recollections in the midst of what is, in fact, a library. In Part I as Nancy Reilly remembers Ann Rower remembering Leary and his associates, the male performers read selections, most of them chosen at random, from the works of Leary and the writers of the fifties and sixties connected with him. As the voices play from side to side across the table, the fabric of memories and readings becomes more and more complex. Rather than being clarified, the reality of the period becomes increasingly elusive as the gap between present and past expands, between Ann Rower's provisional observations and the men's far more assertive texts, their written monuments. Perhaps it is impossible to discover the "truth" of an era, perhaps memory and writing produce only chimeras, events distorted and disfigured, isolated in solitary reflection or in the lonely act of bringing pencil to paper. Perhaps history is only hallucination.

In exploring this "perhaps," *L.S.D.* examines the "flip side" of the "tranquillized *Fifties*,"[2] juxtaposing personal recollections against the writings of the men who spoke out against the quiescence of the Eisenhower years, who questioned the prevailing cultural order, who, as it were, *made* history. By reading excerpts from Arthur Miller's *The Crucible,* it examines Miller's denunciation of the U.S. Government's most repressive project, the Communist "witch hunt" then being conducted by the House Committee on Un-American Activities. For the nine-year period from 1953 until 1962, these texts constitute a kind of counter-history. They record the loudest (and often the most articulate) voices of opposition against an oppressive status quo.

In *L.S.D.* the Wooster Group writes its own fictive history of these oppositional voices, but only by undermining the dialectic of culture versus counterculture. It refuses to produce a closely argued answer to Leary or Miller, in the knowledge that a rebuttal would fall prey to the very patterns of thought and action it is examining. Instead of schematizing events and producing a systematic critique, the Wooster Group's hallucinatory chronicle admits the several points of view that history, even alternative history, represses. It hearkens to the voices of the excluded. It listens to hearsay. It delights in the inconclusive and contradictory, in not putting the pieces together, in fostering dissent. It liberates that which is squelched in written history: the randomness of political and cultural activity, the background "noise" of events. *L.S.D.* thereby challenges the notion of history as systematic development and suggests that the memories and documents by which one hopes to know the past stand not as truth, but as a testament to the inaccessibility of historical truth, to the impossibility of recovering intention, sensation, event. It performs questions, not assertions, structuring the piece to move toward not a final synthesis but a distillation of the questions—in Part IV the many interrogatories are stripped down to one, "What is this dancing?"

By conceiving of history as a confluence of many memories, texts and points of view, *L.S.D.* demonstrates that it is always a fabrication—

both illusion and product of human labor. To visualize the process of fabrication, the Wooster Group begins the piece not with pretense but by acknowledging the concrete reality of the situation. Working from a real base, it shows how theatrical—and historical—illusion is constructed. Illuminating historical context, it reads excerpts from *The Crucible* in Part II, using period costuming for the first time—suggestions of seventeenth-century dress for the women and Matthew Hansell, a fifties suit for Ron Vawter and contemporary street clothes for the other men. The attire does not give the piece the accuracy of a costume drama but puts historical difference on stage: it exposes the play's archeological status, both for Miller and the Wooster Group. The contrast between costumes from three periods acknowledges *The Crucible*'s status in *L.S.D.* as a reading, in the mid-eighties, of a 1950s drama set in the seventeenth century. Like a production of *Julius Caesar* which shows Shakespeare's Romans to be Englishmen, *L.S.D.* envisions Miller's characters not as seventeenth-century personages but as chimeras from the fifties. It uses a white actress in blackface to play Tituba to suggest that Miller's West Indian is more like the Aunt Jemima of fifties television commercials than a seventeenth-century slave.

L.S.D. uses difference, the gap between present and various pasts, between reading and writing, between disparate perspectives, to expose the illusional, manufactured quality of history and the ways in which politics, economics and ideology determine what is recorded and how. Its juxtaposition of varied materials unsettles both official history and the unofficial. Even the frame provided by Nancy Reilly reading Ann Rower is far from an orthodox, deterministic base (what Foucault would call a "regulative mechanism"[3]). Her remembrance of the past is too haphazard, her style too extemporized and her tone of voice too laconic for her observations to be any more than a casual point of reference. Her most important function is to disrupt the assurance and certitude of the other voices, their habit of mythologizing their own activity and categorizing events according to an alleged truth-value—splitting human activity into the real and the unreal, the good and the bad, the free and the enslaved. For Ann Rower, the opposite of a truth is always equally true: not either/or but both/and. Memory blurs her recollection, giving the past many interpretations and her account two titles. She can't even remember exactly how *The Crucible* fits into the piece when she introduces it in Part II: "Ya, and then I think at that same time, um, um, there was a theatre troupe that came to the house or maybe I took Jackie [Leary] and the kids to see them...or maybe they were in it...I don't remember...you could say...you could say they were doing *The Crucible*."[4] *L.S.D.* uses her as the voice that connects illogically, that questions, guesses and doubts. It builds upon her memories a hallucinatory structure that jumps skittishly from one reading or dance to another, unable to offer the audience anything that pretends to the truth.

* * *

The Singular Randomness of Events

Elizabeth LeCompte: When we were working on Nayatt School *Spalding brought in* The Crucible *for someone to read, just one speech, "Elizabeth, your justice would freeze beer." And it stuck with me. And then... we finished* Route 1 & 9 *and our money had been cut. And I thought, why don't we do seven or eight plays? Like one a week. Real plays. Just to do them, what the hell. I can't remember why I re-read* The Crucible, *but I did. And I knew that I wanted that to be one of the plays.* Route 1 & 9 *had gotten terrible reviews. We knew we were going to go "out of business" because that cut really crippled us terrifically. I remembered, I guess, "Your justice would freeze beer," and I found the script and brought it in and we all sat around upstairs and I said, "I want to do this play." Then we started to count the characters and everybody discouraged me, in a nice way. Spalding said, "Look, this is crazy to try to do this piece. It's a huge piece and we don't want to do it in a small way." And I realized I didn't want to do it in a small way, either. I knew that it was attractive because of the witch hunt aspect, and all of that. But that was almost secondary. I think I was most attracted to the play because of the language, the imitation language, and the screaming of the girls. Those attracted me so much that my mouth would water just thinking about doing it.*

Then, at the same time, we wanted to do another quickie record album interpretation. And everybody brought in records. There was one that I'd never heard all the way through, Ken Kobland's record, L.S.D. *by Timothy Leary. I think Spalding had borrowed it many years ago. As soon as I heard Leary's voice and his description of the place in Millbrook, I knew. There was something about his paranoia and something about his quest. As I was working with that material, I suddenly realized that it was all part of the same piece.*

In February 1983 the Wooster Group began performing open rehearsals of a work-in-progress entitled *L.S.D.*: a forty-five minute version of Arthur Miller's play *The Crucible* prefaced by a side of Timothy Leary's record album, *L.S.D.* (1966). The Group presented a reading of the play, reducing Miller's text to "just the high points," accompanied by music and dance.

This first version of the piece began (much like the final version) with all the performers assembled behind the long table. Jim Clayburgh put the needle on the *L.S.D.* record and held up the record jacket as Timothy Leary's voice filled the Performing Garage. Speaking slowly and deliberately, Leary set forth his credo in a hypnotic monotone, his phrases separated by long and sleepy silences. Listening to his voice, one heard a man both enraptured by and detached from the world around him, and totally dedicated to his paranoia:

> This is the home of the Castalia Foundation, a center for research on the scientific and religious implications of consciousness expanding drugs. This is a serene and beautiful place inhabited by serene and serious-minded people who are dedicating their lives and their energies to expanding their consciousness and harmonizing with the energies inside and outside their body. The situation here is not completely serene at the moment because this quiet island is under siege, for the last few days, the last few weeks, the last few months, this peaceful surrounding has been surrounded by government agents, wire-tappers, anxious and angry politicians....
>
> I'm in trouble because I know too much....
>
> By using psychedelic drugs, I became tuned in on a network of neurological signals and cellular wisdoms that radiate hundreds of millions per second within my body. In the last six years I have taken the voyage out of my mind into my head, into my cells, over three hundred times....
>
> We gave these drugs to thirty-six prisoners who looked at the cops and robbers game through the brutal microscope of expanded consciousness, and laughed, and gave up crime....
>
> In this time of hysteria and crisis, you must do what men have always done in such times: listen to your friends and trust your own judgment.[5]

After twenty minutes of random selections from the record, the Group performed excerpts of four scenes from *The Crucible*, casting Kate Valk in blackface as Tituba and Mary Warren and then fourteen-year-old Matthew Hansell as Deputy Governor Danforth. Three wizened older women (Beatrice Roth, Maria Myers and Irma St. Paule) played the parts of the young girls, moving back and forth in the trough in front of the table. Ron Vawter played Reverend Hale, delivering all of his speeches so

Figure 45. *L.S.D.*, Part II
Ron Vawter, Matthew Hansell, Jim Clayburgh, Michael Stumm, Nancy Reilly, Elion Sacker, Peyton Smith, Jeff Webster, Kate Valk. *(Nancy Campbell)*

fast that they became near-gibberish harangues. As in the finished piece, the women wore suggestions of period costumes. Most of the men used microphones while the women did not.

Watching this first version of *L.S.D.*, one witnessed the juxtaposition of two texts produced in response to two different social crises, the one, an allegorical drama about the Salem witch trials and the other, a statement by the man the *L.S.D.* record jacket calls the "Messiah of the LSD cult."[6] Both dramatize an adversarial relationship with a ruling orthodoxy: the former, between John Proctor (and the other falsely accused witches of Salem) and the ecclesiastical and civil authorities of the Massachusetts Bay Colony; the latter, between Timothy Leary (and the other members of the "LSD cult") and the civil authorities of the United States, the "government agents, wire-tappers, anxious and angry politicians."

Placed next to each other, the two texts delineate the major upheavals of two contiguous decades. In *The Crucible* Arthur Miller uses the Salem trials as a dramatic allegory of the "red hysteria" of the fifties in its most malignant manifestation, Senator Joseph McCarthy's communist "witch-hunt." In the printed script Miller makes the parallel explicit: "in America any man who is not reactionary in his views is open to the charge of alliance with the Red hell."[7]

During the next decade drugs became a powerful disruptive force, not simply for their biochemical effects but because they became the basis for a subculture complete with its own economy, politics and art. By the mid-sixties, drug culture had become one of several centers of "underground" activity, attracting those who were, in Leary's words, "alienated from the establishment power centers."[8] Like the witches of Salem, or the "reds" of the fifties, he and his drug "underground" battled a terrified status quo that justified then, as it had in the past, its criminal repression by equating rebellion with demonism:

> Three hundred years ago you'd be sitting here talking with me about the devil. In Salem . . . they were talking about witches. . . . The fear of those who are anti-God—which is what you are—the fear is always expressed in the metaphor of the time: witches, possessions, devils, and so forth.[9]

There are other parallels between *The Crucible* and Leary. Both witch and drug cults begin with forbidden intoxication and carousal, either dancing naked in the wood or ingesting LSD. In both, illegal activity threatens suspicious and fearful authorities who then institute widespread persecution. Both lead to courtroom and prison and from thence, however, to very different ends. The girl's dancing ends with the hanging of the accused witches, while Leary's activity leads to his several arrests and trials and, finally, his release from prison. In the last scene of *The Crucible*, John Proctor refuses to give in to the authorities, he refuses to name names. Leary's honor is more questionable. He has repeatedly denied "ratting on dope-dealer friends and the Weathermen" and maintains that assertions to that effect are simply part of the government's attempt to discredit him.[10] His son, Jackie, takes a different view of the situation: "Timothy has shown he would inform on anybody he can to get out of jail...."[11]

In the making of *L.S.D.*, the Wooster Group did not emphasize the parallelism between the two "plots," i.e., narratives and conspiracies. Instead, it visualized the dynamics of power within each "plot" by highlighting, tacitly but emphatically, the distribution of microphones and roles. By translating the young girls of Salem into old women, it dramatized their exclusion from the exercise of juridical power. By amplifying the men's voices, it underscored the forces of control within the "plots," the fact that each is organized around a dominant central character, John Proctor or Timothy Leary, who plays the part of heroic leader to his followers.

As the hero of Miller's dialectical and polemical tract, John Proctor is fashioned after the hero of Ibsen's social dramas. A loner, standing somewhat outside the community, he is a man of action and principle, the only one to understand the real motive behind the accusations. He struggles against the lies, answering what he believes is a higher power, a supra-legal morality. He even possesses a tragic flaw of sorts, a moral weakness that allows him to become involved sexually with Abigail. Like his dramatic forebears (Doctor Stockmann, in particular), he holds firm against a criminal society and suffers for it.

Timothy Leary, in contrast, cuts a different kind of hero. As a non-fictive personality, he comes without a single drama in which he is a player. Instead, he appears as a character in a number of contradictory histories written by his former associates, the press and Leary himself. Some fifteen years after his heyday, he remains a deeply ambiguous figure, the hero of a movement which, even in hindsight, resists simple moral and political categorization. It is precisely this complexity that *L.S.D.* explores, using *The Crucible* as a lens through which to focus Leary's would-be heroism and Leary himself as a lens through which to focus *The Crucible* and the values it promotes.

The completed piece of 1984, *L.S.D. (...Just the High Points...)*, elaborates on the Leary material and *The Crucible* by placing them in the framework of Ann Rower's recollections. There they loom as documents called forth by memory. Like a hallucination, the Miller play is fragmented with song, dance and *shtick*, its dramatic tension undermined. By being presented as *both* costume epic and dramatization of the McCarthy hearings, it is de-allegorized, set behind a table with microphones and stacks of papers, its two settings evoked simultaneously, Salem and Washington. In *L.S.D., The Crucible* takes its place less as a "timeless" work of art than as a social and theatrical document (quite in accord with Miller's intent), the commemoration of social upheaval poured into the "well-made play" mold, a staple of high school, university and community theatres. LeCompte has explained this process of contextualization in a letter to Miller:

> I want to put the audience in a position of examining their own relation to this material as "witnesses"—witnesses to the play itself, as well as witnesses to the "story" of the play. Our own experience has been that many, many of our audience have strong associations with the play, having either studied it in school, performed in it in a community theatre production, or seen it as a college play. And the associations with the play are important to my *mise en scène.* It is a theatrical experience which has cut across two generations, a literary and political icon.[12]

In contrast with the historicization of *The Crucible,* the Wooster Group uses Timothy Leary's writings and those of his former associates to fictionalize him, to construct a drama in which Leary appears as a protagonist composed of and by discourse. This drama emerged out of the Wooster Group's research and finally relied most heavily on three sources: the interview with Ann Rower (a "participant in the great experiment"[13]), Leary's own writings and John Bryan's "unauthorized" biography, *Whatever Happened to Timothy Leary?* By juxtaposing Leary's words against often contradictory material, the Group focuses attention on the way Leary has been made and has made himself into a mythic figure. It urges the spectator toward a "character analysis" of Leary and an understanding of the relation between his psychological make-up and his political stance. It constructs a discontinuous and hallucinatory drama in which Leary emerges as a hero less valiant and less divided against himself than John Proctor but, in the end, every bit as unreal.

* * *

Reading Timothy Leary

Elizabeth LeCompte: For Part I, I had all the material that everybody had gathered by the different writers involved with Leary. It was academic to try to make a situation where these characters were being "played." So the actors chose books that they wanted to read out loud. It was reading session for me.

I wanted to have a narrator for this piece. It was a dialogue with the audience about Route 1 & 9. *I wanted a comic narration to make fun, in a way. Originally, the narrator was going to be Jackie Leary. But then I got a letter from Ann Rower remembering an episode in the bathroom of the Leary house and I thought, "Ah, the babysitter. That was a voice even further removed." And Nancy Reilly developed as the perfect vehicle for that as she picked out different things she liked from the Ann Rower interview. Although I was cynical about using a single narrator for the piece (I felt forced by the* 1 & 9 *experience to revert back to the narrator "hook" of earlier work), I liked it more and more as we worked.*

David Savran: One night when I saw L.S.D. *in Boston, Richard Alpert was there. He came backstage afterwards and was sort of glowing... I was amazed.*
Elizabeth LeCompte: They see what they want to see.
David Savran: I guess so.
Willem Dafoe: I was most taken by him saying, "Yeah, you really captured the Millbrook days." And I thought, "Man, if those were the Millbrook days.... I mean, you were there, and we captured them?!?"
Elizabeth LeCompte: I watched him during the whole show.
Willem Dafoe: He was beaming. I didn't recognize him, but I picked him up in the audience as... there is a guy that is really liking the show! [Laughter.]
Norman Frisch: It would have been interesting but I'm glad you didn't read the blow job thing that night. 'Cause that might have put him over the edge.
Kate Valk: What blow job?
Willem Dafoe: Leary and Alpert had a fight, took some acid...
Kate Valk: With friends and Jackie around him?
Willem Dafoe: In front of everybody... They did a wrestling match to get out the anger and it ended up with Alpert blowing Leary.
Michael Stumm: Or Leary allowing Alpert to blow him in a benevolent gesture.
Willem Dafoe: Right, right.
Elizabeth LeCompte: [Laughs] Benevolent gesture....
Norman Frisch: But then, didn't he turn on him?
Michael Stumm: Homos, shmomos, I don't care....
Willem Dafoe: That's a recurring thing. That's part of why Alpert started to lose gas as his righthand man, I think, because he found Leary terrifically homophobic. If couples would stay there, he would literally, like someone's parent, separate the gay couples. Not let them sleep together. If two guys came in he'd say, "You get the big room and you get the... But then Sally and Bobby get the...."

Ron Vawter: Certainly in L.S.D. *we were addressing our origins in the Performance Group. Many of the things that were going on in the Millbrook house, the drugs, the breaking down of social inhibitions, all went into the kind of theatre we developed from. It's such a part of all of our pasts that it had to be there. And the guru—Schechner always thought of himself as a guru. Theatre was just a part of it. We never lived together in a collective, but our lives revolved around a kind of guru-follower,* ashram, *sixties experience, which has good and bad memories for me. And one of the reasons why, when we deal with the sixties in the piece, we keep waffling back and forth, is because we feel a great deal of ambivalence.—Were these people inspired? They did change ways of thinking and perceiving.—Were they destructive? They were obviously both. So there's repulsion and attraction, constantly. And the same was true with Richard who had some absolutely wonderful ideas. And some real, out-in-left-field, eccentric ones. And they have continued to affect us. When an emancipation occurs, lots of things are liberated, some good, some bad.*

Part I of *L.S.D.* ("Newton") introduces Ann Rower and reads selections from the works of Timothy Leary and other writers of the fifties and sixties. It thereby provides a slice of the "official" history of the period, a recounting of the experiences and anecdotes of the beat poets and associates of Leary, their values, beliefs and aesthetics. The readings (which Ron Vawter limits to sixty seconds) are punctuated by Ann Rower's memories and the music of Maynard Fergusson (a friend of Leary). The sequence of texts is often surprisingly clearly focused despite (or perhaps, because of) the fact that most of the selections are chosen spontaneously. Indeed, the principal irony of Part I resides in the fact that, most nights, the random selections provide a far more assertive and deterministic frame than the tentative observations that comprise Nancy Reilly's set text. Part I thus reverses the relationship between the arbitrary and the pre-planned, thereby reaffirming what Foucault calls the *singular* randomness of events,[14] the fact that history, composed by a multitude of events that could have happened in a multitude of different ways, instead unfolds (like the evening's performance) as the result of unique and irrevocable, but ultimately random choices. It turns the spectator's attention toward the rigor of the arbitrary, the throw of the dice—or round of Russian roulette—which apportions happiness and unhappiness, wealth and poverty, life and death.

When Norman Frisch reads an Allen Ginsberg letter to Peter Orlovsky from 1961, he provides a vivid sense of the revolution these men envisioned and their own position at its leading edge:

Figure 46. *L.S.D.*, Part I
Jeff Webster, Michael Kirby on monitor, Matthew Hansell, Michael Stumm.
(Nancy Campbell)

> Leary was great here, calmed everyone, Bill [Burroughs] dug him.... They both go to Harvard where Bill will experiment with white noise & sensory deprivation machines etc.
>
> Leary told me he agreed with Bill that Poetry was finished. Because he felt the world was really moving on to a new super consciousness that might eliminate words and Ideas....
>
> I think Bill & Leary at Harvard are going to start a beautiful consciousness alteration of the whole world—actually for real—Leary thinks it's the beginning of a new world.[15]

When Michael Kirby reads the opening of William Burroughs's *Naked Lunch* (1959) he evokes the danger and paranoia which are the dark side of Ginsberg's excitement, as well as the exultation of discovering a new literary language:

> I can feel the heat closing in, feel them out there making their moves, setting up their devil doll stool pigeons, crooning over my spoon and dropper I throw away at Washington Square Station, vault a turnstile and two flights down the iron stairs, catch an uptown A train....[16]

Like many of the other readings, *Naked Lunch* provided a source of inspiration for the sixties drug culture and the reaction against bourgeois values. For its young partisans, the use of hallucinogens was a pointed attack on what Leary calls the "mechanized, computerized, socialized, intellectualized, televised, Sanforized" patterns of the "air-conditioned anthill"[17] in which they had been raised. This revolt was waged by a variety of groups, from flower power hippies to the S.D.S., Weathermen and Yippies. Although their tactics were different, the factions were united by a vision of the sterility of Western culture and by an understanding of the crushing economic and political weight of America's "military-industrial complex."

As the readings continue, the slightly adenoidal, matter-of-fact voice of Nancy Reilly as Ann Rower interrupts to provide personal glimpses of "King Leary"[18] and his family and descriptions of the carryings-on by those who would visit in 1961 for the weekend "trips." Her observations

Nancy Reilly: I was on the panel with the guys and they all had books. And the babysitter was riding shotgun on the outside. So one day Liz said, "Everybody get your materials." And they all took the books. So I grabbed my tape which I had been transcribing. I said, "Well, here's my book."

provide a stark contrast to the effusions of the poets: "I came in, um, and we met Tim. And I just remember him standing there with his arms around the kids, and they all looked very depressed. They were really very down. I guess, I guess the suicide of the wife was, whatever, fairly recent."[19] (Leary's first wife, Marianne, had in fact committed suicide four years earlier.) She describes the focus of the household, the three-tiered ceramic candy dish which held the pink psilocybin pills from Switzerland, and how one weekend the candy dish was empty "and there was this atmosphere of... waiting."[20]

As presented in *L.S.D.*, Ann Rower's attitude toward Leary is highly equivocal, as she explains later in Part III: "He was a liar... he was obviously a psychopath, in many ways... you know... he was a liar... he was uhhh uhh a classic paranoid... ya, but again, you know, like most paranoids he turned out to be right."[21] Steve Buscemi, meanwhile, standing in the trough, presents similarly ambiguous feelings toward Leary, reading Jackie Leary's statements taken from the Bryan book. In Part I these two performers are differentiated from the rest by not being seated behind the long table. They are the two outsiders, the two composers of a history that is unofficial because it is oral, not written. Reilly and Buscemi read from interview transcripts. The men at the table read from books. The former have not taken pen in hand to justify themselves and their actions; their words have simply been intercepted by tape recorders. The others (including Arthur Miller) have purposefully set out to preserve and promulgate their ideas, to compose themselves and their epoch in print, to write history.

By using Ann Rower's casual observations as the scaffolding for the written texts, Part I encourages the spectator to make connections between the readings. Eschewing an interpretive authoritarianism, it opens up options. The nights that I attended *L.S.D.* I heard a wide variety of readings, each of which added to the ambiguous composite picture of the period. I remember one evening Jeff Webster read an excerpt from a 1966 *Playboy* interview with Leary which was so fascinating to me because I'd never heard it before (nor was I to hear it again). *Playboy* asked about his rumored promiscuity and Leary explained it as a necessary consequence of his work.

> ...a charismatic public figure does generate attraction and stimulate a sexual response.
> *Playboy*: How often do you return this response?
> Leary: Every woman has built into her cells and tissues the longing for a hero, sage-mythic male, to open up and share her own divinity. But casual sexual encounters do not satisfy this deep longing. Any charismatic person who is conscious of his own mythic potency awakens this basic hunger in women....[22]

In observing any revolution from afar, one can discern tendencies and practices that seem to negate the goals being fought for. Listening to Webster read, I was struck by what seems the principle contradiction inherent in Leary's project: all the while that he has espoused rebellion, he has in fact, tacitly appropriated vital elements of the ideology he attempts to undermine. His statement is a gauge of his failure to understand that his concept of the heroic and mythic leader perpetuates an autocratic power structure that will, in turn, simply co-opt the social networks of "the establishment," thereby making his revolution into the mirror image of what it is fighting against. Further, he seems unaware of the implications of his identification of political with sexual power and blind to the fact that the patriarchal values he espouses have been a major force in upholding an oppressive status quo.

This random selection provides a striking counterpoint to the first dramatic presentation in *L.S.D.* At the end of Part I, Nancy Reilly reads Ann Rower's description of Arthur Koestler's visit to Leary's house. As she reads, the other performers casually reenact the narrated action, as they might re-create an event before a courtroom, Ron Vawter as Koestler walking in place or slipping his fingers matter-of-factly through his hair. Reilly describes Koestler on LSD going upstairs to his bedroom and seeing Allen Ginsberg and Peter Orlovsky making love there, "on [his] bed... sixty-nine." He screams and runs out of the house, freaking out. Norman Frisch as Ginsberg, a blanket wrapped around him, goes after him and calms him down while Matthew Hansell as Orlovsky, his chest bared, a towel round his waist, stands proudly on a chair at the center of the table, "a radiant dish."[23] As startling as Ann Rower's story appears, it becomes even more so when compared with Koestler's own words, written two years before his "bad trip" in Cambridge.

> As for the "sexual problem," the answer is contained in a remark overheard in a Zurich bookshop, where a girl of about twenty, pointing at a book which bore precisely that title, drily asked her companion, "Why *problem*?"[24]

Which text provides the "true" portrait of Koestler? Or is their very contradiction the source of interest, the operative historical detail?

Some evenings (depending on which selections are read) *L.S.D.* presents Timothy Leary and many of his colleagues as part of the dance of fathers and sons evoked in *Point Judith.* As sketched by the Wooster Group, he is (sometimes) exposed as the producer of a *machismo* in which paranoia and tyranny prey off and reinforce each other. He is a mass of contradictions, the archetypal bourgeois rebel, launching a powerful and trenchant attack against middle-class culture only after interiorizing its values. He is the endlessly reflective subject, the scientist (with a Ph.D. in psychology) pondering his own consciousness while he "freaks out."

Leary, Ginsberg, Burroughs and the other men whose words are read in Part I no doubt believed that their ingestion of LSD would inaugurate a new world (and *L.S.D.* questions less their sincerity than their methods). Certainly, they were promoting some powerful and revolutionary ideas for political reorganization and the rejection of consumer culture. And Leary himself (never one to disparage his own importance) certainly recognized the function of his sect in inspiring political change: "Every historical advance has resulted from the stern pressure of visionary men who have declared their independence from the game."[25] (It is far more than a figure of speech that excludes women from this vanguard.) Despite their insights, however, Leary and the others never realized how deeply they were always a part of the *ancien régime,* how their modes of thought and behavior were to a surprising extent quite compatible with those of "the establishment," and how their revolution was doomed to be co-opted by the society against which it rebelled. By the mid 1970s, the revolutionary potential of "LSD cult" had, in large part, collapsed, both from internal and external pressure. From the perspective of *L.S.D.,* the failure of Leary and his associates is seen as the result both of the contradictions within the movement itself and the sect's persecution (and prosecution) by those ubiquitous "government agents." For the audience cognizant of that failure, the prophecy of Allen Ginsberg resounds with a bitter poignance:

> Peter and I went up to Harvard last week eating synthetic mushrooms—very high—*The Revolution Has Begun*—Stop giving your authority to Christ & the Void & the Imagination—*you are it,* now, *the God....* [26]

* * *

Attempting to Secure Performance Rights for *The Crucible*

Peyton Smith: I heard from a dear friend who's on the scene that she was going to a cocktail party and that Arthur Miller would be there. So I went with her, because we had been trying unsuccessfully to get him to come and see what we were doing. It was the hundredth anniversary of the Chelsea Hotel and he was an honorary guest. And I thought, "I'm gonna go there and get right up next to him and lay the stuff on him." Right. So we get there and it's, like, a cartoon of a bursting room. Absolutely no

way you could get in. And there's about twenty-five video cameras, all the news, all these prestigious guests. It was horrible. I said, "forget it, it's not gonna work."
Elizabeth LeCompte: So she headed for the bar.
Peyton Smith: I might as well have a drink. Anyways, for Christ's sake, I got all the way up here, I'll have a drink, go down and do the show. 'Cause we had a show that night.
Elizabeth LeCompte: You were going to drink before a show?
Peyton Smith: Well. . . .
Jim Clayburgh: She was just having a Perrier.
Peyton Smith: Yes, a Perrier. So I literally elbowed my way to the bar with a person pressed against my back, and I hear, "So, Arthur, what would you like?" I was so excited. I turned around and there he was. He's like six foot six, or something and he was real, like, charming. I had to say, "M-M-Mister M-M-Miller? M-M-My name is Peyton from the Performing Garage. . . . " And he's going, "Well, yes, I do want to come down and see the show."
Willem Dafoe: [Smoothly] My name's Peyton, *I'm a* performer . . .
Peyton Smith: Performer . . .
Willem Dafoe: At the Performing *Garage.*
Peyton Smith: That's not what I did. That's what I was trying to do. [Laughter.] That I was Mrs. Proctor. *[Laughter.] That it's perfectly* pretentious*!*
[Laughter.]
Norman Frisch: Didn't he come, like, that night?
Peyton Smith: He came that night. He wrote it down in his little book and said he'd come. And I went back to the Garage and told Liz. But I couldn't tell anyone else in the Group, 'cause she didn't want people getting nervous.
David Savran: How did he react when he saw it?
Peyton Smith: He looked like he was having a good time.
Michael Stumm: He would have been much happier if it had been a Tennessee Williams play, let's put it that way.
Peyton Smith: He definitely enjoyed it.
David Savran: But then he said no.
Kate Valk: He never said no, he *never said no, did he?*
Michael Stumm: Sure he did.
Kate Valk: He just said, he wouldn't say yes, that's all.
Michael Stumm: What was the tenor of the letter, right after? It looked pretty cut and dried to me.
Peyton Smith: It was that we were not a "first class . . . "

Jim Clayburgh: That means Broadway.
Elizabeth LeCompte: Norm talked with him for a while. He didn't say no.
Norman Frisch: That night, he was very positive. It was clear that if he was going to say no he wasn't going to say it to our faces. He was going to do it through his agent.
Peyton Smith: He didn't leave. He came up and wanted to talk to us.
Norman Frisch: He loved the performances. He thought Matthew was great. He talked with Matthew.
Elizabeth LeCompte: He said, "You're going somewhere, young man."
Norman Frisch: On that evening, he was perfectly charming.
Elizabeth LeCompte: Something happened while we were talking to him.
Norman Frisch: He said something like, "Do you think the audience will think it's a parody?"
Peyton Smith: Because he came on a night when there were only about ten people in the audience. And nobody laughed.
David Savran: So he was afraid that people would laugh at him?
Elizabeth LeCompte: Yes.
Norman Frisch: The whole world was watching....
Michael Stumm: The Day After.
Norman Frisch: So the house is empty.
Elizabeth LeCompte: Because, of course, our audience is so socially conscious.
Norman Frisch: So just before he left, he asked that question, did we think the audience would think it was a parody? And we immediately said "No, no, no." We made it clear that we didn't intend it to be humorous. It wasn't a send-up of the play. So at the moment, he seemed sort of satisfied with that, and went away.
Elizabeth LeCompte: Remember, he said one other thing before he left. He said, "How would this affect a revival of the play," remember that, "on Broadway?" We were standing out on the street.
Willem Dafoe: And Liz said, "Fat chance, Arthur. I read your reviews from '53."
Elizabeth LeCompte: He seemed confused and he was actually ruminating in front of us about how this would affect a big revival of The Crucible. *I had the feeling that he was going to try to bring it into New York. And would this destroy that possibility?*
Peyton Smith: We heard that he didn't want it revived because he didn't want to go through the bad reviews again. Because it's regarded as not such a good play.
Elizabeth LeCompte: He wants to control totally, of course, any production of it because he wants to try to revamp its rep.

Willem Dafoe: You've got to remember, this guy goes to cocktail parties. This guy's living off... you know, he's making deals for his old plays. His new stuff hasn't been received well.
Michael Stumm: He's not had a nice word come his way in a long time.
Peyton Smith: Except revivals.
Michael Stumm: He's already a living fossil. He doesn't want to get shit on and beat up and have a bunch of punks downtown make him look like an asshole.
Elizabeth LeCompte: I think that's really what it was about. Finally he began to get worried about how he would look.
Willem Dafoe: It really stinks, when you think about it, because the way that the world knows The Crucible *is when Appleton High puts it on.*

Elizabeth LeCompte: One thing that's always present in my work is the opposition between high art and low art, high entertainment versus low entertainment, the good artist and the bad artist, the artist and the non-artist. And in L.S.D. *it's Arthur Miller versus our dance at the end, actually all the dances that we do next to the Miller. What I did was to collide Arthur Miller with... I went to Salem and at one of the tourist traps I saw a re-enactment of the trial testimony by two high school girls surrounded by all these mannequins. And it was horribly done. So I took the idea of working on* The Crucible *as a high school play, so to speak, well-done and totally committed, but finally divinely amateur in a way that Arthur Miller sensed, I think. His vision of himself is in the realm of high moral art. But this is a play that most people see in high school productions, with people wearing cornstarch in their hair.*

When the Wooster Group began working on Arthur Miller's play *The Crucible* in November 1982, it immediately wrote to Dramatists Play Service to secure performance rights. The reply that came from the Service's Leasing Department, dated November 9, 1982, read: "I regret to inform you that *The Crucible* is not available for production in New York City and so we cannot grant you permission to perform. Sorry."[27]

On January 15, 1983, Elizabeth LeCompte wrote to Miller's agent at ICM, Luis Sanjurjo, requesting "special permission to use excerpts from *The Crucible*" for a new piece, *L.S.D.*[28] Sanjurjo told her that before making any decision he would have to see the piece with a lawyer. "When you have something ready, call me," he told LeCompte. During the spring and summer of 1983 the Wooster Group was in Europe performing *Route 1 & 9* and developing *North Atlantic,* written by Jim Strahs, which was to be used as Part II of *L.S.D.* When the Group returned to New York, it set to work rehearsing and adapting *North Atlantic* for an

American cast and, in September, resumed performing open rehearsals of excerpts from *The Crucible*. Invited by the Group to attend, Sanjurjo, in discussion after the performance, suggested that Arthur Miller see it.

During the following weeks, the Wooster Group tried in vain to contact Miller. One afternoon in late October, however, Peyton Smith met him at a reception at the Chelsea Hotel and persuaded him to attend the show that night. Afterwards, in conversation with LeCompte, Miller voiced three concerns. First, the audience might think LeCompte's interpretation a parody. Secondly, the audience might believe the piece was a performance of the entire play and not just excerpts. And thirdly, Miller feared that these performances might preclude a "first-class," i.e., Broadway, production. He left saying he would have to think about it. A week later he instructed ICM to write the Wooster Group saying that he would not grant them permission to use excerpts from *The Crucible*. The letter indicated that Miller believed the use would "among other things, tend to inhibit first-class productions" of the play.[29]

Between November 30, 1983 and October 22, 1984 Elizabeth LeCompte sent three letters to Miller and/or his agent. She argued that the production of excerpts in a tiny Off-Off Broadway theatre would not affect the possibility of a "first-class" production. She also declared her serious regard for *The Crucible*, explaining that her work was not intended as parody, and elaborated the reasons for its incorporation into *L.S.D.* Simultaneously, the Wooster Group continued the development of the piece. It retained *The Crucible* excerpts as Part II, reducing them to twenty-five minutes, and noted in the program that only a part of Miller's play was being used. The Group also excised *North Atlantic* (presenting it as a separate piece) and composed three new parts, all based on Leary material. In the spring it added the subtitle *(... Just the High Points...)* and performed the first three parts in New York. On the invitation of Peter Sellars, then artistic director of the Boston Shakespeare Company, the Group took *L.S.D. (... Just the High Points...)* to Boston, where it was opened to the critics, who reviewed it favorably. In the final days of the Boston run, the Group presented Part IV publicly for the first time.

In September the Wooster Group began performing all four parts of *L.S.D.* in New York. LeCompte sent a letter to Sanjurjo informing him of the piece's development and explaining that *The Crucible* excerpts had been conflated to a twenty-five minute sequence. In a collective decision, the Group opened *L.S.D.* to the press at the end of October. On October 31, Mel Gussow panned the piece in the *New York Times*, referring to Part II as a "send-up" of *The Crucible*.[30] Ten days later, the Group received a "cease and desist" order from Miller's attorneys in which they threatened to "recommend to Mr. Miller that he take any and all legal measures against you, including instituting court proceedings."[31] LeCompte wrote Miller on November 15 to explain again her intentions. At the same time, in consultation with a copyright lawyer, the Group reworked Part II so that *The Crucible* section would be performed in gibberish. The incident was reported two days later in the *New York Times*[32] and in the November 27 issue of the *Village Voice* by Don Shewey. According to Shewey, Miller denied receiving any of the letters—his agent refused to comment—and indicated that "The first thing they've gotta do is send me an apology."[33] LeCompte did so in a letter dated November 26 in which she also announced that she had "with great sadness" stopped performances of *L.S.D.* the preceding night.[34]

During the month of December the Wooster Group reworked Part II of *L.S.D.*, substituting excerpts from a text by Michael Kirby for most of Miller's. Kirby's play, *The Hearing*, translated Miller's action back to 1950s suburbia, substituting microfilm for the poppet, drugs for Tituba's brew. The new section thus introduced another narrative layer that followed the shape of the *The Crucible* excerpts and simultaneously dramatized the enforced suppression of Miller's script. When a performer "accidentally" spoke a line of *The Crucible* or made a reference to one of Miller's characters, he or she was silenced by the buzzer. The new version was opened on January 4 for an intended eight performance run. On January 7, John A. Silberman, Miller's lawyer, wrote the members of the Wooster Group to inform them that one of the attorneys in his office had attended a performance on January 5. He told the Group that its current version "continues to constitute an infringement of Mr. Miller's copyright" and demanded that it "cease and desist." He warned them that the playwright could institute court proceedings "based upon all past, present and future performances" and insisted that "blatant and continuing violations of Mr. Miller's rights must not be allowed to continue."[35] On January 8, the day it received the letter, the Wooster Group closed *L.S.D.*

Arthur Miller is certainly acutely aware of the difference between his interpretation and that of the Wooster Group, since he has made the issue paramount in his interviews with the press. In an article from December 1983, Miller is quoted as saying, "The issue here is very simple. I don't want my play produced except in total agreement with the way I wrote it." He objects to the Wooster Group's use because "It's a blatant parody."[36] A year later Miller reiterated his position, explaining that the insistence on a "first-class" production was a smokescreen: "I'm not interested in the money. The aesthetics are involved. I don't want the play mangled that way. Period."[37]

* * *

Elizabeth LeCompte: For L.S.D. *I took the* Nayatt *set and inverted it so that the audience is on the floor looking up at the table. It's just a reversal. That came early in working on* The Crucible. *As I began to work... the difficulty in trying to find the form and the style of that piece with only seven or eight performers was overwhelming. Would I use puppets? Would I have doubled roles? What would I do? It took six months to work all those things through. I wanted it to be a fully cast production. I didn't want the full play, but I wanted a full production. Then I realized that everything would be performed on the table, everything. Originally the courtroom scene was behind the table and the other scenes were played very frontally. And the table would move back and forth. The performers had to be locked into the table for the entire piece.*

The confrontation between Arthur Miller and the Wooster Group over performance rights for *The Crucible* has been the most widely reported dispute in the Wooster Group's history. Although it has been resolved—at least as of this writing—the implications will continue to reverberate. From now on, *L.S.D.* will be in part "about" Miller withholding the rights, in the same way that *Route 1 & 9* is now in part "about" the NYSCA funding cut. Both Miller and LeCompte seem to agree that the fundamental disagreement concerns the Group's interpretation of *The Crucible*. Since Miller never saw the completed version of the piece, he is unable to evaluate the play's function within the larger work. From what he saw, however, he realizes that the *mise en scène* submits the play to an incisive critique, even if he remains unconvinced of its ultimately equivocal attitude toward his drama.

It is clear from the way it is staged that *The Crucible* is not being used simply for the story it tells. If it were, the Wooster Group could have substituted some other version of the Salem witch trials when Miller denied them access to the play. Or it could have chosen other material about intoxication, witch hunting or imprisonment. Its decision to retain the Miller script is indicative of the Group's valuation of the play not simply for its intrinsic value but for the unique network of associations it brings with it. As LeCompte explains in her letter to Miller, the performance is calculated to distance the spectator, to transform him into a "witness" before whom the play becomes an "exhibit," a historical and theatrical document.

Following the pattern of the earlier work, *L.S.D.* submits *The Crucible* to an examination. Like *Nayatt School* it elaborates a pedagogical intention, alternating between the simple act of reading and the acting out of a highly theatricalized mania. It inverts the *Nayatt* set to erect a raised stage on which the long table now sits. The performers either read from behind it, present testimony from one end of it, or parade back and forth in front of it on the platform or in the trough. Their elevation gives them a grandeur, a sense of being larger-than-life. In *Nayatt* the performers descend into chaos, while in *L.S.D.* their pathos, madness and demagoguery tower above the audience, almost heroic in scale.

L.S.D. begins its examination straightforwardly. Even the dramatization of Arthur Koestler's "bad trip" remains cool and presentational, despite the "characters'" impassioned responses. So, too, the reading of *The Crucible* starts quietly, like a congressional hearing, building intensity to the courtroom scene, when it degenerates into a mad and wild spectacle, with witnesses trading accusations, screaming and raving. Led by the girls of Salem and inspired with a lust for revenge, for the blood of the innocent, the entire courtroom freaks out.[38]

* * *

Dancing *The Crucible*

David Savran: What gave you the ideas for Parts III and IV?
Elizabeth LeCompte: After we'd worked on The Crucible *for almost a year, I realized I wanted to break it down slowly in the course of the piece, to let it disintegrate over time. The structure of* L.S.D. *would be the disintegration of* The Crucible, *linguistically. The image that I was working from was a story [from the Bryan book] of a whole courtroom being given acid someplace in California. And jokey, clichéd sixties images of turning on the world. But I didn't know how to do it. I would start, "I'm going to break down the text and take lines that I like." But I can never work that way, from my head. I have to work from watching the performers. It might have been perfectly fine but it was empty for me. So I finally knew the only thing to do was... the worst thing in the world you could do in the early seventies. And that was to take LSD to make art. So I said, "We have to do what was a 'no-no' in those days, especially for the Performance Group." We set a situation where everybody took acid and then I videotaped them doing* The Crucible. *They just picked random parts to do. I was the only one who didn't take any. And it was pretty boring. It was pretty horrendously boring. They couldn't remember their lines. And you know when people laugh at themselves, and they think it's funny? But it's not funny, it's indulgent and... kind of... horrible? Well, I*

recorded all of that. And then I realized that rhythmically it was what I wanted for the next part, a slow tempo, and a lack of concentration. And it left room for other things to come in between.

So then—I didn't know why but I didn't tell the actors because I was a little nervous about it—we set about recreating it second by second, to ten seconds, to twenty seconds, and so on. This goes back again to a real naturalism I'm interested in. They watched the videotape and recreated their actions exactly for this section—fifteen, eighteen minutes. Ken brought in the video... I just knew there was something about landscapes... "That Florida exists" was written real big in neon lights up in my head. So we began working with those images next to what was happening live. I could begin to play around now with the story of The Crucible *coming in and out with lots of other material. And then we made Part I and I realized that Part III was just the continuation of the reading from Part I. And that's when the whole structure fell into place, because the whole piece is a reading that breaks down. The performers, the authors, are still, ten years later, trying to continue this reading. It's the same set-up, almost, and they're at the same table but it's years later. It's like the calender changing on film. And then Part IV was very simple. I had this phrase in my head, "What?—is this dancing?" "What is this?—dancing?" It's what Danforth says to the girls when he hears they were dancing in the woods. "What is this dancing?" He wants to know about it. It was a horrifying thing to him. So in Part III he says, as* The Crucible *is broken down, "What is this dancing?" In Part IV the only thing left of* The Crucible *had to be the line "What is this dancing?" and there had to be a dance.*

At the end of the last scene of *The Crucible,* six of the performers dance an epilogue to the play. The women—Valk, Smith and Kohler—stand at the front of the platform while the men—Vawter, Dafoe and Stumm—sit behind them, all hidden except their legs, hanging into the trough, their pants pulled up to their knees. Latin piano music begins ("Mambo-Jambo" and "Tico-Tico" played by George Feyer, circa 1954) and the women bob and sway to the rhythm while the men move their feet up and down, back and forth in time with the music. The three pairs form a *trompe l'oeil* chorus line: like Mary Warren's poppet or witches in flight, the hanged women of Salem dance together, kicking up "their" heels, blank expressions on their inert faces. Only for a moment does the dance intimate the horror of their death, as bodies shake and legs twitch spasmodically. Afterwards, they list and float as their souls, in a final victory over their persecutors, fly up to heaven, the paroxysms of death transformed into choreographic display.

In *L.S.D.* everything returns to reading and dancing, the two basic performance tasks. Although the one is verbal and the other kinetic and gestural, *L.S.D.* reveals their structural equivalency, the fact that reading is itself a dance—of denotation, connotation, memory and association. Whether the performers are reading from books or *The Crucible,* they dance their way through a series of texts, alternating between the present and the various pasts evoked by the readings, pairing off now Timothy Leary and Arthur Miller, now Leary and G. Gordon Liddy.

All the action of the piece takes place within the framework of this open-ended reading (which is also a dance) in which the performers are gradually infected by the mood of the texts that they are reading. More and more, they become Ann Rower's memories fleshed out, given independent, three-dimensional form and, in Part III, even a kind of plot: a party scene. They start to celebrate in the wake of *The Crucible's* "high" spirits, but in the course of the party, their activity slowly winds down as they become more and more self-absorbed and the accompanying music, more and more melancholy. As the years pass fictively in Parts III and IV, the reading disintegrates, the dance breaks down. Character and text become recognizable for what they are: memories, hallucinations, random fragments, a story here, a line there. In the mouths of the revelers the individual texts become dissociated quotations, losing their "authors," their patronymic identity. The texts and actions, instead, become recognizable as the fragments that collectively constitute history, "with its moments of intensity, its lapses, its extended periods of feverish agitation, its fainting spells."[39] They become the testaments of an age, a party, an unfinished revolution.

* * *

Nancy Reilly: L.S.D. *is so much an encapsulization of the days of my twenties. It's a wonderful feeling to present that play. It's a moving force for me. I remember being so happy when my father was in Boston to see it. I thought that, as a performer, because of the kind of work I've chosen, this is a true moment of autobiographical exchange with him. I can really give him a section of my life, with all the open ends, this loose wire in everybody's history. And I remember one night in Boston, I went through the part: "It was more than a party, I mean... it was more like a revolution... and on a certain level everyone really believed that if you could give this to everyone it would change the world... it's so hard to get back to feeling that now." And somebody in the audience went... it was such a heartfelt and mental collapse of a sigh. He was just, like, "WHOOO!"*

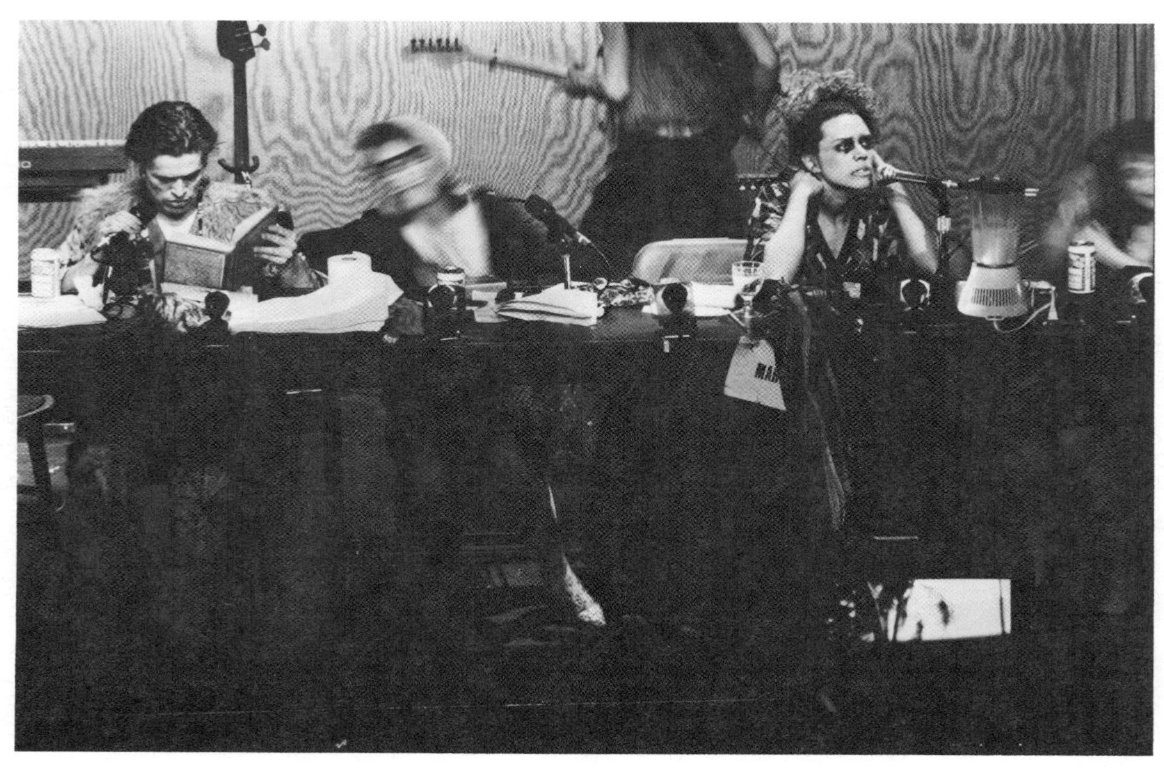

Figure 47A *L.S.D.*, Part III
Willem Dafoe, Nancy Reilly, Jeff Webster,
Kate Valk, Anna Kohler.
(*Paula Court*)

Figure 47B *L.S.D.*, Part III
Jeff Webster, Michael Kirby on monitor,
Peyton Smith, Willem Dafoe.
(*Bob Van Dantzig*)

Part III is titled "Millbrook," evoking the house and commune in New York State where Leary and his followers lived in the mid-sixties. During its first portion, Ann Rower's memories are interrupted by eighteen minutes (with several gaps) of the "LSD version" of *The Crucible* and by Michael Kirby's reading of Alan Watts. (All of Part III is accompanied by Ken Kobland's video.) Duplicating exactly their actions on the videotape, the performers drink, smoke and party while fragments from Act III of *The Crucible* surface in a fitful rhythm. Several minutes into Part III, Willem Dafoe/John Proctor, speaking into the microphone, asks what's going on (his question invariably sparks laughter of recognition): "Umm, are we staying on the play or are we doing Leary stuff too?"[40] Kate Valk/Mary Warren, meanwhile, having applied whiteface make-up over her blackface, talks and laughs with Nancy Reilly/Ann Rower and the other performers seated at the stage left end of the table (their conversations can't be heard because they don't have microphones).

> *Ken Kobland: Watching Part III, as soon as you focus, you're missing something else that's going on, some other silly or gentle or crazy connection.*

After about fifteen minutes of seemingly improvised activity, four of the performers take up musical instruments (Anna Kohler sings) and become a rock'n'roll band, spread out along the platform, while the video continues and the remaining performers become ever more absorbed in their variously obsessive activities.

The narrative climax of Part III occurs shortly before the band starts, when Nancy Reilly reads Ann Rower's description of Alan Watts's visit to Leary's house "not with his wife but with his girlfriend." She explains that "he had just written I think ... *Man, God and Nature*" (in fact, the book, from which Michael Kirby reads, is titled *Nature, Man and Woman*). She continues: "everybody takes pills ... and at one point, you know, there's this scream coming from the bathroom." The performers then rise and act out the story in the same way that they acted out Arthur Koestler's "bad trip" at the end of Part I.

> Everybody's um banging and I come in, and there's this line of people ... huddled outside the bathroom door pulling on the door. "Let us in ... let us in" ... and there's this woman screaming and screaming inside ... um, finally you know, finally ... somebody said to her ... "what's the matter ... what's the matter?" She says, "They're coming, they're after me, they're coming ... they're coming." "Who's coming?" ... that's the men. "They're coming, they're trying to steal my shit." And finally the door, you

> know...they burst, they pulled the door open and she comes out, or something like that...and points to the wallpaper...with these little birds on it, um, that she had hallucinated into these horrible vultures, or something like that, that were coming down trying to steal her shit.[41]

Ann Rower explains that she remembered the scene because of *The Crucible,* with its "scene about the birds."[42] She thus performs another elaboration on the play, a record of a hallucination even more incongruous than Abigail's alleged vision in the courtroom. The story also plays off John Proctor's adultery, casting Anna Kohler as both Abigail Williams and Alan Watts's girlfriend.

With the exception of this story, Part III offers little sustained narrative or dialogue. Instead, it presents kaleidoscopic imagery, the stage composition constantly and subtly shifting as the performers engage in their psychedelic ramblings, both verbal and gestural. It is

> *Ron Vawter: It's a little bit like a divining rod, or passing your hands over a Ouija board's heat. It's staying light on your toes over a lot of material and finding what's possible between them.*

closer to being a mood piece than any work the Group has made since *Sakonnet Point,* striking a tone of subdued revelry, alternately silly and solemn, lucid and incoherent. Near its end, as the band plays stoned, melancholy music ("Pale Blue Eyes" by the Velvet Underground), the performers retreat more and more into their own private worlds as the nostalgic guitars and gentle tambourine hold sway. Although the

> *Elizabeth LeCompte: It's not so much that the piece is nostalgic but that the material is very nostalgic. And the music. Even I get a little bit weepy.*
> *Kate Valk: Really?*
> *Elizabeth LeCompte: Well, not quite. But it plays on that.*

seeming antithesis of *The Crucible,* the ending of Part III in fact provides an ironic re-reading of both Miller's last act and Leary's capture. The imprisonment and isolation of Proctor and Leary becomes, in the Wooster Group's transformation, a series of non-interactive performances: Ron Vawter's solitary perusal of a newspaper or Peyton Smith's muffled sobbing.

During the last section of Part III the most arresting and disturbing of the solitary activities is Kate Valk's "faint dance." It comes directly out of the "LSD version" of *The Crucible* when Jeff Webster as Reverend Parris

Figure 48. *L.S.D.*, Part III, Faint Dance
Peyton Smith, Willem Dafoe, Kate Valk.
(Nancy Campbell)

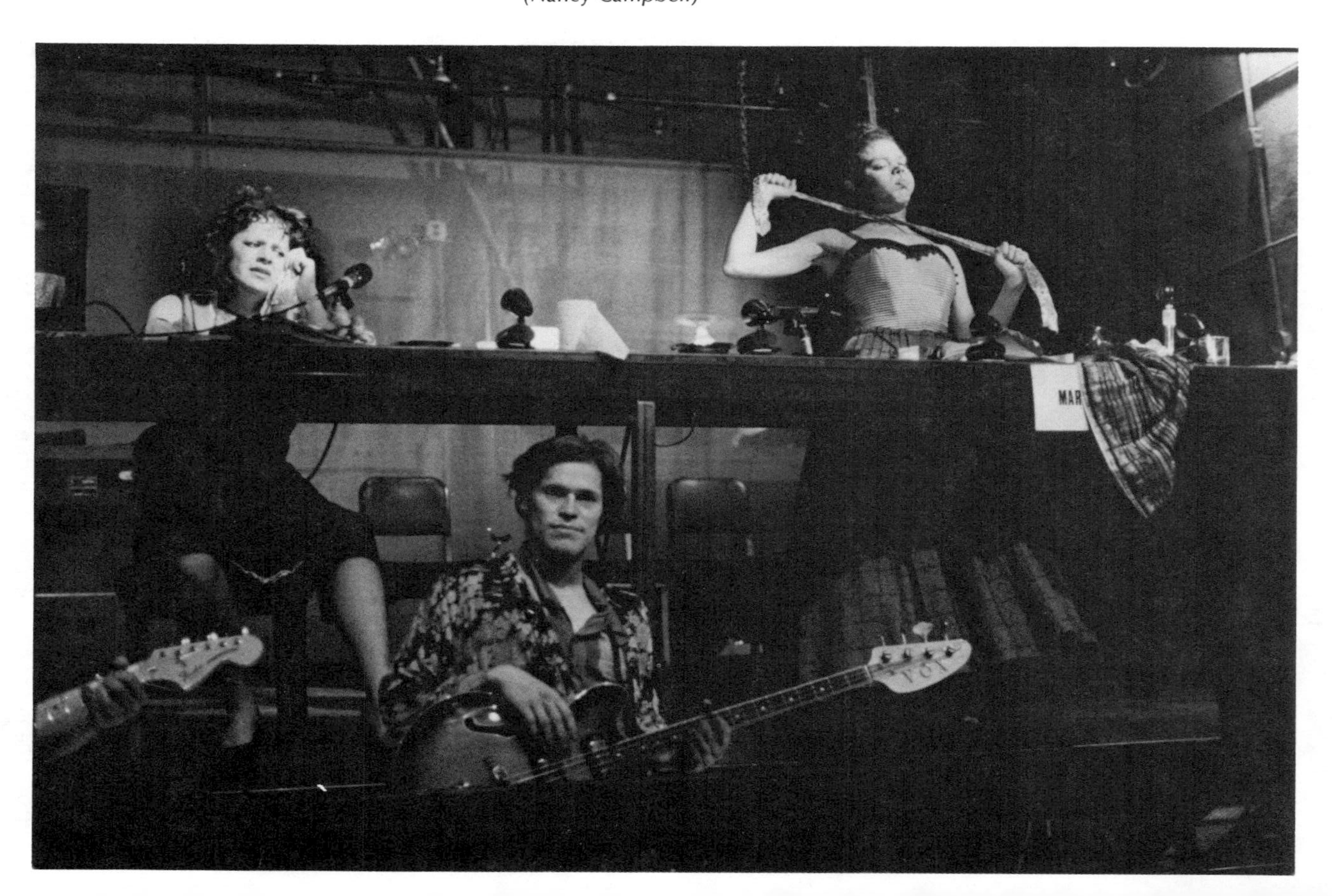

Figure 49. *L.S.D.*, Part II
Kate Valk, Willem Dafoe.
(Nancy Campbell)

questions Mary Warren's recantation and orders her to pretend to faint for the courtroom, as she pretended to faint before: "Let her turn herself cold now, let her pretend she is attacked now, let her faint. (He turns to Mary Warren.) Faint!"[43] While the band is playing Valk does all she can to lose consciousness. She hyperventilates and holds her breath. She spins wildly and again holds her breath. At Peyton Smith's suggestion, she tries pounding her chest with her fist, and finally takes a tie and, while holding her breath, tightens it around her neck. None of these stratagems

Kate Valk: When I was growing up, slumber parties were the big rage and one thing to do was to try to make ourselves pass out. Pre-drug highs. Then we'd tell each other, "Oh wow," what it was like when we were passed out. And we'd do levitation and seances and trances. The faint dance really upset my little sister when she came to see the piece.

succeeds, however, and the "faint dance" never achieves its goal, the ecstatic annihilation of consciousness. Kate Valk just continues to spin, deliriously and beautifully. Half-rapture and half-suicide, the closest thing to real intoxication in Part III, her dance unsettles "Pale Blue Eyes" and draws the sweetness and nostalgia out of the scene.

Far from being an isolated event in *L.S.D.*, the "faint dance" plays off many images of and references to the victimization and self-destruction of women. In *The Crucible* Kate Valk, in Tituba's blackface, plays Mary Warren as a beleaguered black teenage girl, screaming helplessly at her accusers before finally collapsing into cartoon-style unconsciousness. In Part I Ann Rower alludes to the suicide of Leary's first wife and in Part III the performers stage a multimedia reenaction of William Burroughs's murder of his wife, Joan Vollner. (In the early 1950s the couple was living in Mexico, she, addicted to benzedrine and he, to heroin. At a party on September 7, 1951, in a fatal variation on the William Tell trick, the near-sighted Burroughs shot his wife through the head while she balanced a champagne glass. He denied the story the next day, saying the gun went off accidentally, and the Mexican authorities never pressed charges.[44]) In the Wooster Group's presentation, the gap between action and reenactment, between the present and an unknowable past (perhaps Burroughs, as he claimed, was not responsible for her death), is tacitly acknowledged in the gulf between the different media. Having read Burroughs in Part I, Michael Kirby draws a revolver (both "live" and on the video monitor sitting on the table) as Nancy Reilly, stage right, places a glass of water on her head. A gun shot rings out. Reilly slowly removes the glass, looks at it and takes a drink of water. Ron Vawter turns to Kirby and repeats a line allegedly spoken to Burroughs after the shooting: "Bill, you missed."[45]

In picking up themes and images broached in the first half of the piece, Part III freely associates off an array of primary texts. As a result, *L.S.D.*'s "party piece" is less about themes or ideas than it is a performance of history. It enacts associations between present and past; it makes hypothetical connections between people, things and ideas; it

Michael Stumm: Many people mention to me that during the third section, whether they get it or not, they feel a little tinge in the back of their heads, as if they'd taken LSD. At a certain point, it looks like a bunch of people had taken LSD. And it ebbs and flows.

hallucinates characters and texts. It dramatizes the affinity between theatrical experience and drugs, transforming the willing spectator into a member of Leary's "underground," inspiring in him (to paraphrase Leary) an array of possible sensations: curiosity, sensuality, shamelessness, freedom, mischief, rebellion, humor, play, spirituality.[46] It performs the inability of historical discourse to comprehend and describe the feelings aroused during several hours of unfamiliar experience. It performs the fact that history, like theatre, is always a dance of absence and substitution, a dance of death.

* * *

Reading The Crucible

Kate Valk: We read The Crucible *over and over. And we edited it. That's how it started. And the blackface was a different experience compared with* Route 1 & 9 *because it was yet another distancing. It wasn't as risky because it's historical and so costume-y. Ron's not a minister. We're not Salem. It's so obviously placed in another time. Liz just didn't want to let go of the blackface, after* Route 1 & 9. *And the play was interesting to us because Arthur Miller wrote it as a moral play. He took responsibility, social responsibility. There was a hero. And everyone's contention was that* Route 1 & 9 *wasn't a moral play, that we were irresponsible.*

Ron Vawter: L.S.D. *is still such a problem because of Arthur Miller and the whole notion of theatrical property. That's interesting to us, that words can be owned, and that you can trespass even by the way you interpret them. It's also very much about the great American play, the chestnut, and the reverence in which one holds it.*

Elizabeth LeCompte: I think at the very core of L.S.D. *is a discussion about "meaning" and responsibility for what you make. What people are calling responsible art is work that illustrates a theme toward which you already have a clear-cut "moral" attitude. But that's not the way we work.*

Arthur Miller wrote *The Crucible* as an allegory to expose the ruthlessness and injustice of the McCarthy hearings. In the printed script, his parenthetical notes interrupt the dialogue to draw attention to the similarities between Salem of 1692 and America of the 1950s:

> The times, to their eyes must have been out of joint, and to the common folk must have seemed as insoluble and complicated as do ours today. It is not hard to see how easily many could have been led to believe that the time of confusion had been brought upon them by deep and darkling forces.[47]

In *The Crucible* Miller demonstrates that the "deep and darkling forces" of witchcraft are a sham, used only as justification for persecution. He shows that charges of wickedness, whether levelled against witches or communists, always serve to justify the suppression of those less powerful, the innocent victims on whom other people's frustrations are vented. He shows that witch-hunters manipulate the law to consolidate their power and profit from their enemies' economic ruin. He plumbs the characters' real motives and exposes Abigail's accusations as a ruthless attempt to snare John Proctor and destroy his wife. He shows that Reverend Parris's moral and religious crusade is a paranoid response to those, like John Proctor, who are critical of "him and all authority."[48] He shows that an accusation of witchcraft is an effective means of obtaining the property of one's adversaries. As Giles Corey points out to the court: "This man is killing his neighbors for their land!"[49]

There is no doubt of the acuity of Miller's understanding of witch-hunting or of the play's importance in 1953 (or 1986, for that matter). What *L.S.D.* calls into question is not the playwright's intentions but the way he has realized them, the way he has designed the drama and colored characters and action. By juxtaposing *The Crucible* against the psychic violence of "Millbrook," the *mise en scène* exposes the play's implicit structure of values, its "unconscious" promotion and deprecation of certain characteristics and beliefs. It examines the play's contradictions, noting silently (while the girls of Salem scream) Miller's tendency to justify his own beliefs by using the same device he denounces, by laying the blame for the witch hunt on yet another set of "deep and darkling forces."

Taking its place in *L.S.D.* as Part II ("Salem"), *The Crucible* provides another portrait of the rebel-hero and another (and less equivocal) example of a man's valiant struggle against the forces of tyranny and repression. From his first entrance, John Proctor has the mark of heroism upon him. He is described by the playwright as being independent of spirit and having a "sharp and biting way with hypocrites." He is "powerful of body, even-tempered, and not easily led," the kind of man who "instantly" would make a "fool" feel his "foolishness." But he is also a man who has fallen prey to temptation who, despite his "steady manner," remains a "sinner"—a divided man—lacking a way of "washing away" his "sins."[50]

Miller tries and proves John Proctor's heroism by dramatizing his relationship with two women, one bad and the other good. To his shame, Proctor has committed "fornication"[51] with the impassioned Abigail Williams, his former serving girl, and is plagued with guilt for having betrayed his "cold"[52] but "honest"[53] wife, Elizabeth. He has been driven to adultery because his marriage has been an uneasy union, frustrating both for him and Elizabeth because she is unable (or unwilling) to offer him the passion he craves:

> Proctor, with a grin: I mean to please you, Elizabeth.
> Elizabeth—it is hard to say: I know it, John.
> (He gets up, goes to her, kisses her. She receives it.
> With a certain disappointment, he returns to the table.)[54]

In contrast with his honest wife, Abigail is characterized as vengeful, deceptive and pitiless. She once "drank a charm to kill John Proctor's wife,"[55] and covers up her activity with a string of lies, hoping to dispatch Elizabeth and take her place. She is a creature of passion, the woman who looks into Proctor's eyes "feverishly,"[56] who makes him sweat "like a stallion"[57] whenever she is near. A wild, reckless, dangerous woman, a "mad... murderous bitch,"[58] she unleashes the "deep and darkling forces" in the play: the destructive power of female sexuality.

To dramatize John Proctor's ruin at the hands of the ruthless Abigail, Arthur Miller makes use of a highly emotional dramatic style unique among the plays the Wooster Group has appropriated. Writing a kind of agit-prop tragedy, he portrays John Proctor's heroism of spirit through a series of confrontations with the authorities (and less conventionally, confrontations with himself). The Wooster Group's performance, however, does not induce the audience to empathize with Proctor's

Willem Dafoe: If someone's got to cry, they know I'm going to do that. And I like that role. I weep during Proctor's last speech and it has to sound like an aria—the rhythm and sound are very important.

emotional upheavals. The wild and grotesque performance of Willem Dafoe (quite in line, however, with Miller's stage directions) points up the playwright's highly manipulative and inflammatory style. The overacting distances the spectator so that he is able to contemplate the hysteria from a detached perspective and to recognize it as a device that is used to disguise a political situation even more disturbing than it initially appears.

Although the historical John Proctor was indeed hanged in 1692 for witchcraft, the action of *The Crucible* is Miller's invention. As Paul Boyer and Stephen Nissenbaum explain in *Salem Possessed,* Proctor was sixty years old and a rich tavernkeeper at the time of the hysteria. Like many of the accused witches, he was a successful businessman who had enjoyed a swift rise in economic fortunes. Being "wealthier than any of his accusers,"[59] he became an inevitable target of the witch-hunt and, according to Boyer and Nissenbaum, was the victim less of "a whore's vengeance"[60] than of an economic revolution:

> The social order was being profoundly shaken by a superhuman force which had lured all too many into active complicity with it. We have chosen to construe this force as emergent mercantile capitalism.... Salem Village...called it witchcraft.[61]

Although Miller does not ignore the economic basis of the witch-hunt, he clearly subordinates it to Abigail's lust, thereby burying historical and economic reality in a psychosexual fiction.

Throughout *The Crucible* John Proctor refuses to recognize the economic force behind the witch-hunt, even after it is exposed by Giles Corey in Act III. Instead, at the end of the play, the man who has courageously refused to name names subordinates his innocence to his pride. He signs a confession but balks at the thought that it should be published lest it destroy his name. "You will not use me! I am no Sarah Good or Tituba, I am John Proctor! You will not use me!"[62] He shudders to think the authorities will have had the satisfaction of manipulating him to their ends the way they have manipulated those weaker than he: the woman and the black slave. "I have three children—how may I teach them to walk like men in the world, and I sold my friends?"[63] Proctor fears that his humiliation will endanger his progeny and jeopardize their pride, as well as their inheritance. "Tell them I confessed myself; say Proctor broke his knees and wept like a woman...."[64] To make his demoralization more vivid, Willem Dafoe puts glycerine in eyes and blubbers away, his power lost, his pride shattered. But he will not sacrifice his name, reputation and racial identity. His wife may have willingly abandoned her own name on her marriage day but he will insure that his redeemed patronym be passed on to his children.

> (with a cry of his whole soul): Because it is my name! Because I cannot have another in my life! Because I lie and sign myself to lies! Because I am not worth the dust on the feet of them that hang! How may I live without my name? I have given you my soul; leave me my name![65]

By insisting on his innocence and his name, John Proctor secures honor and property for his wife and children. In caring thus for his heirs, he unwittingly reinforces the social and economic system based on inherited land and wealth, to which he has fallen victim. Even in his final—and truly tragic—refusal, John Proctor fails to recognize that his heroism serves to safeguard the status quo and he dies a martyr to the economic system that has destroyed him.

* * *

Haphazard Conflicts

Ken Kobland: For the L.S.D. video we began with the notion of the Leary–Liddy opposition. And we began with a geographic opposition, too, between the New England woods and Miami. The tropical atmosphere was one of cheap, kind of Cuban intrigue. And the woods, having all those New England mystical associations. I went down to Miami in January 1984 with Ron to make the film. We had the idea to make some kind of film noir or intrigue, with a covert agent. And I wanted to use a lot of the filmic terms that go with that—details of things, drawers opening, faces appearing out of focus against backgrounds, lots of half-distorted images, looking out of windows, venetian blinds. So I worked along a line or scenario of coded images that, in repetition and formal structure, could play in lots of ways, depending on what live, physical things were going on. So we worked out highly defined images of waiting, secrecy, searching, hiding, all the things that circulate around the idea of a Liddy character, of intrigue and mystery. Set against abstracted Miami: tropical landscapes in which things were just gestures, a hand reaching for something, a cigarette smoking, waiting.

We shot a great deal and edited the tape in New York, building in congruences with the live action. Because the third part was very intricately timed, we were able to say at 20.5 seconds we want to have a particular gesture come in. It would often happen that way, especially around pauses and caesuras in the piece, and around the story of the woman getting locked in the bathroom. There was a section of Ron's hands on the tiles. Either he was searching for something behind the tiles, knocking to find the hollow tile or else he was just spacing out. You can't really tell because the tape is too blank a screen to have any direct narrative meaning. But it's either someone waiting or someone cracking up. And there are moments of erratic snowy television images that come in. But this searching, this feeling over the tiles and the story of the woman in the bathroom freaking out on acid became a central point.

The strength of the third part is so much in visual and verbal gesture and detail, in refined, repeated gestures. And the monitors offer another dimension of image, of depth, of narrative. In terms of meaning, it's hard to say. It has visual meaning, providing pleasure for the eye and for the ear. We wanted the television to stand as a kind of wallpaper, that's why we neutral densitied, toned down the screen, to push it back and make it as flat as possible. It should be like a picture hung in the space. It shouldn't have that TV brightness. I've often thought of it as a kind of basso continuo, *a continuous undercurrent that's drawing you in but that you can easily escape from. I'm constantly drawn into the sheer beauty of the live images against the flatness and depthlessness of the long table. It's as if the televisions were holes through which you can look out into the world. It's funny, it's a contradiction. The television which is obviously a depthless image gives us this sense of a hole in the space through which we look out into the world.*

David Savran: And then, while the band is playing, there's the video of the woods.

Ken Kobland: For me, the music is a kind of funky sixties remake, and the woods are an image, very crudely, of a back-to-nature experience—the whole thing of Leary in the woods and Millbrook, and the sixties fascination with the natural environment.

David Savran: Which also connects with The Crucible, *the dancing in the woods.*

Ken Kobland: Exactly. And the fear that surrounds the mysticism of the woods. There's an element of a horror film in it, too, the traditional horror code of trucking through the woods. The camera's handheld and it's crashing through the grass and looking around. Very traditionally in

horror films there's the perspective of the monster walking through the woods. But you don't know how to connect it. Is it some kind of secret agent or some kind of horror, like the Devil? Or is it a trippy home movie, someone on acid walking through the woods and just looking at a tree and tripping out? It's hard to find out where it connects. There's also the climate opposition, from the sunny tropic to the cold wood.
David Savran: Where was that filmed?
Ken Kobland: Cape Cod, at Wellfleet. The footage of Ron in Miami has a sinister quality and this has another sinister quality. But with the music it almost becomes a kind of floating, trippy homage to the sixties.
David Savran: I also saw the romantic desolation.
Ken Kobland: As I said, it depends on where you connect it. There's a lot of that for me when I connect it to the bad rock 'n'roll, the funky, amateur quality of the music. That takes on a wonderful melancholy. And the woods are so barren. Depending on what you're reading, there are a lot of different feelings you can get from it.

The video in Part III introduces an opposition between Timothy Leary and G. Gordon Liddy, to be developed further in Part IV when excerpts from a 1982 debate between them are read. (In fact, their historical connection goes back many years. In 1966 Liddy was the Assistant District Attorney for Dutchess County and was, in large part, responsible for "busting" Leary at Millbrook.[66]) The video contrasts less the two men than the associations they bring with them. It pits the bare, cold Northern woods against the sunny tropics, the inhibited and guilty New England conscience against the freedom and laxity of Hispanic/American culture, the academic against the secret agent, the natural world against the commercial, monochrome against garish color, the subtle against the tawdry, Cape Cod against Miami Beach. It opposes two romanticisms, the horror movie and the *film noir,* exploiting and enlarging upon the mystery and ambiguous tonality of each.

The antithesis between Miami and New England brings a new formal and imagistic parameter into the piece. However, it also plays off and visualizes one already inscribed in both *The Crucible* and the Leary material (and in *Route 1 & 9*). In each it is evident in the opposition between the pressure and constraint of everyday life and the longing for freedom, pleasure and release. In *The Crucible* this longing envisions a tropical island on which Puritan values have no place, a paradise that the imprisoned Tituba in Act IV recalls to Sarah Good in her drunken revery:

> Oh, it be no Hell in Barbados. Devil, him be pleasureman in Barbados, him be singin' and dancin' in Barbados. It's you folks—you riles him up 'round

here; it be too cold 'round here for that Old Boy. He freeze his soul in Massachusetts, but in Barbados he just as sweet and—(A bellowing cow is heard, and Tituba leaps up and calls to the window:) Aye, sir! That's him, Sarah![67]

As if elaborating on Tituba's vision, Leary describes Mexicans and Puerto Ricans as part of the "underground"[68] with which he identifies. Elsewhere, John Bryan explains that Leary is drawn to the tropics and its people as a means of escape from a repressive culture:

> Mexico always loosened Timothy Leary up.
>
> Hispanic culture appealed to the romantic, poetic side of his nature and, down there, the constraints of home evaporated and he no longer had to play the part of the charming widower and the overpoweringly brilliant social scientist.
>
> Cheap booze. Plentiful whores; those warmblooded little women who appealed to his old Catholic double-standards, reverent Earth Mothers who said a Hail Mary before fucking for cash beneath a color litho of the Virgin of Guadalupe.[69]

The tropics, however, are only a paradise in part. They have more menacing associations as well, linked in *L.S.D.* to G. Gordon Liddy. As he confesses in his autobiography, he recruited and worked with Cuban-Americans from 1971 to 1973 on intelligence gathering operations and

Ron Vawter: Liddy was down in Miami, training a bunch of Cubans. It's another stream in the piece. He is this odd man. Busting Leary, the Cubans, Watergate, then joining with Leary again. It's a great American portrait.

domestic sabotage. (The latter included a foiled attempt to spike Daniel Ellsberg's soup with LSD before he was to deliver a speech.[70]) The program note for Part IV ("Miami") quotes an excerpt from the Leary/Liddy debate in which he describes the "natural order" he observed off the coast of Honduras:

> And I saw the barracuda attacking the yellow tail (inaudible), devouring him. I looked a long time and I did not see a yellow tail attacking, devouring a barracuda. And all the preaching you can possibly do is not going to reverse that natural order. And if you think it doesn't apply to human beings, ask the Poles.[71]

Although introducing a festive and paradisiac strain into the piece, the evocation of the tropics also suggests a more disturbing context: an indifferent and impassive natural world, social Darwinism and poverty, espionage and revolution. As a segue into Part IV Steve Buscemi reads Jackie Leary's description of his trip to Antigua with his father in 1963 and their stay (until they were thrown out) at a hotel called the Bucket of Blood where they saw a man who had "flipped out on acid."[72]

In the midst of its hallucinatory fragments, Part III introduces a crucial plot element that follows through into Part IV. Several minutes into the party Ron Vawter telephones Kate Valk, sitting at the other end of the table.

> RON VAWTER: Hi, it's me.
> KATE VALK: Where are you?
> RON VAWTER: Miami.[73]

She giggles and immediately hangs up, laughing with Peyton Smith (his video image *is* in Miami). Later, he calls again and she talks to him.

> RON VAWTER: Listen, there's gonna be a no-show at the Shelbourne tomorrow night. Donna Sierra and the Del Fuegos aren't gonna make it. You think we can get the old Cuban act together?
> KATE VALK: Uh, huh.
> RON VAWTER: Take the 12:01 and I'll pick you up at the airport.
> KATE VALK: OK. I'll bring the shoes. How many?
> RON VAWTER: Oh, six of one, half a dozen of the other.[74]

In Part IV everyone heads toward Miami, toward sun, freedom, azure waters and hungry barracudas.

* * *

David Savran: I loved the final dance, the Cuban one...
Kate Valk: With the shoes.
David Savran: The sneakers, all the sneakers hanging from your dress, like extra pairs of feet, that the guys smash down on the platform.
Kate Valk: That was inspired by Jack [LeCompte and Dafoe's then two-year-old son].
David Savran: Yeah?
Kate Valk: We were working on the dance, on rolls over the table, just thinking of Ron and Willem and me as the entertainment, the dancers, the Del Fuegos. And then one morning Jack had his shoes, was doing a dance with his shoes hanging from the shoestrings. And Liz thought, what a great idea. First, we all had the shoes, then it was just me, with the boys running them.

David Savran: And Part IV, "What is this dancing?"
Ken Kobland: It ties in with the whole thing Liz has elaborated for Ron, for the dance troupe. And suddenly the dancing in the woods—one aspect of The Crucible *and one icon of liberation in the sixties—becomes this cheap, seedy dance troupe.*
David Savran: And when they punctuate the dance by crashing all the pairs of sneakers down on the platform, the TV...
Ken Kobland: The TV image smashes, goes wild, yes. That's wonderful.
David Savran: And that just happens naturally in performance?
Ken Kobland: That actually happens because the connections get smacked.
David Savran: And the violence is being inflicted all around, on the people performing, on the spectators, on Earl Sandle, even on the equipment.
Ken Kobland: Exactly. The television freaks because of the violence being inflicted on the stage... it snaps.

Willem Dafoe: I had the sense that the final dance was the ultimate entertainment after all of that, because it had the tone of the whole show wrapped up in it. It was kind of irresponsible, amateurish but absolutely correct.
Michael Stumm: You could almost take it on the Ed Sullivan Show and do it right after Topo Gigio.

David Savran: Why does everyone end up in Miami? A vacation?
Ron Vawter: Yeah, being a tourist in a lackluster resort. It's the place you'll eventually arrive at. Miami. The elephant's graveyard, at the same time, infused with this Latin energy—vibrant, third world, Central American, jazzy, energetic. It's a kind of metaphorical place. But because of Liz's suspicion of metaphor, she doesn't let it operate that way. She doesn't weigh it, in any way. It's just a place, the last place, where the piece ends.

Part IV of *L.S.D.* brings Ann Rower's memories up to date, it flips the pages on the calender to 1982, to a debate between Timothy Leary and G. Gordon Liddy. While excerpts are being read, Kate Valk, Ron Vawter, Willem Dafoe and Matthew Hansell fill-in for the absent Donna Sierra and the Del Fuegos, straddling both the gap in the platform and the gulf between imitation and the real thing—the "real" performers never show up, only their substitute. Valk stands center stage, at the very front of the platform while Vawter and Dafoe stand next to and behind her in the

Figure 50. *L.S.D.*, Part IV, Shoe Dance, Rehearsal Shots
Ron Vawter, Kate Valk, Jeff Webster.
(Nancy Campbell)

trough. She wears a red and black Cuban/Mexican dress, sombrero and black sneakers. The men have their chests bared, wearing Mexican hats

> *Kate Valk: After* The Crucible *I smudge the blackface and put chalky stuff over it and blush and lipstick. It comes from a book Liz was looking at one day of the prostitutes of India, with the dark skin, that paint their faces white.*

and painted mustaches. Hansell carries a rifle and stands behind her on the platform. The other two hold three sneakers each that are tied to the hem of Valk's dress. When the Latin pop music begins ("Franjas de Agua" by the Trio Armonica[75]), Valk proceeds with a dance that is a combination of ballet exercises and flamenco, an arched arm over her head, kicking her feet up and down, forward and back from the ankles and knees. The men manipulate the extra sneakers, keeping them alongside her own feet, as if impersonating two absent dancers next to her, following her own steps exactly. At each cadence Valk jumps and the men, in time with her, smash their sneakers down on the platform, shaking it so violently that the brightly colored image on the television monitors ("What is this dancing?") almost disappears into video snow. After each section (or *raga*), the three pause, stepping out of character momentarily to adjust themselves and prepare for the next round.

During the first several minutes of the dance, excerpts are read from the question period following a Leary/Liddy debate. Peyton Smith reads the part of the moderator while Ron Vawter and Jeff Webster fill in for Liddy and Leary, respectively. First, a young man (read by Michael Stumm) notes that although both of them "talk of power," they "disregard the power of the Lord." (Substituting for the real audience at the debate, the performers boo and hiss.) He continues: "Let us learn to love one another and not preach power and greed and escape through drugs so on and so forth." (Applause.) Liddy answers with "a brief poem," his own porno-theology:

> May the bleeding piles possess thee.
> May thorns adorn your feet.
> May crabs as big as [inaudible] turds
> Crawl on your balls and eat.
> [inaudible]
> [inaudible]
> May a [inaudible] crawl through your asshole
> And break your fucking neck.[76]

This is followed by loud applause and laughing.

Finally, from the end of the table Norman Frisch, wearing "blind" glasses, raises his hand and reads the final question from the text he holds before him.

> EARL SANDLE: My name is Earl Sandle and, ah, my question is directed at Dr. Leary.... Let me inform you that I did serve in Vietnam with the Marine Corps and I came back and was shot in the face with a shotgun. I have over 130 pellets left on my brain, my eyes are made of plastic and the people that did this got the false courage to do it because they followed the teachings that you put in your books,... they were high, high on LSD and because of LSD they got the false courage to do what they've done.
> TIMOTHY LEARY: Well, I'm certainly opposed to that and I think that's the most terrible thing I've ever heard. I denounce the people that did this to you. ... I have done more to serve than anyone in history, to warn people, to prepare people, ah, to do exactly the opposite of what you're talking about. I'm very sorry this happened and I assure you that no teachings of mine that would ever... I'm a pacifist... I've always been that and no one that ever took up a gun, drunk or sober, can say they were a follower of mine.
> EARL SANDLE: They were following teaching... they were looking for a cheap thrill in drugs—they used LSD. The false courage that LSD gave them they got, and they were under hallucinations, and were under some kind of trip that that house was there because of the colors, because the bushes were jumping around at them and all, that they have to start shooting. And here I am, sir. So thank you, and I hope you can sleep very peacefully when I bump my face on the walls, when I stumble and trip. God bless you. Good night.
> TIMOTHY LEARY: God bless you and good night.
> (Pause.)
> MODERATOR: Dr. Leary, how do you feel?
> TIMOTHY LEARY: I feel very sad.[77]

At the end of the excerpts, the long table moves five or six feet upstage on the hydraulics and the fake Del Fuegos perform their dance finale. Kate Valk lies down on the now vacated platform and Matthew Hansell, carrying his rifle, straddles her, his feet stretched behind him invisibly. He seats his torso on top of her hips so that her legs appear to be his own. The two thus unite to comprise a single *trompe l'oeil* entity, a squatting dancer, miraculously propelling "his" outstretched legs. Vawter and Dafoe, meanwhile, continue to follow "his" feet with their sneakers, as "he" spreads "his" legs wide, bends "his" legs at the knees in time to the music, and smashes "his" feet down on the platform. The other performers, silhouetted in the low light, wave their arms slowly, following the dance, as Michael Stumm whistles sweetly into the microphone. At its end, there is a last moment when the dancers, their work finished, take a final siesta, a last moment of rest, and the piece is over.

Elizabeth LeCompte: For Part IV we created a dance that for me represents all that I've done in my work. The reading is still going on, but now the locale has changed. Is it Miami? Is it south of the border? Where is it? It's southern, it's emigres, people who have left New York and moved south... to die? Old age homes? And the performing team is still performing. And the questions are still being asked. The reading is from Leary's most recent work. And it culminates in the question, "Dr. Leary, how do you feel?" And "What is this dancing?" from The Crucible.

* * *

The Choreography of Persecution

David Savran: Why is there no Kennedy assassination material in L.S.D.*?*
Elizabeth LeCompte: The same reason it's not in Nayatt School. *It's too loaded. I know too unambiguously what it is for me. So it becomes boring very quickly.*
Willem Dafoe: It's why we'd never do a play on nuclear disarmament.
Michael Stumm: It's too small.
Elizabeth LeCompte: It's too specific.
Michael Stumm: It's like Monopoly. There's no choreography of persecution.
Elizabeth LeCompte: We tried it in Nayatt. *We abstracted the Zapruder film and took away its recognizability, but it lost its potency. And when we played it straight and everyone knew what it was, I hated it.*
Michael Stumm: There's nothing truly paranoid about it unless you know what it is.
Elizabeth LeCompte: Exactly. And it couldn't take on any more meaning.
Michael Stumm: You found it much easier to invent situations that acquire their own paranoia.

As the readings that comprise *L.S.D.* move fictionally through time toward the present, the problems of writing and interpretation remain. *L.S.D.* provides no answers. It only asks questions. "Dr. Leary, how do you feel?" Are you responsible for what has happened? Have your writings encouraged criminal activity? Have you, in attempting to bring about peace and understanding, effected destruction instead? But what of this "effect"? Is a writer responsible for the way others have interpreted his texts? Is not writing, by definition, cut off from the living hand, from the active, creative consciousness? Isn't it always cast adrift, always open to interpretation, always potentially dangerous?

L.S.D. demonstrates that every reading is a political act; every interpretation, an exercise of power. It dramatizes the process that bestows the force of "truth" upon certain cultural voices and interpretations. It shows how isolated points of view are subordinated to more systematic perspectives allied with institutional power, be it the power of the state or the literary and cultural establishments. It visualizes the play of meaning across a table, across a field of knowledge, among a group of intimates who have systematically, if not premeditatedly, suppressed those perspectives that threaten to subvert their control of the field. It visualizes the process that grants certain aggressive voices the status of cultural history and excludes the voices of the disenfranchised. It dramatizes history's reliance on the written text and its exclusion of those points of view, tentative and impermanent, which are not written down, not subject to the linearity of writing. It challenges the assumption that history in the theatre means fictionalized costume drama. It suggests instead that theatre, on account of its pretense, its use of simultaneous actions and its separation of role from actor, is the most suitable medium in which to "write" history.

Quite by accident, Arthur Miller's threat of legal action has proven the veracity of the Wooster Group's demonstration. It has confirmed the suggestion that the sphere of interpretation is not a pure, aesthetic realm but the world of political power. In this world, Miller's own reading of the play is distinguished from all others not because it is more correct but because it is empowered with the force of law. By insisting on his own interpretation, Miller has, ironically, aligned himself with the very forces that *The Crucible* condemns, those authorities who exercise their power arrogantly and arbitrarily to ensure their own continued political and cultural dominion. Miller's act of condemnation exacerbates what, in the play, he so clearly recognizes to be the hazards of a "divided empire in which certain ideas and emotions and actions are of God, and their opposites are of Lucifer." In place of this destructive dualism he urges the less judgmental conception of a "unity... in which good and evil are relative, ever-changing, and always joined to the same phenomenon,..."[78] a description that perfectly characterizes *L.S.D.* The Wooster Group there realizes, by undermining the opposition between good and bad, culture and counterculture, precisely those free-floating dynamics that Miller envisions: a semantic utopia in which meaning is liberated to circulate exuberantly and incessantly, without coming to rest upon any conclusive evaluation.

L.S.D. dispenses with the idea of history as dialectical development and conceives it instead as hallucinatory dance, a choreography of persecution, an "endlessly repeated play of dominations."[79] The piece brings this choreography into focus, this interplay of constantly shifting power relations (the dancers constantly swapping partners), both on a microscopic level—in the minute interactions between participants—and on a grosser cultural level—in the struggles between ideologies and interpretations. The choreography coalesces the paradisaic and the tyrannous, the free and the enslaved, into a dance in which each step is at once oppressive and radiant. It produces the beatific vision of the souls of the hanged flying up to heaven in the "poppet dance" and the sheer exhultation and delirium of Kate Valk's spinning in the "faint dance." It animates the final *ragas* of Donna Sierra and the Del Fuegos: Kate Valk dancing and Matthew Hansell straddling her, while the men smash the sneakers down on the platform, sending shock waves through the television cables. As if in horror and disbelief, the screens ask, "What is this dancing?" But they, too, succumb to the dance, as the very words dissolve into a shimmer of green and magenta snow.

Afterword

Looking back at the history of theatre, one sees that much of the most important and certainly all of the most radical work has been deconstructive—from the indecorous tragedy of Euripides which ridicules and indicts the gods, to Büchner's demonic comedy, to Brecht's non-"Aristotelian," non-cathartic Epic Theatre. The work of these three playwrights was so revolutionary—and remains so—not because it tried to create something wholly new but because it worked within history, and within metaphysics, to launch a trenchant critique of the ideology spoken through history and through metaphysics. Each manipulated preexisting forms to reveal their mode of operation, to expose the theatrical and dramatic devices on whose "invisibility" they traditionally relied. By exposing the forms (whether making ludicrous or strange, using *ostranie* or *Verfremdung*), the three playwrights challenged the entrenched theatre that demanded their silence and efficiency.

During the 1970s and 1980s the most important experimental theatre has likewise been deconstructive in strategy, performing a more or less trenchant critique of theatre and culture from within. Besides the Wooster Group, notable American practitioners include Richard Foreman, Lee Breuer, Richard Nelson, Meredith Monk. Among the aforementioned artists, the Wooster Group is perhaps the most politically radical, not because it pursues a revolutionary agenda, but because it is so deeply aware of the "chain of brutality" of which it is a part. Unlike the dominant liberal art of the period, it does not seek a moral high ground, knowing that it cannot detach itself from the process it examines: it recognizes that its activity will always produce the very objectification it deplores. As a result, the Wooster Group's work describes an urgent moment of politicized deconstruction which is in no way compromised by Elizabeth LeCompte's refusal of commitment. On the contrary, the work performs a skepticism that is so deeply political not because its material is political (what material isn't?) but because the Group's working process, its confrontation of the material, disentangles and exposes the political dynamics (relations of force) that are so finely and deeply inscribed in all cultural products. The Wooster Group visualizes the circulation of power, both in theatre and society, through a deconstruction (more Nietzschean than Marxist) that refuses to align itself with political dogma. Eschewing the certitude of the liberal critic or the authoritarianism of the proselyte, it questions from a position of doubt.

Because the Wooster Group's work refuses simply to illustrate a political position or a predetermined theme, its meaning is always provisional and open-ended, always, like the pieces themselves, in the process of being revised. As I write, in April 1986, the Group is developing a new piece with the working title *St. Anthony* to conclude its second trilogy, *The Road to Immortality,* which also includes *Route 1 & 9* and *L.S.D.* (The trilogy's title is taken from a 1932 book by British psychic Geraldine Cummins which purports to be a description of the afterlife as communicated to her by the deceased Frederic W. H. Myers, author of *Human Personality and Its Survival of Bodily Death.*) The screenplay to Ingmar Bergman's *The Magician* provides the main story line for the piece which seems, at this point, to be about a theatre troupe (and Flaubert) working on Flaubert's dramatic poem, *The Temptation of St. Anthony*; about the development of cinema out of magic shows (and the Group getting more and more involved with film); about Maury Hayden's recollections of Lenny Bruce's obsession with *The Road to Immortality* during his last days. It is about dancing and reading; death, theatre and history; salvation, vision and faith.

When *St. Anthony* is performed it will provide a new perspective from which to view the other pieces in the second trilogy. It will, in effect, re-read *Route 1 & 9* and *L.S.D.*, urging perhaps a re-examination of the sterile afterlife given Wilder's dead, of Leary's paranoid visions and of the departed playwrights' attempts to control their orphaned creations. It will certainly overlay the Wooster Group's consideration of the past with another layer of hallucinations, in which the field of history may appear, perhaps, as a seance, and historical discourse as the clairvoyant communications of the dead. But the operative word here is "perhaps," since no meaning is ever final. Interpretation must tread carefully lest it attempt to freeze the object of its examination with a conclusive *Q.E.D.* It must recognize itself to be as much the victim of time and mutability as the memories of Spalding Gray or Ann Rower. It must acknowledge and delight in the certainty that as soon as it is written, it is out of date.

Notes

Part I

1. Memo from Rob Marx to Mary Hays, December 18, 1981, p. 1.
2. The Wooster Group, *Route 1 & 9 (The Last Act)* in *Benzene,* Nos. 5/6, Spring/Summer 1982, p. 5.
3. Ibid., p. 5.
4. Don Shewey, "Playing Around," *Soho Weekly News,* March 25, 1981, p. 64.
5. *Route 1 & 9,* p. 6.
6. Ibid., p. 5.
7. Thornton Wilder, Preface to *Three Plays,* p. viii.
8. Ibid., p. ix.
9. Ibid., p. x.
10. The Wooster Group, *Point Judith* (Documentation), *Zone,* No. 7, Spring/Summer 1981, p. 23.
11. Ibid., p. 23.
12. *Route 1 & 9,* p. 5.
13. In conversation with the author, February 1983.
14. Quoted in John S. Patterson, "Route 1 & 9: Director Liz LeCompte Talks about What the Play Says to Her," *The Villager,* January 21, 1982.
15. Wilder, Preface, p. xii.
16. *Route 1 & 9,* p. 7.
17. Elizabeth LeCompte, quoted in Tish Dace, "Setting the Record Straight," p. 6.
18. Quoted in Leonora Champagne, "Always Starting New: Elizabeth LeCompte," p. 23.
19. Dace, "Setting the Record Straight," p. 5.
20. Ibid., p. 5.
21. Ibid., p. 6.

22. Thornton Wilder, *Our Town* in *Three Plays,* p. 6.
23. *Route 1 & 9,* p. 10.
24. Ibid., p. 10.
25. Ibid., p. 11.
26. Ibid., p. 12.
27. Ibid., p. 13.
28. Dace, "Setting the Record Straight," p. 5.
29. Ibid., p. 5.
30. *Our Town,* p. 58.
31. Ibid., p. 56.
32. Ibid., p. 64.
33. Ibid., p. 46.
34. Ibid., p. 47.
35. *Route 1 & 9,* p. 14.
36. Ibid., p. 61.
37. Dace, "Setting the Record Straight," p. 5.
38. Jeffrey M. Jones, *An Appeal of the Decision of the New York State Council on the Arts to Withhold Funds from the Production of Route 1 & 9,*" p. 18.
39. Memo from Rob Marx, p. 1.
40. Patterson, "*Route 1 & 9 . . .*"
41. Don Shewey, "Elizabeth LeCompte's Last Stand?" p. 75.
42. *Our Town,* p. 62.
43. Dace, "Setting the Record Straight," p. 6.

Part II

1. Eugene O'Neill, *Long Day's Journey into Night,* p. 98.
2. T. S. Eliot, *The Cocktail Party,* p. 175.
3. Kenneth Burke, "Psychology and Form" in Burke, *Perspectives by Incongruity,* ed. Stanley Edgar Hyman (Bloomington: Indiana University Press, 1964), p. 28.
4. Spalding Gray, "About *Three Places in Rhode Island,*" *The Drama Review,* p. 36.
5. Spalding Gray, "Playwright's Notes," *Performing Arts Journal,* p. 89.
6. Ibid., p. 87.
7. Spalding Gray, quoted in Florence Falk, "Autobiographical Theatre," *The Soho Weekly News,* p. 21.
8. Ibid.

9. Ibid.
10. Elizabeth LeCompte, quoted in Arnold Aronson, "Sakonnet Point," *The Drama Review* T68, p. 35.
11. Gray, "About *Three Places*," p. 35.
12. Ibid., p. 35.
13. Gray, "Playwright's Notes," p. 87.
14. Spalding Gray and Elizabeth LeCompte, *Sakonnet Point*, unpublished manuscript, p. 1.
15. Elizabeth LeCompte, quoted in Robert Coe, "Making Two Lives and a Trilogy," *Village Voice*, p. 119.
16. Elizabeth LeCompte, quoted in Aronson, p. 34.
17. Gray, "About *Three Places*," p. 42.
18. Ibid., p. 39.
19. Spalding Gray, *India and After (America)*, Video by Dan Weissman and Brad Ricker, 1979.
20. Gray, "Playwright's Notes," p. 89.
21. Ibid., p. 89.
22. Elizabeth LeCompte, quoted in Leonora Champagne, "Always Starting New: Elizabeth LeCompte," *The Drama Review*, p. 22.
23. See Richard Schechner, *The End of Humanism*, p. 84.
24. Libby Howes, quoted in Roderick Mason Faber, "The Road Taken," *Village Voice*, December 12, 1977, p. 95.
25. Spalding Gray and Elizabeth LeCompte, *Rumstick Road*, in *Performing Arts Journal*, pp. 103–104.
26. Ibid., pp. 95–96.
27. Ibid., p. 95.
28. Ibid., p. 99.
29. Ibid., p. 100.
30. Ibid., p. 106.
31. Ibid., p. 108.
32. Ibid., p. 111.
33. Roland Barthes, "On *The Fashion System* and the Structural Analysis of Narratives," interview with Raymond Bellour, in Barthes, *The Grain of the Voice: Interviews 1962–1980*, trans. Linda Coverdale (New York: Hill and Wang, 1985), p. 47.
34. Ibid., p. 55.
35. Gray, "About *Three Places*," pp. 38–39.
36. See Ted Hoffman, "The Obies: Raw Deal on *Rumstick Road*," p. 13.

37. *Village Voice,* April 21, 1980, p. 84.
38. *Village Voice,* April 28, 1980, p. 29.
39. *Rumstick Road,* p. 112.
40. Ibid., p. 112.
41. Ibid., pp. 114–15.
42. Gray, "About *Three Places,*" p. 42.
43. Spalding Gray and Elizabeth LeCompte, in collaboration with Libby Howes, Bruce Porter and Ron Vawter, *Nayatt School,* unpublished manuscript, p. 5.
44. *The Cocktail Party,* title page.
45. Arthur Pollack, quoted in *Nayatt School,* p. 1.
46. *Nayatt School,* p. 2.
47. Ibid., p. 4.
48. *The Cocktail Party,* pp. 29–30.
49. *Nayatt School,* p. 27.
50. *The Cocktail Party,* pp. 30–31.
51. Ibid., p. 61.
52. Ibid., p. 133.
53. Ibid., pp. 136–37.
54. Ibid., p. 139.
55. Ibid., p. 139.
56. Ibid., p. 141.
57. Ibid., p. 145.
58. Ibid., pp. 174–75.
59. *Nayatt School,* p. 37.
60. Ibid., p. 183.
61. *Nayatt School,* p. 32.
62. *Rumstick Road,* p. 108.
63. *The Cocktail Party,* p. 175.
64. Gray, "About *Three Places,*" pp. 41–42.
65. *The Cocktail Party,* p. 147.
66. Ibid., p. 184.
67. Ibid., p. 101.
68. *The Cocktail Party,* p. 181.
69. Ibid., p. 183.

70. Ibid., p. 184.

71. Ibid., p. 175.

72. *Nayatt School*, p. 15.

73. Elizabeth LeCompte, "An Introduction," *Performing Arts Journal*, p. 86.

74. The Wooster Group, *Point Judith* (Documentation), *Zone*, No. 7, Spring/Summer 1981, p. 16.

75. Ibid., p. 23.

76. *Long Day's Journey into Night*, p. 130.

77. Ibid., p. 102.

78. Ibid., p. 72.

79. *Point Judith*, pp. 16–17.

80. Ibid., p. 19.

81. Ibid., p. 17.

82. *Long Day's Journey into Night*, p. 166.

83. Ibid., p. 64.

84. Ibid., p. 111.

85. Ibid., p. 118.

86. Ibid., p. 147.

87. Ibid., p. 7.

88. *Point Judith*, p. 17.

89. Ibid., p. 19.

90. Ibid., p. 15.

91. *Long Day's Journey into Night*, p. 97.

92. *Point Judith*, p. 26.

93. Ibid., p. 26.

94. Ibid., p. 27.

95. Ibid., p. 26.

Part III

1. Wooster Group interview with Ann Rower, 1983, used in Part I of *L.S.D.*

2. Robert Lowell, "Memories of West Street and Lepke" in *Life Studies and for The Union Dead* (New York: Noonday Press, 1964), p. 85.

3. Michel Foucault, "Nietzsche, Genealogy, History" in *Language, Counter-Memory, Practice*, ed. Donald F. Bouchard (Ithaca: Cornell University Press, 1977), p. 154.

4. Wooster Group interview with Ann Rower, used in Part II.

5. Timothy Leary, *L.S.D.*, Pixie Records CA 1069, 1966.
6. Ibid., Carol Arket, liner notes.
7. Arthur Miller, *The Crucible*, p. 31.
8. Timothy Leary, "Drop Out or Cop Out," in Leary, *The Politics of Ecstasy*, p. 134.
9. Timothy Leary, "M.I.T. is T.I.M. Spelled Backwards," in Leary, *The Politics of Ecstasy*, p. 244. LeCompte did not want this quote to be read in Part I of *L.S.D.*
10. Timothy Leary, *Flashbacks: An Autobiography* (Los Angeles: J.P. Tarcher Inc., 1983), p. 355.
11. Jackie Leary, quoted in John Bryan, *Whatever Happened to Timothy Leary?* (San Francisco: Renaissance Press, 1980), p. 273.
12. Elizabeth LeCompte, Letter to Arthur Miller, November 30, 1983.
13. Wooster Group interview with Ann Rower, used in Part III.
14. Foucault, pp. 154–55.
15. Allen Ginsburg, Peter Orlovsky, *Straight Hearts' Delight: Love Poems and Selected Letters, 1947–1980*, ed. Winston Leyland (San Francisco: Gay Sunshine Press, 1980), pp. 205–7.
16. William Burroughs, *Naked Lunch* (New York: Grove Press, 1959), p. 1.
17. Timothy Leary, "She Comes in Colors," interview with *Playboy* Magazine, in Leary, *The Politics of Ecstasy*, p. 117.
18. Wooster Group interview with Ann Rower, used in Part I.
19. Ibid., used in Part I.
20. Ibid., used in Part I.
21. Ibid., used in Part III.
22. Leary, "She Comes in Colors," p. 110.
23. Wooster Group interview with Ann Rower, used in Part I.
24. Arthur Koestler, "The Silent Generation," in *Drinkers of Infinity: Essays 1955–1967* (New York: Macmillan Co., 1968), p. 98.
25. Leary, "She Comes in Colors," p. 117.
26. *As Ever, The Collected Correspondence of Allen Ginsberg and Neal Cassady*, ed. Barry Gifford (Berkeley: Creative Arts Book Co., 1977), p. 205.
27. James Behan of Dramatists Play Service Inc., Letter to Jeffrey Jones, the Wooster Group, November 9, 1982.
28. Elizabeth LeCompte, Letter to Luis Sanjurjo of International Creative Management, December 29, 1982.
29. Stephen Sultan of ICM, Letter to Elizabeth LeCompte, November 29, 1983.
30. Mel Gussow, "Stage: Wooster Group," *New York Times*, October 31, 1984.
31. John A. Silberman of Paul, Weiss, Rifkind, Wharton and Garrison, Letter to the Wooster Group, November 9, 1984.

32. Samuel G. Freedman, "Miller Fighting Group's Use of Segment From 'The Crucible,'" *New York Times*, November 17, 1984, p. 14.

33. Arthur Miller, quoted in Don Shewey, "Miller's Tale," *Village Voice*, November 27, 1984, p. 123.

34. Elizabeth LeCompte, Letter to Arthur Miller, November 26, 1984.

35. John A. Silberman, Letter to Arthur J. Greenbaum, Esq. of Cowan, Liebowitz and Latman, P.C., January 7, 1985.

36. Arthur Miller, quoted in Robert Massa, "Arthur Miller Clings to 'The Crucible,'" *Village Voice*, December 27, 1983.

37. Arthur Miller, quoted in Don Shewey, p. 123.

38. Compare, "Another pair of oddball Californians (known as Bernie and Barnie) brewed up their LSD in sickly-looking brown batches and bottled it in rubber-stoppered vials which they handed out along the road until busted by observant cops in a small village.
    During the trial, the two somehow managed to dose the judge, the jury, the prosecutor and all the cops. They disappeared into the sunset while the whole courtroom freaked out." Bryan, p. 106.

39. Foucault, p. 145.

40. The Wooster Group, *L.S.D.*, Part III.

41. Wooster Group interview with Ann Rower, used in Part III.

42. Ibid., used in Part III.

43. *The Crucible*, p. 102.

44. John Tytell, *Naked Angels: The Lives and Literature of the Beat Generation* (New York: McGraw-Hill, 1976), pp. 39–46.

45. The Wooster Group, *L.S.D.*, Part III.

46. Leary, "Drop Out or Cop Out," p. 134.

47. *The Crucible*, p. 4.

48. Ibid., p. 28.

49. Ibid., p. 92.

50. Ibid., p. 18. Compare Leary's self-description: "an arch-Romantic Alchemical Rebel, passionate, irascible, guilt-ridden but unrepentent . . . the lonely hero who, in proud moral hauteur, defends his indomitable self against all social and bureaucratic encroachments. . . ." Bryan, p. 280.

51. *The Crucible*, p. 145.

52. Ibid., p. 131.

53. Ibid., p. 107.

54. Ibid., p. 48.

55. Ibid., p. 17.

56. Ibid., p. 19.

57. Ibid., p. 20.

58. Ibid., p. 145.

59. Paul Boyer and Stephen Nissenbaum, *Salem Possessed: The Social Origins of Witchcraft* (Cambridge: Harvard University Press, 1974), p. 209.

60. *The Crucible,* p. 106.

61. *Salem Possessed,* p. 209.

62. *The Crucible,* p. 137.

63. Ibid., p. 137.

64. Ibid., p. 137.

65. Ibid., p. 138.

66. See G. Gordon Liddy, *Will: The Autobiography of G. Gordon Liddy* (New York: St. Martin's Press, 1980), pp. 107–18.

67. *The Crucible,* p. 117.

68. Timothy Leary, "Hormonal Politics: The Menopausal Left-Right and the Seed Center," in Leary, *The Politics of Ecstasy,* p. 144.

69. Bryan, p. 35.

70. *Will,* p. 170.

71. Leary/Liddy debate, State University of New York at Albany, 1982; excerpt printed in *L.S.D.* program.

72. Jackie Leary, quoted in Bryan, p. 77.

73. The Wooster Group, *L.S.D.,* Part III.

74. Ibid., Part III.

75. From *Bomba!,* Monitor presents music of the Caribbean, MFS-355. The liner note for the song explains that it is a Mazurka, "one of the dance rhythms imported from Europe and bent to the demands of gentile Puerto Rican society of the late 19th Century. It conjures up pictures of gentlemen in cutaways and wasp-waisted ladies dancing into the dawn."

76. Leary/Liddy debate, used in *L.S.D.,* Part IV.

77. Ibid., used in Part IV.

78. *The Crucible,* pp. 30–31.

79. Foucault, p. 150.

Bibliography

Primary Sources

Gray, Spalding. "Perpetual Saturdays." *Performing Arts Journal* IV (1): 46–49.
______. "Playwright's Notes." *Performing Arts Journal* III (2): 87–91.
______. "About *Three Places in Rhode Island.*" *The Drama Review* 23 (1): 31–42.
Gray, Spalding, and LeCompte, Elizabeth. *"Rumstick Road."* *Performing Arts Journal* III (2): 92–115.
______. *Sakonnet Point.* Unpublished manuscript.
Gray, Spalding, and LeCompte, Elizabeth, in collaboration with Libby Howes, Bruce Porter and Ron Vawter. *Nayatt School.* Unpublished manuscript.
Howes, Libby. *Nayatt School Notebook.* Unpublished manuscript.
LeCompte, Elizabeth. "An Introduction." *Performing Arts Journal* III (2): 81–86.
______, from the notebooks of. "The Wooster Group Dances." *The Drama Review* 29 (2): 78–93.
______. "Who Owns History?" *Performing Arts Journal* IV (1): 50–53.
The Wooster Group. *L.S.D.(... Just the High Points...).* Unpublished manuscript.
______. *Point Judith. Zone* 7: 14–27.
______. *Route 1 & 9 (The Last Act). Benzene* 5/6: 4–16.

Secondary Sources

Aronson, Arnold. "The Wooster Group's *L.S.D.(... Just the High Points...).*" *The Drama Review* 29 (2): 65–77.
Bierman, James. "*Three Places in Rhode Island.*" *The Drama Review* 23 (1): 13–30.
Champagne, Leonora. "Always Starting New: Elizabeth LeCompte." *The Drama Review* 25 (3).
Coe, Robert. "Everybody's Autobiography." *The Soho Weekly News,* December 27, 1979.
______. "Making Two Lives and a Trilogy." *The Village Voice,* December 11, 1978, 119–20.
Dace, Tish. "Plywood and Electronics: Designer Jim Clayburgh of the Wooster Group." *Theatre Crafts,* February 1984.
______. "Setting the Record Straight." *Other Stages,* January 14, 1982, 5–6.
Eliot, T.S. *The Cocktail Party.* New York: Harcourt, Brace and World, 1950.
Falk, Florence. "Autobiographical Theater." *The Soho Weekly News,* June 1, 1978.
Hoffman, Ted. "The Obies: Raw Deal on *Rumstick Road.*" *Villager,* June 9, 1977.
Leary, Timothy. *The Politics of Ecstasy.* London: Paladin, 1970.
Leverett, James. "Mapping Rhode Island." *The Soho Weekly News,* December 21, 1978.

———. "The Wooster Group's 'Mean Theatre' Sparks a Hot Debate." *Theatre Communications,* July/August 1982, 16–20.
Levine, Mindy N. "An Interview with Elizabeth LeCompte." *Theatre Times* 3 (8).
Miller, Arthur. *The Crucible.* New York: Bantam Books, 1959.
O'Neill, Eugene. *Long Day's Journey into Night.* New Haven and London: Yale University Press, 1956.
Rabkin, Gerald. "Is There a Text on This Stage: Theatre/Authorship/Interpretation." *Performing Arts Journal* IX (2/3): 142–159.
Savran, David. "The Wooster Group, Arthur Miller and *The Crucible.*" *The Drama Review* 29 (2): 99–109.
Schechner, Richard. *The End of Humanism.* New York: Performing Arts Journal Publications, 1982.
Shank, Theodore. *American Alternative Theatre.* New York: Grove Press, 1982.
Shewey, Don. "Elizabeth LeCompte's Last Stand?" *The Village Voice,* November 11, 1981.
———. "The Wooster Group Stirs Controversy with an Avant-Garde Series." *The New York Times,* May 16, 1982.
Wilder, Thornton. *Three Plays.* New York: Avon Books, 1957.

Formal Interviews

Savran, David. Interview with Jim Clayburgh, September 11, 1984.
———. Interview with Jim Clayburgh, Willem Dafoe, Norman Frisch, Anna Kohler, Elizabeth LeCompte, Peyton Smith, Michael Stumm, Kate Valk, Jeff Webster, September 7, 1984.
———. Interview with Willem Dafoe, August 24, 1984.
———. Interview with Norman Frisch, September 14, 1984.
———. Interview with Spalding Gray, July 27, 1984.
———. Interview with Spalding Gray, Elizabeth LeCompte and Ron Vawter, October 22, 1984.
———. Interview with Matthew Hansell, August 24, 1984.
———. Interview with Ken Kobland, June 25, 1985.
———. Interview with Elizabeth LeCompte, July 30, 1984.
———. Interview with Elizabeth LeCompte, July 31, 1984.
———. Interview with Elizabeth LeCompte, October 24, 1984.
———. Interview with Nancy Reilly, August 31, 1984.
———. Interview with Peyton Smith, August 23, 1984.
———. Interview with Kate Valk, August 28, 1984.
———. Interview with Ron Vawter, August 21, 1984.
———. Interview with Ron Vawter, April 13, 1985.

Index